GCSE media studies

GCSE

Julian Bowker

Orders: please contact Bookpoint Ltd, 78 Milton Park, Abingdon, Oxon OX14 4TD. Telephone: (44) 01235 827720, Fax: (44) 01235 400454. Lines are open from 9.00–6.00, Monday to Saturday, with a 24 hour message answering service. Email address: orders@bookpoint.co.uk
A catalogue record for this title is available from The British Library

ISBN 0 340 730366

First published 1999
Impression number   10 9 8 7 6 5 4 3 2
Year   2005 2004 2003 2002 2001 2000

Copyright © 1999 Julian Bowker

All rights reserved. No part of this publication may be reproduced or transmitted in any form or by any means, electronic or mechanical, including photocopy, recording, or any information storage and retrieval system, without permission in writing from the publisher or under licence from the Copyright Licensing Agency Limited. Further details of such licences (for reprographic reproduction) may be obtained from the Copyright Licensing Agency Limited, of 90 Tottenham Court Road, London W1P 9HE.

Selected cover photos from ITN and BBC Photolibrary/Gala Films
Typeset by Fakenham Photosetting Ltd, Fakenham, Norfolk
Printed in Great Britain for Hodder & Stoughton Educational, a division of Hodder Headline Plc, 338 Euston Road, London NW1 3BH by JW Arrowsmith Ltd, Bristol.

Contents

Introduction	1
Questionnaire	2
1 Asking questions: what is media studies?	5
2 Languages and categories	10
3 Producers and audiences	33
4 Messages and values	53
5 Music industry	68
6 Film industry and promotion	85
7 Television and radio news	107
8 Newspaper tabloids and broadsheets	121
9 TV hospital dramas and documentaries	141
10 Magazines	154
11 Advertising: standards and controls	171
12 Sport, game shows and chat shows	186
13 New media and old	199
14 Practical production guide	207
15 How much do I know?	217
16 Resources	219
Glossary	222
Appendix	224
Index	232

Acknowledgements

This book is dedicated to Fiona and Lily.

The author would like to thank the following:
Students of Varndean College, Brighton – Alex Hill, Anne-Marie Illingworth, Sarah Morland, Judah Shostak-Reilly and Rachel Stone. Staff of Varndean College, Brighton – Caroline Fryer and Martin Sohn-Rethel.

The author and the publisher would like to thank the following for permission to reproduce copyright text and illustrative material:

©Newsweek, Inc. All rights reserved. Reproduced by permission, pg. 64; Advertising Standards Authority, pgs 175, 176, 177; Associated Press Ltd., pg. 17, 94; Audit Bureau of Circulation, pgs 47, 130, 156; BARB, pg. 36; BBC Education Publicity, pg. 35; BBC Photograph Library, pg. 193; BBC: BBC Online site information and BBC job advert reproduced by permission of the BBC, pg. 39; BBFC, pg. 43; BFI, pgs 16, 22, 24, 25, 26, 27, 92, 93, 95, 98, 110; Black Echoes Ltd., pg. 18; British Sky Broadcasting Group plc, pg. 37; BRMB/Mintel, pg. 164; Burger King Corporation, pg. 90; By permission of The Press Standards Board of Finance Limited, pg. 134; Channel 4, pg. 26; Dobsons Agency, Scarborough, pg. 54; Emap Èlan, pgs 46, 51, 160, 161; Emap Metro (*Smash Hits*), pg. 78; Emap Online, pg. 165; Fourth Estate, pgs 138, 203; *Guardian Review* / Willem, pg. 64; Guzelian photography, pg. 15; H. Bauer Publishing, pg. 146; *Independent on Sunday,* pgs 7, 49, 74, 142; IPC Magazines, pg. 159; ITC, pgs 177, 178; Kobal Collection, pg. 26; Mojo/Alpha Pictures, pg. 78; Music Week, copyright of Miller Freeman UK, pg. 69; Nestlé, pg. 179; Northern & Shell plc, pg. 168; Press Complaints Commission, pg. 136; Ronald Grant/BBC, pgs 22, 23; Ronald Grant, pgs 26, 95; Screen International, pg. 102; Soccer-fanzine.co.uk, pg. 194; The Advertising Archives, pg. 60; *The Guardian*, pgs 55, 79, 86, 194, 204, 205; *The Independent*, pg. 124; *The Mirror*, pg. 122; The Press Association, pgs 18, 187; The PressWise Trust, pg. 135; *The Voice*, pg. 125; TM Ragdoll, Productions (UK) Ltd., Licensed by BBC Worldwide Ltd., pg. 39; Tony McHale in *Radio Times*, pg. 145; Twentieth Century Fox, pg. 93.

Every effort has been made to trace copyright holders but this has not always been possible in all cases; any omissions brought to our attention will be corrected in future printings.

Introduction

HOW TO USE THIS BOOK

This book is designed to match the requirements of AQA (formerly SEG) and OCR (formerly MEG). To use the book to its best advantage the student should obtain the current examination syllabus from the board they are studying. These can be obtained from the addresses at the back of the book. Teachers and centres should also have copies of these.

The book is divided into the following sections:

▶ Concept chapters 1–4.
▶ Media topic chapters 5–13.

Topics such as Film Promotion, Pop Music, Science Fiction Films, Television and Sport and Television News have been set by one or more boards for the timed examination papers. It is therefore worth finding out what the set topics are for each year to help plan your study.

The chapters can be read in any order, once the first four conceptual chapters have been read. Key words (KW) and technical words (TW) are included in each chapter to highlight key terms. Practical activities, a glossary of terms and resource listings are included at the end of the book to aid the development of knowledge and to support research.

The questionnaire which follows is designed to start you thinking about what media you use and produce. When you finish the book it might be worth comparing what you have said at the start with what you know once you have finished. Completing the questionnaire will provide an ideal opportunity for making this comparison.

Julian Bowker
September 1999

Questionnaire
MEDIA CHECK-UP

This questionnaire is designed to help you assess how much and what type of media you consume. It also may surprise you to discover how much media you produce yourself, when you assess what you produce across the whole range of media. Keep this information for a year and see if it changes during that time. You could also compare your results with someone else in your year or with someone much older or younger than yourself to see what differences you find.

Fill in all the questions by ticking the appropriate answer, unless instructed otherwise.

Age

Surname and first name

Year

1. What media do you watch/read/listen to? Circle the appropriate number.

No. hours per week

Television	0–1	1–5	5–10	10–15	15–20	20–25	more than 25
Films	0–1	1–5	5–10	10–15	15–20	20–25	more than 25
Computer games	0–1	1–5	5–10	10–15	15–20	20–25	more than 25
Music	0–1	1–5	5–10	10–15	15–20	20–25	more than 25
Photography	0–1	1–5	5–10	10–15	15–20	20–25	more than 25
Fiction books	0–1	1–5	5–10	10–15	15–20	20–25	more than 25
Non-fiction books	0–1	1–5	5–10	10–15	15–20	20–25	more than 25
Internet – general search	0–1	1–5	5–10	10–15	15–20	20–25	more than 25
CD-ROM – general knowledge	0–1	1–5	5–10	10–15	15–20	20–25	more than 25

2. Top five

List the top five media by the number of hours you spend on each.

1.
2.
3.
4.
5.

3. Television

a) How many television sets do you have in your house?

None
One
Two
Three
Four
Five
More than five

b) Where are the television sets located?

Bedrooms
Sitting room
Kitchen
Bathroom
Other places (please state)

c) What type of television programmes do you like to watch?

                                                        Yes   Don't Mind   Don't Like

Comedy
Sport
Films
Soaps
Police drama
Hospital drama
Music shows
Quiz shows
Confessional programmes (Vanessa, Oprah Winfrey, Trisha Goddard)
Documentaries
Advertisements
News and current affairs
Cartoons

QUESTIONNAIRE

4. Film

a) What type of popular mainstream films do you like to watch? Tick as appropriate.

Horror
Science fiction
Romance
Action
Comedy
True stories
Musicals
Western
Thriller
Fantasy
Cartoon
Martial arts and other (please state)

b) How much media do you produce?

                                                            Once   More than once   Often

Photographs (e.g. holiday snaps)
Video
Computer (letters, homework, photo-scanning, T-shirts)
Music compilations, soundtracks, mixing, etc.
Newsletter, magazine or fanzines
Stories
Web page

Evaluation

1. How many hours per week do you spend using media products?
2. How many hours do you spend making media products?
3. What percentage of time in an average day do you spend on media consumption and production? (For example, if you have an average of 13 hours awake in an average day)
4. What conclusions do you draw from your media questionnaire about you and the media?

1 Asking questions

WHAT IS MEDIA STUDIES?

KW

Text ■ languages ■ categories ■ producers ■ audiences ■ messages and values

This chapter explains the type of texts studied in Media Studies courses and provides a general introduction to the concepts which will be discussed in Chapters 2, 3 and 4.

You will analyse some cartoons and questions are given to start you off on learning how to analyse images. You are then given general outlines of responses to these questions to check against your interpretation.

T W

Print run ■ layout and design ■ tabloid ■ broadsheet ■ leader ■ editorial

WHAT IS MEDIA STUDIES?

Studying the media involves looking, watching, listening and participating in, discussing and producing a range of media products. The study is more than just about the products themselves. It entails investigating the people who made them and thinking about what type of people consume them and what they gain from them.

What is a media text?

A media text is any modern media product which is the object of study. It could be a radio news bulletin, a family photograph or a music CD. The media texts covered in this book are:

► film
► television
► radio
► newspapers and magazines
► books
► computer software
► video
► advertisements
► CD-Rom
► internet

Media studies involves the analysis of the content of media texts, their producers, audiences,

ASKING QUESTIONS

the technologies used, the social and economic context in which they were made, and what they mean.

Media studies concepts

Media studies concepts apply equally to the making of the product and to its analysis. There are six main concepts which are useful to learn and apply in media studies. These inform the learning activities of analysis, creativity and media culture. Chapters 2, 3 & 4 have been divided into the following three pairs of concepts. For each concept pairing there are some key questions and these questions can be applied to any text.

1. **Languages and Categories** – What type of text is it and how does it communicate?
2. **Producers and Audiences** – Who made the text, who consumes it and how?
3. **Messages and Values** – What is the idea behind the text? What are the ideas in the text? What worth or value does the text have?

In the rest of this chapter the aim is to introduce you to the different media concepts and begin to discuss some of the theories about media texts, production processes and practices, their institutions and audiences.

LANGUAGES AND CATEGORIES

1. Why is the cactus the wrong way round in the picture within the cartoon below?
2. How do we know this is a cartoon? What are the typical features of a cartoon?
3. What point is the cartoonist trying to make?

Analysis of the cartoon

1. The image in the cartoon is the wrong way round because the author of this cartoon wanted to make a joke. There is however, a serious point being made, in that paintings can never be exactly the same as the reality on which they are based. Every painting, television programme, film, etc, is only a representation of the real world.
2. A typical cartoon contains:

- Fine line drawings.
- Caricatures – humorous portraits of people; exaggerated body parts and facial expressions.
- A major concept expressed as an unusual visual idea or situation.
- A humorous setting.
- A caption of dialogue or a short single-line statement.

3 The point the cartoonist is trying to make is that there is no such thing as an accurate version of reality. The painter or the photographer selects a part of the real world and recreates it in their mind before reproducing that idea on paper and placing a frame around it.

PRODUCERS AND AUDIENCES

Source: The Independent on Sunday, 14 June 1992

1 Who made this cartoon?
2 Why was the cartoon produced?
3 What type of person will have read it?
4 In what type of media text, and where in that text, would you find this cartoon?
5 How did this cartoon reach its intended target?
6 What is the cartoon saying about all newspaper editors?

Note: The phrase 'to cry crocodile tears' means to pretend to cry, while secretly not have any feelings.

Analysis of Cartoon

1 The person who drew the cartoon is called Riddell, as they have signed it in the top right-hand corner. Getting the final image to the public is the work of several other people who were also involved in the process of reproducing the image. The picture editor of the newspaper, *The Independent on Sunday* (IOS) commissioned the cartoonist to draw it. The cartoon is then scanned into a computer and positioned on a page of the newspaper by a layout designer. Finally, the image is reproduced a few hundreds of thousands of times as part of the newspaper's print run. A print run is the number of copies printed.
2 The newspaper wanted a cartoon that could tell the story of tabloid newspapers' (see Chapter 8) overuse of Lady Diana to sell their papers. An IOS editor then decided to create a cartoon mocking the national press' apparent declaration, that from then on, they would not intrude on Lady Diana's private life.
3 The typical reader of *The Independent on Sunday* is a reader of broadsheet newspapers (see Chapter 8) and is usually educated. They are likely to have political views: and reader political party affiliation ranges from liberal Conservative, Liberals through to democrat Labour.
4 You would normally find a cartoon like this on the front page or inside the home pages of a serious broadsheet newspaper. The cartoon might be next to a leader column or editorial on the inside home pages or on the front page next to the main article.
5 Newspapers are usually passed from the printers to the wholesalers who distribute them to local depots. The newspaper shops (retailers) then receive the number of copies they hope to sell, based on previous

ASKING QUESTIONS

sales. The public then buy it from the shops.

6 The image contains the following: a chart showing rising circulation figures, an editor depicted as a crocodile crying with a mischievous grin on its face; a desk covered in small format newspapers (*The Sun, The Express*, etc.) and a large desk chair. The meaning of the whole image is a comment on the ruthless way the tabloid newspapers used the stories about Lady Diana's private life to sell copies.

The number of papers sold rose when Lady Diana was the subject of the newspaper. When the story was tragic, such as the information about how unhappy she had privately been in her marriage to Prince Charles, the papers pretended to be sorry — the crocodile tears. However, the fact that the newspapers still used the information to sell copies implied that they may not have been truly sorry.

Occasionally questions were asked about the harassment and intrusion of the press into her private life, simply to get a picture of Diana. Several newspaper editors did express their sympathy for Lady Diana, but one must question their sincerity when so many papers had been sold in the months when Diana was placed in the spotlight.

It is possible to comment on the IOS's cartoon that the serious newspapers used the stories which the tabloid's created in order to sell their own newspapers.

MESSAGES AND VALUES

Study the image above and answer the following questions:

1 What do the images on the cave wall illustrate?
2 Do you agree with the statement, 'First, we look at these violent pictures and then go out and kill something'? Give reasons for your answer.
3 In your opinion, for what reasons did cave people draw images on walls?

Analysis of cartoon

1 The images on the wall are typical of paintings discovered around the world of cavemen killing animals. They depict pre-historic humans hunting animals.
2 The point of the cartoon is to state that violence is a part of society and that paintings are not the direct cause of violence —

pictures tell us something about how humans live their lives. The statement, "First we look at these violent pictures, then we go out and kill something" is meant to be sarcastic. In the real world, people are not usually driven to violence by simply looking at pictures – the aggression and the need to hunt depicted in this image is illustrating a social factor.

3 Why do humans need art or some form of expression?

Effects of media images

It has been argued that 'the media' (usually television) causes violence in society. This is known as the 'effects' debate. The effect television has on society has not yet been conclusively proven. It is possible to argue that depicting violence in art is a positive experience. It is a form of fantasy and therapy. We can see the consequences of violence if we see the effects and dangers dramatised in front of our eyes. In reality, it is too long ago to prove what cave dwellers thought when they drew or looked at such drawings. Perhaps we can say that by painting these scenes they served as a mirror to their hunting activities, as a source of comfort, or to instil a sense of superiority over the animals in their successful kills.

2

Languages and categories

HOW DO MEDIA FORMS COMMUNICATE?

KW

Text ■ forms and conventions ■ codes ■ signifiers ■ denotation and connotation ■ anchorage ■ genre ■ narrative ■ *mise-en-scène*

In this chapter you will learn about the concepts of languages and categories across various types of media. You will also analyse and create ideas for still and moving images.

TW

Cropping ■ enlargement ■ captions ■ headlines ■ typeface ■ close up ■ medium and long shot ■ track ■ zoom

THE LANGUAGES OF THE MEDIA

In the study of the modern media, we call any media product a 'media text'. Media texts include radio, television, film, newspapers and magazines, music tapes and CDs, advertisements, computer games and books.

From an early age, a child responds to and interprets visual and sound texts. Each medium has a different way of communicating to us, depending on its technology and format. For example, radio news is purely aural, whereas television news combines sound and vision with typed text. We can describe each medium's method of communication as a 'media language'. Like the world of many cultures and languages the modern media exists in a variety of forms.

We gain information and ideas from newspapers quite differently than we do from television. Newspapers are made from paper; they consist of newsprint and are laid out in columns with computer word processed type, and they also contain electronically reproduced photographs. A reader of a newspaper can pick it up and read it in any order, as selectively as they like. Television programmes are electronically broadcast via air waves or by cable. The transmitting signal consists of sounds and images which are sequenced and shaped into a combined visual/sound narrative. Unless we use a remote control we therefore watch the television in a fixed sequence.

The language of each medium is learnt at a very young age by repeated reading, viewing and listening. By sharing ideas with others about what we have experienced we make sense of these different media languages. In the early days of film people were very alarmed to see trains appearing to come at them from the screen. Today we are rarely surprised if we see half a person appear on the screen – we do not think, as did some of the early film viewers, that the person's legs had been chopped off.

Each media language has what are known as a set of codes, forms and conventions.

Codes

The use of slow motion in films is an example of codes. A slow motion action sequence, as in the film *Chariots of Fire*, is code for a moment of fantasy and wonder. Throughout that particular film there are slow motion sequences depicting 'heroic' competitive running, and these scenes are set to grand orchestral music.

Another example of a code is in drawn cartoons where the convention of using italics marks indicate that the subject is moving through the air.

The way we learn these codes is curious as children are not taught to 'study' television or cartoons with the same intensity that they are taught to learn to read books by being read to or instructed at home. Somehow through familiarity, we pick up what each medium's language is and what the codes mean.

Conventions

A typical television soap opera convention is a cliffhanger. This dramatic moment often takes place at the end of an episode, where we are given an important piece of information, such as when a new character appears announcing: 'I am your long lost brother'. The surprise leaves the audience in suspense, waiting to find out what happens next – and they have to wait until the next episode is broadcast.

A convention of a newspaper front page is to have the most important piece of news announced in large typeface with a short headline, for example, 'Prime Minister Resigns!' A

LANGUAGES AND CATEGORIES

typical convention of an hourly radio news programme is to have a sound of a clock bleeping or a pre-recorded piece of dramatic music to indicate that the words we are about to hear are important and serious.

MEDIA LANGUAGES: HOW DOES EACH MEDIUM COMMUNICATE?

Discuss the following questions. If you wish, draw and annotate your responses to the questions.

1 Film – What types of images and sounds do we usually expect to see and hear if the film is a thriller and danger is present?
2 Television – What is the difference between a typical studio set for a television news programme and a game show? List or sketch out differences in who is present, the layout, the studio set and props.
3 Magazines – What is the difference in looks (i.e. form) and content between a front cover for a fanzine and a music magazine like *Smash Hits*?

Figure 2.1 Example of a fanzine

A fanzine or 'Zine' is usually produced on a very low budget, made at home by the fans. A very small number are distributed amongst friends and clubs. There a variety of types of fanzines – specialist music and football 'zines are common. We can describe a fanzine as being non-mainstream or an alternative to the mainstream product.

Form

As well as different kinds of media, within each medium there are different forms of the same product or text. For example, all newspapers consist of printed text, photographs, headlines and captions, columns, pugs ('ears'), headings and sub-headings.

The form of newspapers

There are two main forms of newspaper: tabloid and broadsheet. A tabloid usually has a four column width and a broadsheet has a seven column width. A tabloid is A3 size and a boadsheet is twice as long.

Historically tabloids tended to be simpler to read and aimed at an 'easy read' audience, with large photographs and more pictures. Tabloids tended to be less 'wordy', while broadsheets often had a higher word content and were targeted at the more literary reader.

In recent times more newspaper editors have chosen to use the tabloid form. This is perhaps because the tabloid form suits a magazine style of content and is easier to hold and carry about. The *Daily Mail* and the *Daily Express*, for example, which used to be termed as broadsheets, are now often described as 'tabloids'. Most Saturday and Sunday newspapers now have tabloid or magazine supplements, even if the main paper is a broadsheet.

Figure 2.2 Tabloid

Figure 2.3 Broadsheet

LANGUAGES AND CATEGORIES

Image analysis

The photographic image is the major component of newspapers, magazines, CD covers, and print-based advertising. Creating an image involves selecting real objects and presenting them in a way that means something to the viewer. To appreciate this the viewer has to be able to interpret visual signs and symbols.

There are four aspects of analysing an image:

- Analysis involves explaining what the images selected and represented from the real world mean.
- Analysis also involves studying what words have been used to accompany the image and how their content, style of lettering and layout changes its meaning.
- The analysis of images involves looking at how images are presented technically to create effects.
- Analysis of images also involves identifying where the image is placed, who has placed it there and for whom?

Symbols

> **Discuss in pairs and write down or draw and annotate your responses to the following question:**
>
> What ideas do you associate with the following images?
>
> 1 red ribbon
> 2 red poppy
> 3 red nose
> 4 red rose

It is possible that you discussed the association of AIDS World Day with the red ribbon; Armistice Day with the red poppy, clowns and Comic Relief for Africa with the red nose and romance, or perhaps the Labour Party, with the red rose.

Signifier and signs

Each of the images mentioned previously mean something else, aside from their meaning as real objects. A red rose is a flower, but is also associated with romance and so is a commonly recognised symbol of this. When objects signify other meanings, then these objects become what are known as 'signifiers of meaning'.

Meaning also depends on culture and country. In Japan or Brazil, a red poppy or a red nose would not have the same meaning as they do in the UK – why do you think this is?

> **Draw or describe objects which are signifiers of:**
>
> 1 American culture
> 2 New York
> 3 British nationality
> 4 Youth culture
>
> Discuss what your images are and explain what they signify.

Icons

The word icon is another term used to discuss the ideas associated with pictures and photographs of people and objects. Literally, an icon means 'to resemble', from the Greek. Paintings of Christ in the Eastern Christian Church were often painted onto panelled wood and displayed in churches for worship. Different religions have their own icons to pray to. However, in many religions creating a likeness is viewed as blasphemous, and taints the god-like with the human.

In modern Britain, an icon is more likely to refer to a pop star, a soap celebrity or royal family figure. An icon is someone or something worshipped by devoted admirers or believers. The icon is usually given a special significance verging on the religious or cultish.

Discuss the following:

1 Princess Diana, when she was alive and after she died, became an icon for people in Britain. In your view, what is Princess Diana an icon of?
2 What associations do the Danger Mine signs and the trainers create? How do the Danger Mine signs and trainers relate to Princess Diana?

Figure 2.4 Modern iconography

Source: © Guzelian Photography

| LANGUAGES AND CATEGORIES |

Icons in culture

In recent film and pop culture history Marilyn Monroe (50s and 60s), Debbie Harry (70s and 80s) and Madonna (80s and 90s) have all been icons in the shape of sex symbols. They have all become icons of female sexuality in different ways, in different decades.

One major reason why these women have become so important is because their images have been mass-produced and circulated so frequently.

Icons as objects

We can also use the word icon to describe objects. For example, in the Western film

Figure 2.5 Marilyn Monroe: an icon of her era
Source: © BFI

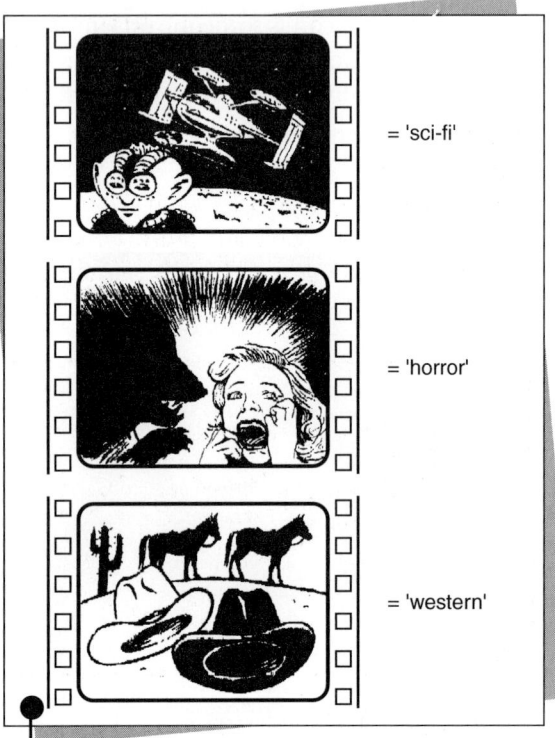

Figure 2.6 Using icons to describe films: sci-fi, horror and the western

Discuss and research images of icons in the music or film industries.

1 Who in the music, film or celebrity world would you describe as being contemporary icons?
2 Ask an adult who they would describe as their five most significant twentieth century icons from the world of politics, sport or pop culture.
3 Identify four icons of American culture.
4 Identify one person who defines themselves as a rebel in the film or music industries.

genre there are a number of typical images of real objects. These are not simply parts of the scenery, but over many years films have come to signify what we recognise as a western: the gun, the hats and boots and spurs, cacti, the horse, the desert and rocky outcrop and the tumbleweed.

Examples of icons in a science fiction film are: futuristic technology and settings, space crafts and robots. All of these icons have become well established over the years. In film studies the word 'iconography' is used to cover a whole collection of icons belonging to a particular type of film genre, be it the Western, the science fiction movie or the horror film (see Figures 2.6).

RECOGNISING THE IMAGE

What can you recognise or identify when you look at an image? A famous line drawing tested people to see what they thought they were seeing. Look at Figure 2.7 and see what you can recognise. What is this an image of?

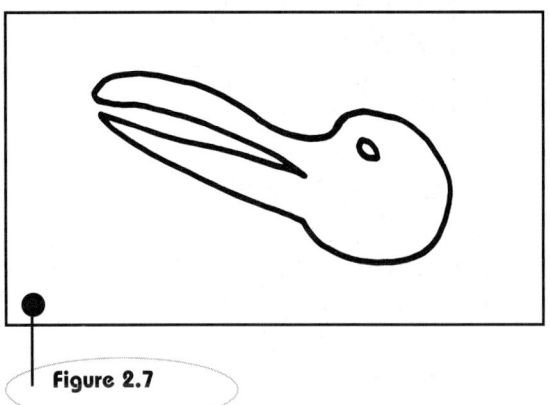

Figure 2.7

It is possible that you saw the line drawing as a duck or as a rabbit. This illustrates two points:

1 Images can sometimes contain more than one meaning.
2 What they associate with the image will depend on that person's background and experience.

An image that has the potential to mean several things is said to be 'polysemic', that is it has many meanings. Advertisements in particular often contain several meanings. Even newspaper photographs about real events are capable of having several meanings. The photo in Figure 2.8 was taken on 20 April 1998, at an event held to mark the occasion of Israel's 50th anniversary. It was printed in *The Guardian*. The image of the Israeli national flag combines the image of war with the innocence of the boy. The flower symbolises peace. To a Palestinian, this peace may not be associated with the Israeli flag.

Figure 2.8 An image with many possible meanings
Source: © Associated Press Ltd.

LANGUAGES AND CATEGORIES

Facial expression, posture and gestures

We can analyse images of people and how someone looks in terms of their facial expression, body posture and gestures with their hands.

PHOTOGRAPHIC IMAGE ANALYSIS

Study the picture opposite of Armand Van Helden. It was taken for the front cover of *Inside Trax*, a garage, house and club supplement to *Echoes*, the 'Black Music Weekly'.

Task 1

a Describe the expression on the face of Armand Van Helden in the photograph.
b Describe his pose and posture. How natural or posed do you think he is?
c Analyse the hand gestures and clothes.
d What angle is the photograph taken from and why?

Denotation

Source: Black Echoes Ltd.

Figure 2.9 Clare Short: image denotation and connotation

Source: The Press Association

The image of Clare Short, International Development Secretary, (Figure 2.9) conveys several ideas associated with the objects featured:

▶ Weapons of war – landmines.
▶ Sign with a skull and cross bones.
▶ She is wearing protective clothing usually worn where explosives or guns are involved.
▶ The sea is in the background.

This description of ideas contained in the image is known as denotation. If we then start to draw some conclusions about what these objects mean and interpret the image and the ideas that are associated with it – these are connotations of the image.

Connotation

In Figure 2.9, the manner in which Clare Short is holding up the landmines suggests that she considers them to be objects which are offensive. She knows the photographers are looking at her and the way the image is composed suggests that she has co-operated with them. In other words, she has not been snapped without her permission, rather the reverse.

In fact, Clare Short has set up the whole photographic event to draw attention in the newspapers to the world problem of unexploded landmines. Referring back to the late Princess of Wales' campaign against landmines, you will recognise the protective clothing is the same as Diana wore when she was drawing attention to the same issue. Clare Short's serious facial expression suggests that she is unhappy about the landmines. The familiar danger signs of the symbol of the skull and cross bones indicates that these are indeed very dangerous objects.

When the image in Figure 2.9 was printed in *The Guardian*, in October 1997, the original caption below the image gave us to understand that the sea behind is in Brighton; the southern coastal location where the Labour party conference was held in 1997. At this event, the issue of the world's sites of unexploded landmines was discussed. In the light of this information we can recognise that where Clare Short is standing is not the location of the mines she is holding up.

IMAGE IN CONTEXT

Create three fictional captions to place under the image of Clare Short for each of the following:

a a film poster
b a local newspaper article
c a government health warning to be displayed on billboards

Discuss for each example how the meaning of the original image and words has changed, i.e. not the words but the image itself.

Anchorage

'Anchorage' is the term given for placing words next to an image. The words convey the meaning of the image. Very few images appear in commercial advertising or government information promotions without words attached. In the captioning activity opposite you were fixing the meaning of the image in three different ways, even though the image itself remained the same.

LANGUAGES AND CATEGORIES

IMAGE: TECHNIQUES ANALYSIS

Following are three examples of how a student has changed the Clare Short image and the context of the images. You will now see that the image's meaning has been fixed in three different ways. The converted image is no longer polysemic, as with the captions and headings it has a limited range of meanings – it has been anchored.

Task 1

Analyse the techniques and processes used to produce images 'A' 'B' and 'C' (coursework by Anne-Marie Illingworth).

Examine lighting, colour, camera angle and type of shot, and the size and shape of the edited image.

In image 'A' the student has used techniques of cropping, enlargement on a photocopier, captioning and wordprocessing headlines. They have also used different font sizes and typefaces, to suit their sci-fi magazine.

The same techniques have been used in image 'B' for this newspaper or billboard advertisement for a documentary on television.

Image B

Image 'C' has not been cropped. Aside from this however, the same techniques have been used for this front page of a newspaper. The name of the newspaper is in a font and typeface which suits a broadsheet newspaper like *The Observer*.

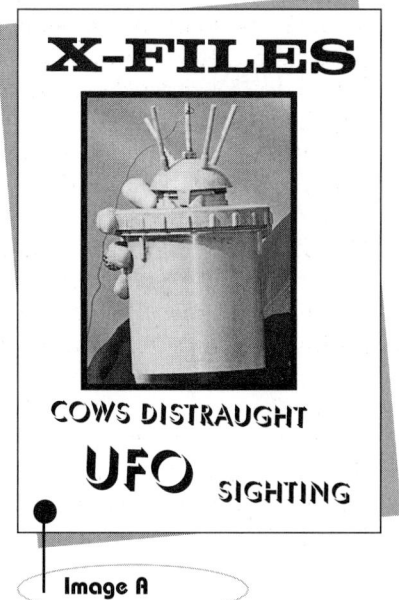
Image A

IMAGE PRODUCTION

In this exercise you will crop, format and analyse a chosen image. Select an image from a newspaper or magazine which is interesting and can be divided into two more images.

Task 1

Remember to keep the original captions or headings from your chosen image. Now place these three images into new contexts, for example, a newspaper, a magazine or an advertisement.

Task 2

Start with the whole image but without the words. Invent new headings or captions, or overlay words on the image. In doing this, you will change the meaning from the original meaning of its original newspaper/magazine context – explain how this has occurred.

Task 3

Next crop the image into two more parts. You will now have invented two more different contexts, for example, newspaper, advertisements or film poster. You may need to enlarge your cropped image. These new images should be completely different from the whole image idea that you created in Task 2. Make the image either landscape or portrait, to suit the place where it will be seen.

Task 4

Write about each of the three images and their new captions, headings or overlays of printed words, in a critical commentary. You should aim to write about 250–400 words.

Critical commentary

A critical commentary is a piece of analytical writing. A 'commentary' involves explaining the process of how you came to produce your images and what you are trying to suggest (or connote) in their new formats. The 'critical' part of the commentary means you can show that you have reflected on and analysed the process and meaning of the images you have produced. You will also have to explain why you changed the shape and size of your images and how you produced them in their new versions.

Use the following headings to guide your written analysis of each image produced:

1 Analysis of process: these are decisions made in producing different captions, headings, lettering, typeface and fonts, and for cropping and enlarging.

2 Image analysis: this includes the terms denotation and connotation. One must ask what is included in the image and what does this mean? How is the meaning conveyed, for example, is it conveyed by signifiers or symbols?

3 Anchorage: how do the captions alter the meaning? What forms and conventions are used in the image?

4 Photographic techniques: analyse the original image, i.e. lighting, colour, camera distance, angle, framing and focus.

5 Institutions: who made the image? How do the two different contexts affect the image content?

6 Audience: who is it targeted at? How many different types of audience might look at these images? How might people react differently to the same images and text?

| LANGUAGES AND CATEGORIES |

MEDIA CATEGORIES

This section deals with identifying various media text categories.

Discuss the following in pairs:

a Name a television programme. What type of programme is it?
b Do you think the following programmes are fiction or factual? Explain your reasons.
   ▶ Friends
   ▶ Crimewatch UK
   ▶ TFI Friday
c Examine the photographs below – is it possible to tell simply by looking at these, which are factual or fictional? Give reasons for why you think you know.
d What type of fiction programme is Friends?

Source: © BFI.

Source: © Ronald Grant/BBC

Source: © BFI

GCSE MEDIA STUDIES

Categorising media texts

We can usually categorise media texts in at least three ways:

1 Categorisation as the labelling and identifying of the different types of media (radio, television, film, newspapers, magazines, etc.).
2 Media forms can be divided within one medium into genre categories. For example, television can be divided into documentary, fiction or news.
3 Types of film or television genre can be further subdivided into groups. For example, film fiction can be subdivided into comedy, sci-fi, musical or western. Alternatively, television factual programmes can be subdivided into quiz, soap or sport, for example.

A further subdivision of the above categories is a sub-category where you can describe a comedy such as *Red Dwarf* as a sci-fi satirical drama.

Figure 2.10 *Red Dwarf*
Source: © Ronald Grant/BBC

TELEVISION

When you switch on the television and flick across the channels, how do you know what type of programme you are watching? Is it a film, a quiz show, a sports programme or a children's drama, for example? We know how to identify a quiz show because there is a host/ess, there are contestants, a panel and a studio audience. These elements are known as the forms and conventions that have become the accepted shape and format of the programme type.

List at least two forms and conventions of the following television programmes:
▶ Holiday travel consumer advice
▶ Saturday morning children's entertainment shows

It is usually possible to immediately identify what type of programme (or media text) it is, as we have seen them before and we recognise the elements which make each type of programme distinctive.

LANGUAGES AND CATEGORIES

FILM

Introducing this section on film genre are short summaries of four films, for which the titles have been deliberately left out. Try to identify the genre of each film from the descriptions.

a Shakespeare's famous love story meets the busy modern media in this violent and sexy romance depicting the fate of the two ill-fated lovers, Romeo and Juliet. When they meet on Verona Beach, the sands of time trickle out as the ruinous hatred is played out between their two rival families, the Montagues and the Capulets.

b Vincent has a heart defect. It helps him survive in this futuristic world, where geneticists design babies free of imperfection. The future is bright for perfect ones who rule over the invalids. With clever deception, Vincent passes as one of the elite, until a murder is committed and DNA evidence points to him.

c The Musketeers are sworn to fight for each and for France to the death. A mysterious French prisoner leads them to embark on their most dangerous mission ever, to save France from certain downfall. They must be strong to defend their friendship, France, and the prisoner whose identity threatens to destroy not only their lifelong friendship but also the throne the Musketeers have sworn to serve.

d 007's brief is to find out the real truth behind the fastest growing news network owned by the evil media mogul, Eliot Carver. There's also the mysterious business of the wreck of the Naval frigate Devonshire, apparently lost in territorial waters – all in a day's work for Bond, James Bond.

Genre

It is not always easy to find a single word to label a film. You may have found in the previous activity, that you could either explain a film with one word or that you had to use several words to explain the type of film exactly.

The word used to describe different types of films is 'genre'. It originally was used to define books into different categories: such as romance, gothic or comedy. When applied to films the word genre also means type or category.

Modern films often combine genres and create their own unique labels and categories. For example, *Mary Shelley's Frankenstein* (1994) combines horror, adventure romance, science fiction and period costume drama.

Mary Shelley wrote the original

Figure 2.11 *Mary Shelley's Frankenstein*: horror film

Source: © BFI

Frankenstein, a gothic novel in the nineteenth century. The word gothic is often used to describe a dark, melancholic mood and setting:

Figure 2.12 *Mary Shelley's Frankenstein*: period costume drama

Source: © BFI

gloomy castles, shadowy corridors and misty graveyards. The director Kenneth Branagh gave his *Frankenstein* the title *Mary Shelley's Frankenstein* because he wanted it to appear to be a faithful rendition of the original story.

The horror genre

The 1935 *Frankenstein* film directed by James Whale started the type of horror movies we now associate with Count Dracula, haunted castles, bats, vampires, possessed females and reconstructed humans. Although the Hammer horror films with Boris Karloff, Peter Cushing and Christopher Lee are old fashioned, the typical ingredients of a horror film today remain similar and are immediately understood by audiences. Even modern films such as the horror-comedy *Scream* series are packed with moments of suspense and terror, just as we saw in the Hammer films.

The violence usually contains some blood letting, an obsessive scientist or psychotic, an out of control monster and the slave or victim who is controlled or killed by the demonic character who craves power over other people. There is also often a monster who carries out the master's wishes, several exciting and scary chases, and the themes of good versus evil and natural versus supernatural.

Sub-categories

Today, there are sub-categories of horror films, such as 'slasher' movies. There are also more modern types of genre such as Kung Fu films. These were created mainly in Hong Kong, and use manga animation, which is Japanese.

FILM GENRE

Task 1

Study the titles of the films listed below and research their genres.

- **a** *King Kong* (1935)
- **b** *Stagecoach* (1939)
- **c** *Star Wars* (1977)
- **d** *Brassed Off* (1996)
- **e** *The Full Monty* (1997)
- **f** *Godzilla* (1998)

Task 2

List the genre of each film. (If you are unsure of any, try researching in a library or resource centre: Cinemania CD-ROM or a *Halliwell's Film and Video Guide* are useful resources).

Task 3

Now that you have studied the titles of the films, look at the film stills pictured overleaf. All of the films in the list were box office

LANGUAGES AND CATEGORIES

Figure 2.13 *King Kong*
Source: © BFI

Figure 2.14 *Stagecoach*
Source: © BFI

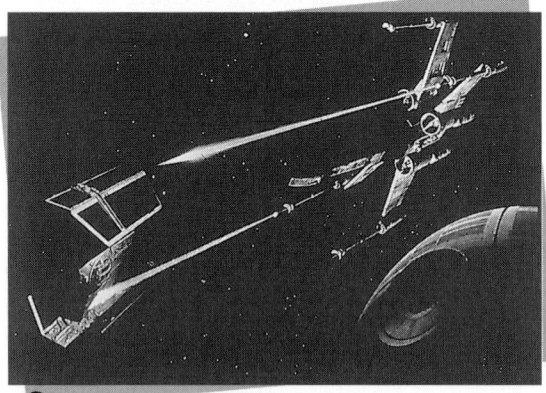

Figure 2.15 *Star Wars*
Source: © Ronald Grant

Figure 2.16 *Brassed Off*
Source: © Channel 4

Figure 2.17 *The Full Monty*
Source: © Kobal Collection

Figure 2.18 *Godzilla*
Source: © Kobal Collection

successes except *Brassed Off*. Make a list of reasons reasons why some films are more successful than others. For example, the film *Brassed Off* is set in Northern England and its theme is unemployment. However, *The Full Monty*, with the same area and general theme, raced away to become the biggest selling film in the UK ever, up to that date, in 1998.

Task 4

Is there a difference between 'good' and 'popular' films?

EARLY FILM NARRATIVE

In the 1890s Britain, along with France, Germany and America was in the forefront of experimenting with the new medium of film. UK film pioneers such as Willamson and Hepworth filmed in the open air due to lack of sufficient indoor light or artificial lighting. They used very simple camera shots and angles.

Audiences usually saw the films projected on a large scale onto walls in theatres, music halls or village halls and in disused shops or specially constructed mobile peep shows, where people would have to pay to view.

Music, live stage effects such as smoke and bombs, and actors would often accompany the moving images. These films tended to be simple drama and used real footage, for example of trains coming into stations, and basic special effects to create illusions. A narrator would often accompany the screening in person to explain what was in the film and make up for the pieces that needed linking together.

Films would sometimes be replayed several times. They were even played backwards for fun, as they were very short. Films aroused a great deal of curiosity in people and in the early years were included as part of the fun of a range of entertainments. As with video games and the Internet today, the potential of films was barely recognised at this time.

Rescue by Rover

Rescued by Rover (1905) by the British film maker, Cecil Hepworth, became a public favourite because it starred a dog as the main character. The dog finds a baby who has been stolen by a poor woman, and is seen running

Figure 2.19 *Rescued by Rover*: a popular film in 1905

Source: © BFI

LANGUAGES AND CATEGORIES

from scene to scene, linking the different scenes together. As a piece of fiction it is fairly slight, but for the time when it was made it is quite a long piece of film drama, at 6 minutes 25 seconds duration. Perhaps for the audience it held the same kind of curiosity as a piece of Jeremy Beadle's Home Video programmes, where members of the public send in videos of the absurd antics of their pets.

FILM STRUCTURE

There is a formula for writing a film script which Hollywood films tend to follow. One page of script equals one minute of film time, and most features run for 90 or 110 minutes. The basic structure of most films breaks down into three acts:

- The Set-Up (script pages 1–30).
- The Confrontation (pages 31–90).
- Finally, the Resolution (pages 91–110).

Between pages 10 and 15 there is a disruption which displaces the normal order of the drama. This event sets the hero or heroine on their quest. By the last act the quest must seem impossible, however, somehow in the final chase scenes (pages 80–110) the hero/heroine manages to find a way out by using force or logic. They succeed in their quest by defeating the enemy and winning the object of their heart's desires.

Where do stories for films come from?

Ideas for films come from a variety of sources. The main ones are:

- Adaptations from plays, short stories and novels (for example, *Great Expectations*, 1998).
- Fairy stories, myths and legends (for example, *Cinderella* or *Little Red Riding Hood*).
- Real life events (for example, *Malcolm X*, 1992, or *Ghandi*, 1982).
- Remakes of tv serials into films (for example, *Star Trek*, 1979, or *The Avengers*, 1998).
- Original screenplays. For example, *Spice World the Movie*. This was wholly created around the Spice Girls phenomena. The style of the film was similar in spirit to *Hard Day's Night* which followed the Beatles as a successful band constantly hopping from place to place besieged by their fans.

CREATING FILM IDEAS

Task 1: Adaptations

Following is an example of a colourful outline of a film, which would be included in a press pack:

Charles Dickens' classic nineteenth century novel, *Great Expectations*, is now adapted as a modern-day, sexy and provocative film set in New York and Florida. The story follows the journey of a young Finn Bell, whose father and mother died when he was very young. He is now an artist who hopes to make his way in the world, but this is dramatically changed by three separate strangers: a sinister convict named Lustig (Robert De Niro); the cool and aloof Estella (Gwyneth Paltrow); and the old, wealthy and definitely cracked Miss Nora Dinsmoor (Anne Bancroft).

Cinderella lives with her father and two ugly stepsisters. Her stepsisters hate her and make her do all the cleaning and cooking while they lie about having a good time. When an invitation arrives for the prince's ball, the two stepsisters insist that the invitation is for them only and that Cinderella has to stay behind to clean the house. And so Cinderella has to stay behind and do the cleaning, but she wishes that she too could go to the ball. Her fairy godmother appears and grants her wish with one stipulation – that she must leave the ball by midnight.

At the ball, Cinderella is a hit, especially with the Prince, who is entranced. However, Cinderella almost forgets her fairy godmother's warning and escapes just in the nick of time, accidentally leaving her tiny glass slipper behind.

The Prince combs the kingdom looking for the woman whose foot fits the shoe. Finally, after much searching and even interference from the ugly sisters, he discovers Cinderella. They get married and live happily ever after.

Write a short press statement for a remake of a classic story by William Shakespeare, Charles Dickens, George Eliot or Jane Austen. Explain the modern settings and the cast.

Task 2: original fairytales, myths and legends

a Turn the fairy story *Cinderella* into a modern film drama, using contemporary themes and settings. If you want to select and cast famous actors and actresses, try to ensure that they will suit the parts you give them.

b Read the story of *Cinderella* opposite and then write a new version. You should try to keep to writing 300 words maximum.

c Now plan the opening scenes of a film version of your story and how you will establish the characters and the settings. Write out in detail what you will see and what dialogue and soundtrack you will hear in the first three minutes of the film.

FILM LANGUAGE AND NARRATIVE STRUCTURE

Films communicate through a series of images and sound combined together. There are camera shots of different sizes and angles and framings. The camera shots are composed by a camera director and artificial lighting is used to emphasise dark and bright areas. The soundtrack consists of speech, sound effects, atmospheric sound and music.

| LANGUAGES AND CATEGORIES |

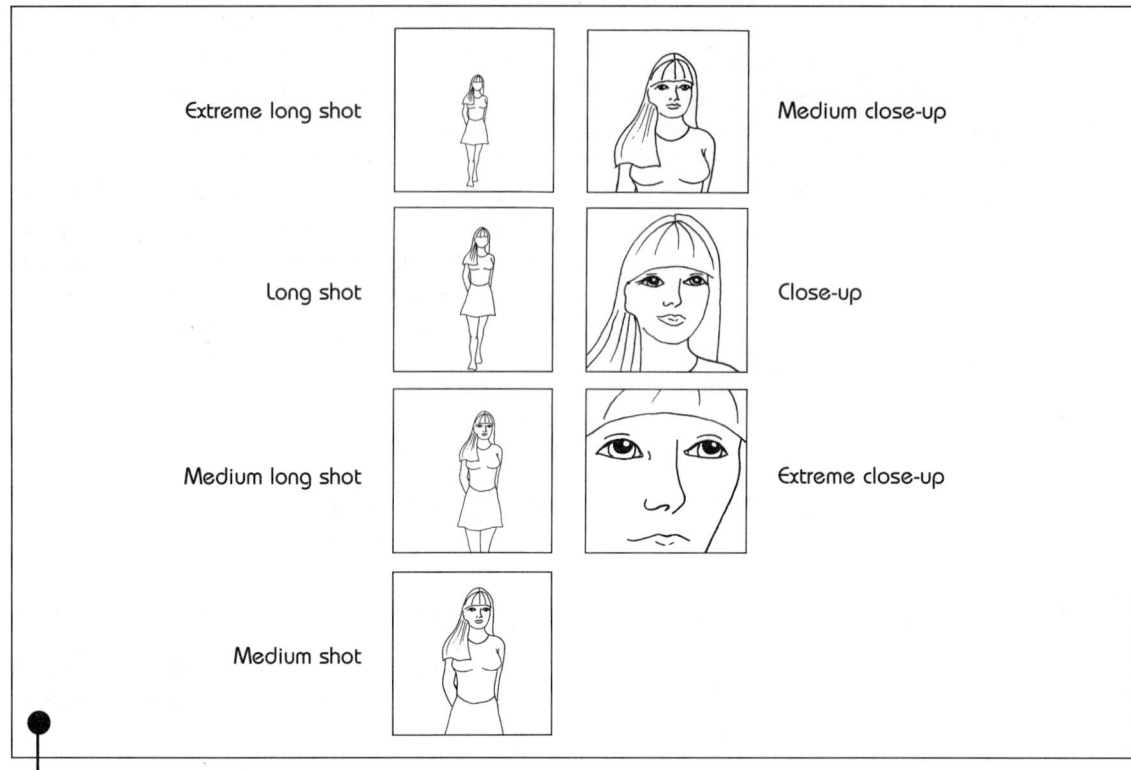

Figure 2.20 An illustration of various shot types
Source: © Advanced Level Media, Mark Joyce, Angela Bell and Danny Rivers, Hodder & Stoughton Educational, 1999

Narrative structure

The narrative structure of a mainstream film usually starts with normality (equilibrium) and then something happens to disrupt that normality (disequilibrium) then the rest of the film is about how normality is once more restored. Some film narratives develop the plot on many levels and can be quite complex.

A simple and often used narrative technique is to have parallel plots running simultaneously so that we see different events and characters occuring in what appears to be the same time. Films today use space and time in a unique way, in contrast to the early days of cinema when it was considered confusing to keep switching between locations and seeing the action unfold in two separate places.

One technique for achieving the parallel plot effect is by editing the film through cross-cutting. Cross-cutting is where the image is switched from one place to another, making the actions appear simultaneous. An example of parallel plot action is when two people talk together on the phone and there is some action going on in the background of each setting.

Editing

Editing techniques are used to place the narrative in sequence and also to shape time and space. Imagine how a boxing match has to be filmed and then edited to make it feel like we the audience are in the ring with the fighters, as well as including the spectators' point of view. A range of close-ups, medium and long shots are needed to achieve this effect.

Other editing techniques are as follows:

▶ Dissolves – to mix from one scene to another, for example to show that time has passed in the same place.

▶ Wipes – to make a narrative transition from one place to another, for example to move from a scene in London to one in New York.

▶ Cuts – a direct interruption and switch to another place or time, to keep both action and narrative moving quickly and sharply.

▶ Fades – emerging or disappearing scene creates the effect of slowly departing or arriving into the place or mood of the narrative.

STORYBOARD SIMULATION

Task 1

a Invent and present an opening sequence to the film you wrote out in Creating Film Ideas: Task 2 (see page 29).

b Produce a storyboard of between 6–10 frames of the opening scene(s) of your modern fairy story. Include the following information:

▶ Lighting
▶ Setting
▶ Soundtrack – music, atmosphere and special effects
▶ Speech
▶ Camera angle
▶ Camera shot size

Task 2

Write a critical commentary on your film of approximately 300 words. Discuss the following:

a Genre – what film is it like or unlike?
b Narrative style – is it a flashback, a drama or a mood you have created?
c Camera composition – is there any particular style or point of view conveyed in the way you have positioned your camera?
d Editing – are the shots dissolves or cuts?
e Signifiers – have you used signifiers, for example, urban concrete landscapes and smoke-filled bars for a gangster film?

Extension Tasks

1 Research a range of newspapers on the same day and collect examples of photographs, captions and headlines about the same event or persons, which can then be compared. Compare and contrast how much space is given to each item and why you think the amounts vary.

2 Produce a storyboard of a title sequence (10–15 frames) for a new crime genre police series. Give a critical account (250 words) of how the sequence would be typical or untypical of current police series.

3 Produce a radio advertisement for a film that is about to go its video rental release.

Include a short dramatic excerpt from the film, either by taping it or reconstructing the soundtrack. The film can be one that you have made up. Write a commentary (300 words) on the effects used and how the narrative for the advertisement was composed. State who the film is aimed at and where the trailer will be heard and seen.

Examination Skills

Textual Analysis

Students will need to produce a detailed textual analysis employing a range of technical and conceptual vocabulary and demonstrating a degree of knowledge of forms and conventions, including the importance of categorisation and genre.

All GCSE examination boards' coursework and examination components require a competent ability to analyse all media forms and their genres, for example, the Science Fiction Film genre or Films and their Promotion.

Students should have an idea of how to analyse the denotative level of meaning and the connotative level of meaning in still and moving image media. Ideology, explored in Chapter 4, Messages and Values (see page 60), is another aspect which should be tackled.

Knowledge and Understanding

Essays in OCR and Welsh boards' examinations demand knowledge and understanding of a range of media forms and conventions, in particular film, television news and drama, radio, newspaper, and magazines, and including advertisements and all promotional texts in any medium. Both technical (for example, close-ups) and conceptual (for example, narrative structure) vocabulary should be used to indicate a level of conversance with the medium in both its practical and theoretical aspects.

Practical Work

Students will need to show an understanding of some of the ways meaning is constructed through form. They will need to show competence in their skills of organisation, attention to detail and a polished finish in creative tasks. Critical commentaries will demonstrate the understanding of technical processes and problem solving. Theoretical writing should reflect a sound awareness of how the student product is similar to or different from mainstream and alternative forms and conventions.

3

Producers and audiences

WHO BY, FOR WHOM, FOR WHAT PURPOSE?

The aim of this chapter is to develop a knowledge and understanding of the producers of media products and the audiences who consume them. There are various types of producers who own, make, control and distribute media products – these range from the large global media organisation to the one person producer of fanzines. You will also learn about what influences the content and the output of media products and become familiar with different ideas about audiences, for example how they enjoy and gain information and consume mass and niche media products.

KW

Institution ▪ producer ▪ distributor ▪ broadcaster ▪ exhibitor ▪ point of interaction ▪ active and passive ▪ uses and gratifications

T W

Ident ▪ licence ▪ subscription ▪ watershed ▪ codes of practice ▪ TV schedules ▪ pre-echo ▪ hammocking ▪ inheritance ▪ identification

Discuss the following:

1. Discuss your opinion of the channels listed below:
   - BBC1
   - BBC2
   - ITV
   - Channel 4
   - Channel 5
   - Sky TV (any channel within Sky's package)
2. Discuss the types of programmes you associate with each of those channels.

Particular programmes can lead you to either like or dislike a channel. To give an example, many young people used to associate BBC2 with adult programmes such as the Open University, however, during the 1990s programme directors have tried to change this image to suit younger audience by broadcasting more comedy programmes. Would you consider BBC2 to be a fun channel to watch? Whatever your opinion may be, you will no doubt have been thinking about the various channels as organisations, as they all produce certain types of programmes which together give each its identity. These channels belong to media institutions.

MEDIA INSTITUTIONS

A major media institution is organised around the three different stages of making a product:

- pre-production
- production
- post-production

Pre-production for television documentaries involves people such as researchers and directors preparing the script and finding locations and people to interview. Production involves all the technical staff such as the lighting, camera and sound operators, the interviewer and the director, filming the product. The post-production stage brings in the editors of the images and the sound. One must not forget the publicists who inform the rest of the media about the programme, or the transmission engineers who ensure the programmes are broadcast to the homes of the viewers.

Finance and promotion

Large media institutions have the finance to pay for advertising and the promotion of their company's services and products. They either use their own publicity and marketing departments or employ independent companies to do this.

Idents

An example of promotion on television would be the floating red globe and the logo of the BBC which is shown frequently between programmes on BBC1. The image of the BBC as a global force in television and radio is created by the floating red balloon of the world floating over parts of the UK landscape.

This type of moving image sequence is known as an 'ident'. An ident is a short animation or piece of film which links programmes. It usually consists of a moving image which brands the channel's identity, and usually includes the institution's logo.

Study the channel logo for the ITV channel in your region. Discuss and make notes on the following:

a What does the image(s) and logo convey about the region and its identity?

b Do you think it is effective? If so, discuss why or why not?

1 Produce a rough sketch of a design for an ident, logo and soundtrack advertising a new cable community channel which is starting in your district. Write notes explaining the colours, images, graphic style, audience and institution.

- What is the institution?
- Invent a name for the logo.
- What type of audience is the ident aimed at?
- Will the image reflect who might watch it?
- Make notes on artwork and ideas.

Consider the target audience carefully before you start on the idea. If people in your audience are over 50 years of age then you will need to create something that is in a style which will appeal to them. If the audience is

under 30 years of age then the style of the graphics, music and images will be different again. If it is a family audience then there will have to be something for everyone.

2 Think of the main landmarks in your area (for example, a building, bridge or a park) and perhaps incorporate one or more of them into the overall image created in question 1. Consider the type of programmes you might have on the channel and whether you want to reflect their content in the ident. Will the letters of the logo move and change? The images and logo will only be on screen for a maximum of 10 seconds, therefore it will need to be simple and striking. What music will accompany the image?

Press release

Press releases are another way of raising the profile of a media institution in the public mind.

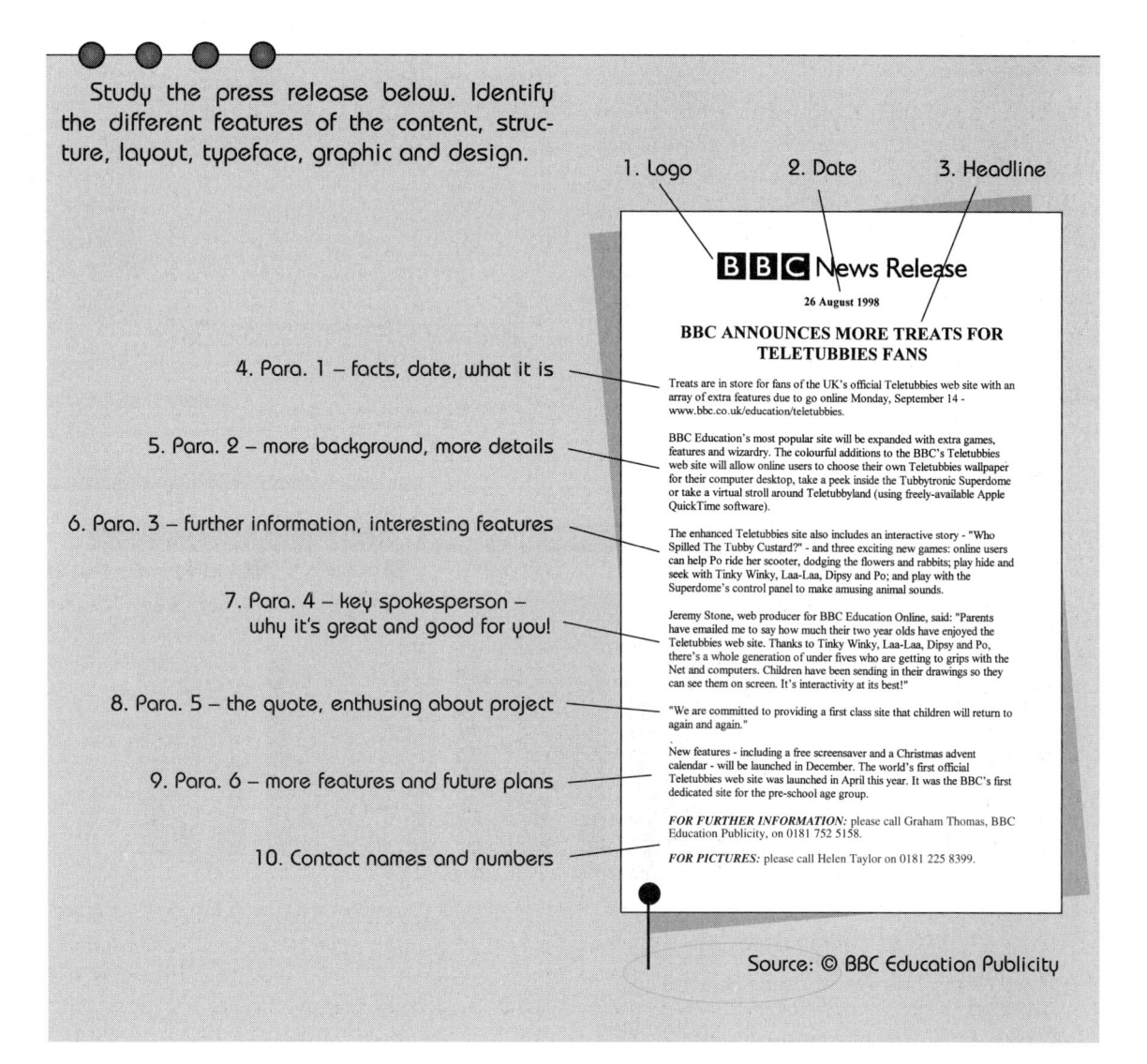

Study the press release below. Identify the different features of the content, structure, layout, typeface, graphic and design.

1. Logo
2. Date
3. Headline

4. Para. 1 – facts, date, what it is
5. Para. 2 – more background, more details
6. Para. 3 – further information, interesting features
7. Para. 4 – key spokesperson – why it's great and good for you!
8. Para. 5 – the quote, enthusing about project
9. Para. 6 – more features and future plans
10. Contact names and numbers

BBC News Release

26 August 1998

BBC ANNOUNCES MORE TREATS FOR TELETUBBIES FANS

Treats are in store for fans of the UK's official Teletubbies web site with an array of extra features due to go online Monday, September 14 - www.bbc.co.uk/education/teletubbies.

BBC Education's most popular site will be expanded with extra games, features and wizardry. The colourful additions to the BBC's Teletubbies web site will allow online users to choose their own Teletubbies wallpaper for their computer desktop, take a peek inside the Tubbytronic Superdome or take a virtual stroll around Teletubbyland (using freely-available Apple QuickTime software).

The enhanced Teletubbies site also includes an interactive story - "Who Spilled The Tubby Custard?" - and three exciting new games: online users can help Po ride her scooter, dodging the flowers and rabbits; play hide and seek with Tinky Winky, Laa-Laa, Dipsy and Po; and play with the Superdome's control panel to make amusing animal sounds.

Jeremy Stone, web producer for BBC Education Online, said: "Parents have emailed me to say how much their two year olds have enjoyed the Teletubbies web site. Thanks to Tinky Winky, Laa-Laa, Dipsy and Po, there's a whole generation of under fives who are getting to grips with the Net and computers. Children have been sending in their drawings so they can see them on screen. It's interactivity at its best!"

"We are committed to providing a first class site that children will return to again and again."

New features - including a free screensaver and a Christmas advent calendar - will be launched in December. The world's first official Teletubbies web site was launched in April this year. It was the BBC's first dedicated site for the pre-school age group.

FOR FURTHER INFORMATION: please call Graham Thomas, BBC Education Publicity, on 0181 752 5158.

FOR PICTURES: please call Helen Taylor on 0181 225 8399.

Source: © BBC Education Publicity

PRODUCERS AND AUDIENCES

THE TELEVISION SECTOR

The television sector in the UK is divided into two types of institutional operations: public and commercial.

Public

The BBC

The BBC is an organisation which has grown into a large institution over seventy years (since 1926) to provide programmes which 'educate, entertain and inform' the British public. The organisation is run by an executive committee of ten people and they form part of a management committee of a further five directors. Overseeing general policy is a body of 12 governors.

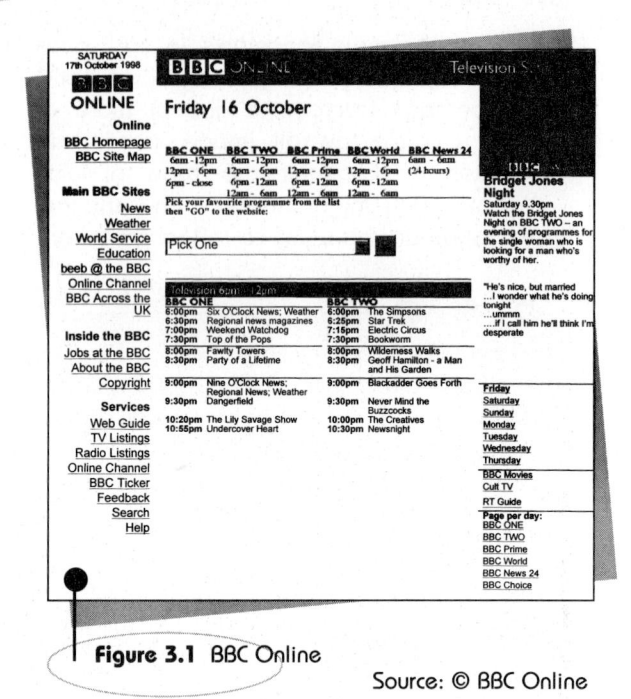

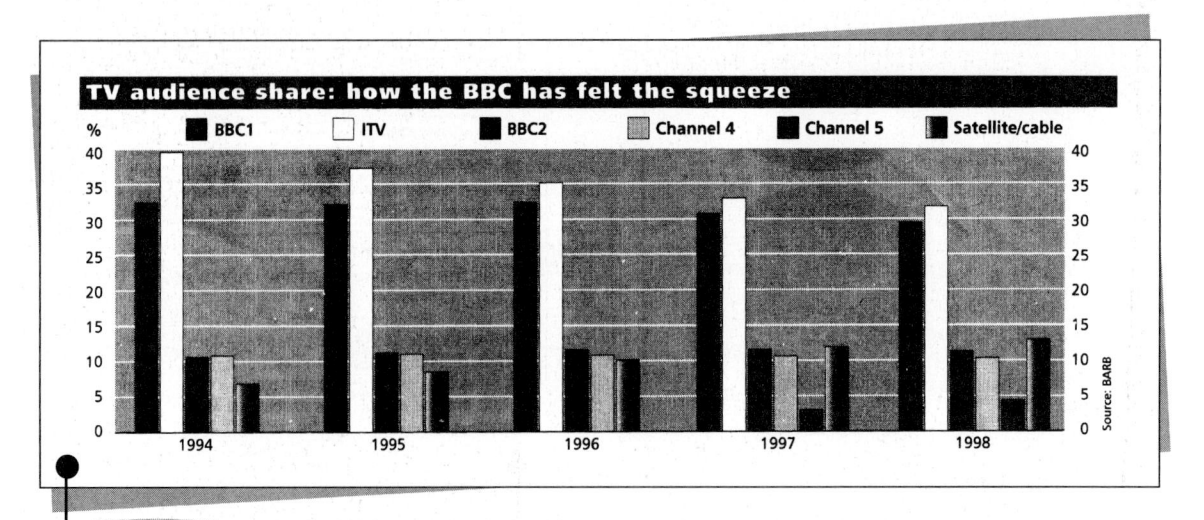

Figure 3.1 BBC Online

Source: © BBC Online

Figure 3.2 Broadcaster's Audience Research Board (BARB) provides statistical research on audience figures

Source: BARB

SkyDigital Channel Line-Up

Sports

Three sports channels offer around 20,000 hours of sports each year, up to a third of total programming is live:

SKY SPORTS 1
Sky Sports 1 - All the top sports, all the time.

SKY SPORTS 2
Sky Sports 2 - Football, cricket, rugby union, golf - live.

SKY SPORTS 3
Sky Sports 3 - The sports fan's bonus 12 hours a day.

Two new services launched on SkyDigital:

SKY SPORTS NEWS
Sky Sports News - Europe's first 24 hour sports news service.

MUTV
MUTV - The inside track on the UK's most glamourous football club.

General Entertainment

Sky One - No.1 for family entertainment.

Bravo - Lads' nights in with compelling movies, action, horror and drama series.

ChallengeTV - Quizzes and competitions. Participate in gameshow heaven.

Sci-Fi - Provoking the imagination with popular Sci-Fi films and action series.

Discovery Home & Leisure - Entertaining 'how to' television.

Granada Plus - Hit programmes from both sides of the Atlantic which have captured the heart of the nation.

Tara Television - All-round entertainment, from Ireland for Britain.

Paramount Comedy - Every night is comedy night.

UK Gold - The very best of British comedy and drama.

UK Gold Classics - Classic favourites to complement UK.Gold at the weekend.

QVC - Britain's first and only home shopping channel.

UK Play - A subversive, populist and witty mix of music and cult comedy coming soon.

Documentary

Discovery Channel - A unique blend of adventure, science, history and nature.

Discovery Channel +1 hour - Discovery Channel's high quality programmes shown one hour later.

Discovery Travel and Adventure - Thrilling explorations of the world.

Discovery Civilisations - The crucial events that shaped the past and present.

Discovery Sci-Trek - Innovative pacy programming showing how science is changing our lives.

Discovery Animal Planet - Devoted to animals, from whales and elephants to cats and dogs.

The History Channel - Intelligent and educational channel covering history from the ancient world to the 20th century.

The National Geographic Channel - Award winning factual, entertaining and enlightening documentaries.

UK Horizons - Outstanding factual entertainment from the BBC's archives.

[.tv] - All about IT for everyone: novices, netsurfers, games freaks and computer buffs.

Movies

Sky Premier - The must have movie channel with blockbusters, award winners and Barry Norman.

Sky Premier Widescreen - The ultimate in-home cinema experience shows two movies every evening.

Figure 3.3 Part of Sky's operation

Source: British Sky Broadcasting Group plc, Annual Report 1998

PRODUCERS AND AUDIENCES

The BBC's channels 1 and 2 do not have advertising between programmes and the organisation is financed largely by a licence fee raised from the public. The BBC has four other channels: BBC 24 hour News, BBC Choice, BBC Prime and BBC World.

The increased competition from ITV and the introduction of Sky TV and Channel 5 has led to a decline in the BBC's share of the total number of people who watch the television. The BBC aims to hold onto around 30% of the ratings despite all the new digital channels.

Commercial

Channels 3 (1955) and 4 (1982) belong to the Independent Television network (ITV) and represent the commercial sector. Their revenue comes largely through advertising. Channel 5 (1996) is the most recent channel and it too is dependent on advertising. All of these channels are also required by law to provide certain public services, broadcasting news, community issues, information and debate. As with the BBC, these channels are terrestrial channels – they can all be received by a standard aerial attached to a high point near the television set, which receive signals from land based transmitters.

Satellite and cable

The other commercial channels are satellite channels, such as Sky TV, and require special dishes to be received, as they transmit via satellites in space thousands of miles above the earth's surface. A cable line is sometimes also used to feed whole communities although these are linked centrally to a satellite reception point. These non-terrestrial channels do not have to provide any public service programmes as they were allowed freedom from the regulations as set out in the Broadcasting Act of 1990. They are financed by advertising and subscriptions. Subscription television means that the viewer pays a fixed amount of money for specific channels or even single programmes, such as important football matches.

MASS MEDIA CONTENT

Factors

There are seven major factors that affect the content of any mass media product, such as television. These are as follows:

1 Ownership and finance – who owns and pays for it?
2 Production – who actually makes the product?
3 Distribution – who delivers the product and in what form (e.g. broadcast, video rental or sale)?
4 Exhibition/Broadcast/Point of interaction – where is the product consumed, and technologically, how does the consumer receive it (e.g. cinema, television, newspaper)?
5 Controls – what rules and constraints exist concerning suitability for public consumption, and who decides on these controls?
6 Promotion and marketing – what methods are used to inform audiences about the content of the product and how to buy it? Who does the promotion and the marketing?
7 Audiences – how socially, personally, and technologically do audiences use, select, enjoy or reject the products they receive, purchase or consume?

GCSE MEDIA STUDIES

Study the video cover of the Teletubbies below. Note down your answers to the questions posed in factors one to five listed previously on page 38. Then compare your answers to the sections on Mass Media Content.

Source: © Ragdoll/BBC.

Ownership

If you study the cover of a Teletubbies video you can see that the BBC own the video. The BBC letters are designed into a logo and it is positioned on the top right of the front page. The BBC is clearly associated with the Teletubbies programme which is broadcast on the terrestrial UK television channel BBC2. The BBC paid for its production and distribution.

Production

If you look closely on the back page of the video you will find that the BBC did not actually make the programme. It was made by an **independent** company called Ragdoll, for the BBC. Ragdoll is a company that specialises in children's television programmes. Ragdoll have been very successful with Teletubbies, which now has worldwide popularity and high commercial profits.

Distribution

One commercial section of the BBC, which sells and distributes products is BBC Worldwide Limited. BBC Worldwide licenses the video from Ragdoll, who then earn further money from the sales.

Exhibition/Broadcast/Point of interaction

Teletubbies programmes are initially broadcast on air twice a day, every weekday morning on BBC2. Once they have been broadcast they are then duplicated to be sold in the form of a video. Teletubbies videos can be bought in a range of shops, including supermarkets and newspaper retailers.

Controls

On the back of the video cover, there is a 'Uc' certificate issued by the British Board of Film Classification (BBFC), who decided that the video is suitable particularly for young children. The spine of the Teletubbies video cover also states that it is a 'Children's Video', so there is a clear message that this is for young children.

Internal controls

No television programme maker can ignore certain rules which exist both within the BBC and outside it. Within the BBC there is a code of practice called *Producer's Guidelines (1996)*. These guidelines cover such areas as the depiction of violence, sex or bad language on television and radio.

Study any video (film/TV) cover. Discuss and make notes in answer to the following:

1. Note down who made the film/programme and who distributed it.
2. Are they the same company or different ones?
3. Find out what you can about the company/companies (try the local library or resource centre or the Internet). What else do they make or sell? For example, Blockbuster video hire shops, MTV and Paramount Film Studios and Nickleodeon are all owned by Viacom, who are also well-known as film distributors. Viacom is in fact part of a much larger company owned by an American family, Redstone, whose US operation is called National Amusements.

For information, institutions like the BBC have many departments dedicated to the production of television. These cover television, radio and a range of genres such as news, comedy and sport. There are also several departments which deal with matters such as finance, copyright, education, digital developments and administration.

The Watershed

There is a period of time called the 'Watershed', which is 9pm. All programme makers must ensure that no bad language, graphic sex or violence is contained in a programme broadcast before this time. The period of time leading up to 8.30pm–9pm is considered to be family viewing time.

> 'The BBC has a well-established policy of making 9pm the pivotal point of the evening's television, a Watershed before which, except in exceptional circumstances, all programmes on our domestic channels should be suitable for a general audience including children. The earlier in the evening a programme is placed, the more suitable it is likely to be for children to watch on their own. However, the BBC expects parents to share the responsibility for assessing whether or not individual programmes should be seen by younger viewers.'
>
> Source: BBC Producer's Guidelines, BBC, 1996

Taste and decency

The following quote is taken from the *BBC Producer's Guidelines (1996)*.

> The BBC is required in the agreement associated with its Charter not to broadcast programmes which 'include anything which offends against good taste or decency or is likely to encourage or incite to crime or lead to disorder, or be offensive to public feeling'. The BBC seeks to apply this requirement to all its broadcasting, whether to a domestic or international audience.
>
> Taste and decency raise sensitive and complex issues of programme policy for the BBC. We broadcast to a much more fragmented society than in the past; one that has divided views on what constitutes good taste. People of different ages and convictions may have sharply differing expectations. Research suggests that while people have become more relaxed in recent years about the portrayal of sex and sexual humour they remain concerned about the depiction of violence.
>
> BBC Producer's Guidelines, BBC, 1996

Audience loyalty

Television schedules are printed in the newspapers every day. Creating a running order of the programmes is a fine art which programme directors organise. Many thousand of pounds can be gained by the channel if advertisers see that their product will be watched by their audiences. For the BBC, the importance of audience figures lies in justifying the licence fee to the taxpayer.

Scheduling techniques

In television, once the viewer has sat down and decided to watch a programme there are three techniques which schedulers use to keep audiences loyal to their channel:

1. **Hammocking** is when a less interesting programme is placed between two more interesting programmes.
2. **Inheritance** is where a viewer will stay with the same channel because they simply do not want to change to another channel.
3. **Pre-echo** is where viewers switch on early for their favourite programme, so they end up viewing a preceding programme which they might not have otherwise have watched.

PROGRAMMING BODIES AND AGENCIES

Further controls on television and radio programme makers come from government bodies, agencies and pressure groups, social opinion and commercial factors. These include:

- **ITC** – Independent Television Commission
- **BSC** – The Broadcasting Standards Commission
- **Oftel** – The Office of Telecommunications
- **ASA** – The Advertising Standards Authority
- **VLV** – Voice of the Listener and Viewer
- **IRA** – Independent Radio Authority

Independent Television Commission (ITC)

The ITC is responsible for licensing and regulating Channels 3, 4, and 5, public teletext, cable and satellite services. In the year 2002 all the regional ITV licences come up for renewal. Each company must show that it has fulfilled certain quality criteria if they are to be renewed over others who want to buy the right to broadcast in that area.

Current licence holders may be asked if they have produced enough local news or information services to the community.

For example, in 1998, there were complaints about a documentary on drugs smuggling called Connections, produced by ITV's Central and Carlton companies. The documentary makers who produced the programme paid people to pretend they were drug smugglers. This sort of practice is considered to be unfair and cheating the public. The ITC made the companies issue an apology in the papers and on the television, and also fined them £2 million.

The Broadcasting Standards Commission (BSC)

The BSC was set up in 1996 to produce guidelines which all programme makers must follow. These are called 'codes of practice'. If a viewer complains, the BSC has to decide if the producer has broken a code of practice.

OFTEL

The Office of Telecommunications is in charge of monitoring telecommunications which include telephone lines, cable and satellite. Now that the Internet has become more widely used, OFTEL's role in television and Internet communication covers more than just the technical and financial markets.

As more people are linking the use of their telephone line to their computers and televisions, there are new controls and freedoms for OFTEL to monitor. Telephone lines are capable of transmitting signals cheaply which can then be converted back into images and sounds, and the use of this form of communication is used by many media institutions to relay their products and services (for example, cable TV, online television and image, or sounds and text such as cartoons and music).

The future of the control of the Internet and the role of the media institutions using these forms of networking is monitored by OFTEL. OFTEL is a government body whose aim is to decide whether the companies who control the lines are operating fairly between each other and in the best interests of the public.

Advertising Standards Authority (ASA)

The ASA regulate the advertising industry. If any advertisement causes offence and there is a complaint then an investigation is made by ASA. For example, Bennetton was reputed to have upset many people because it used a man dying of AIDS to advertise its clothes. Tango, a fizzy orange drink, advertised people surprising other people and ambushing them with a can of drink, with a voice saying, 'Have you been Tangoed?'. This was subsequently deemed too dangerous by the ASA in case other people imitated it. The authority has a right to make the advertiser withdraw the advertisement.

Independent Radio Authority

The Independent Radio Authority monitors the licences for radio stations and ensures that quality criteria are maintained.

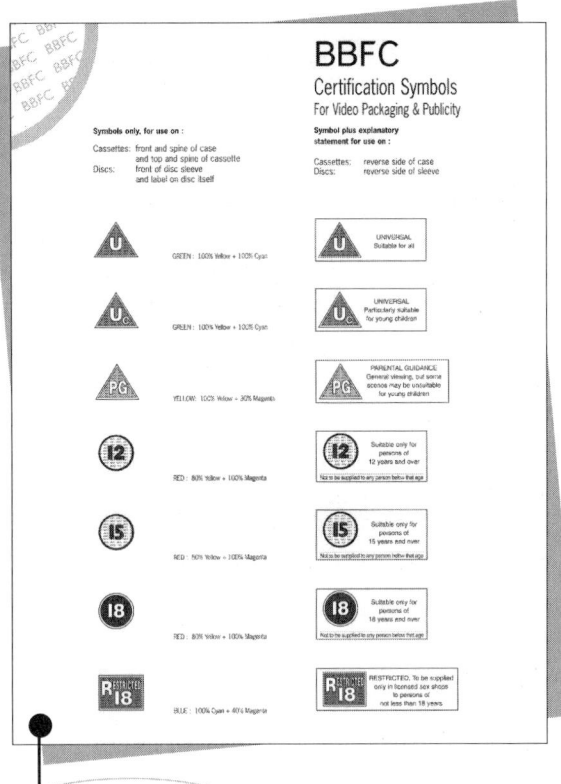

Figure 3.4 BBFC Classification Symbols
Source: © BBFC

Voice of Listener and Viewer (VLV)

VLV is a lobby organisation of unpaid enthusiasts who believe in the public's interest being served by the television and radio media. They produce small leaflets and write to the BBC when it is appropriate about programme content and the running of the institution.

British Board of Film Classification (BBFC)

Other media industries pay their own governing bodies to create guidelines for controlling the content. In the film industry, for example, each distributor pays the BBFC to certificate their films for showing in cinemas, or video rental and hire.

Press Complaints Commission

The Press Complaints Commission was set up to investigate the complaints made about newspapers who may harass or go into people's private affairs, intrusively. In 1998, the 14 year old daughter of a woman who had served a prison sentence discovered through the newspapers that her mother was Mary Bell. Mary Bell had murdered a child many years previously. The daughter's mother had been paid by a writer to sell her story, which was then serialised in *The Times*. When the press found out about the payment the mother and daughter were tracked down.

In theory, newspapers are not supposed to intrude and expose children under sixteen years of age to the spotlight of the media. In the latter case a press 'pack' of hounds hot on the chase of a story meant that the PCC guidelines were ignored. Furthermore, unless someone is prepared to pay for the legal pursuit of the case, then the PCC is limited in how it can act. The PCC did however comment on the case, and they declared that, though regrettable, the press were not at fault for allowing the child to be caught up in the media coverage.

British Videogram Association

The British Videogram Association oversees the certification of the videos for hire and sale, in association with the BBFC in its capacity as the classifier of the certificate.

> **Discuss the following scenario:**
>
> A councillor is rumoured to have helped to sell off council property to his friends, in exchange for money. Is it fair that the press should be allowed to interview him against his will in the following places?
> 1. In an NHS hospital.
> 2. Outside a school gate, where he picks up his children.
> 3. In a restaurant or café.
> 4. On a walking holiday.

MEDIA PRODUCTS

Mass Media

Mass media products are intended for a large population and can be shared as a film in a cinema or in the home on the video.

Many media products are designed for mass consumption across all the social groups which already exist in society. A mass media product is designed to appeal to a wide range of people spanning age, gender, class, race, etc. A mass market does tend to be family oriented.

Niche media

Niche media products are targeted at an existing group, for example, by age, gender, race or lifestyle. A niche product is aimed at a specific interest or social group, for example, a motorbike magazine is aimed at motorbike enthusiasts. Another example is business television news which is aimed at the financial market.

Alternative media products

Some media products are made for non-commercial reasons. These can be intended for the public benefit, for alternative cultures such as 'zines or take the form of music loaded onto the Internet for free use. These products are created by enthusiasts not institutions, and they are interested in the product for its content, more than for its ability to sell. Their distribution is very small and often limited.

AUDIENCES

The word 'audience' carries with it the picture of a group of people assembled together in a space like a cinema or theatre to listen or watch a performer on stage. With modern media this idea is no longer a fixed one.

Members of an audience in a theatre or cinema come into the hall, sit down and laugh, cry or are silent. It is essentially a captive audience – all share the same moments of drama on the stage or screen in front of them. In the case of modern media (television, cinema, videos and video hire, magazines, newspapers, Internet on-line, CD ROMs) there are now hundreds of public places where we can see or hear media products. We can also watch television or read a magazine or listen to a walkman on our own due to technological advances.

An 'audience' ranges from the individual watching a video in the bedroom, to the passer-by seeing an advertisement on the side of the bus, to the group watching a large screen projection of a music video in a club, to the student with a walkman secretly listening to a favourite piece of music in the classroom.

EastEnders and *Coronation Street* regularly reach over 17 million people from all walks of life but there are also products which are targeted at specific audiences by age, class, gender or racial groups. Most media products can be seen or bought in many different venues, for example the *TV Times*. Magazines, comics and male and female interest magazines may be aimed at small sectors of the market. For example, *Minx* is a magazine targeted at women aged 21–23 yrs, who are either in further education or employment.

PRODUCERS AND AUDIENCES

Compare these *Minx* and '*B*' profiles, as printed in the advertiser's handbook BRAD. Discuss the following:

1 What are the target ages of each magazine?
2 What lifestyle does each group have?

minx

Launched last September by Emap Elan, **minx** is a monthly magazine aimed at a slightly older audience than sister title more! **minx** readers are intelligent, ABC1 single women between the ages of 18 and 28, either in further education or full time employment - the core readership will be 21-23.
minx readers live life to the full and want a magazine which reflects their optimistic outlook on life. Research suggests that this attitude is being catered for - with the tagline "For girls with a Lust for Life" and articles on celebrities, travel, nights out, clubs and the latest venues, food, entertainment and relationships.
Given the glossy production values and a monthly frequency, **minx** aims to attract more! readers as they grow older. The preview issue had a total print run of 650 thousand, 50 thousand of which were included in university Fresher welcome packs. Priced at £1.95 **minx** is now firmly placed in a previously unfilled gap in the women's monthly magazine market.

Minx

B

From the publishers of the successful teen magazine Sugar, Attic Futura launched **B** in the first week of May. Aimed perhaps at the grown up Sugar reader, **B** is also published monthly but targeted towards a slightly older audience comprising of young women aged 16 to 24, a similar audience to the Emap Elan weekly publication More!
With the subtitle 'It's Absolutely You' **B** magazine features entertainment, real life and celebrity features, questions and answers, relationships, clubbing information, fashion, beauty and travel. In essence **B** magazine aims to cover 'everything a young woman looks for in a magazine'. Generally, the average reader will either be in further education or starting her first job, but all will have a zest for life and enjoy their independence, believing these are the best years of their lives.
B is published on the first Wednesday of every month and has a cover price of £1.80.

B

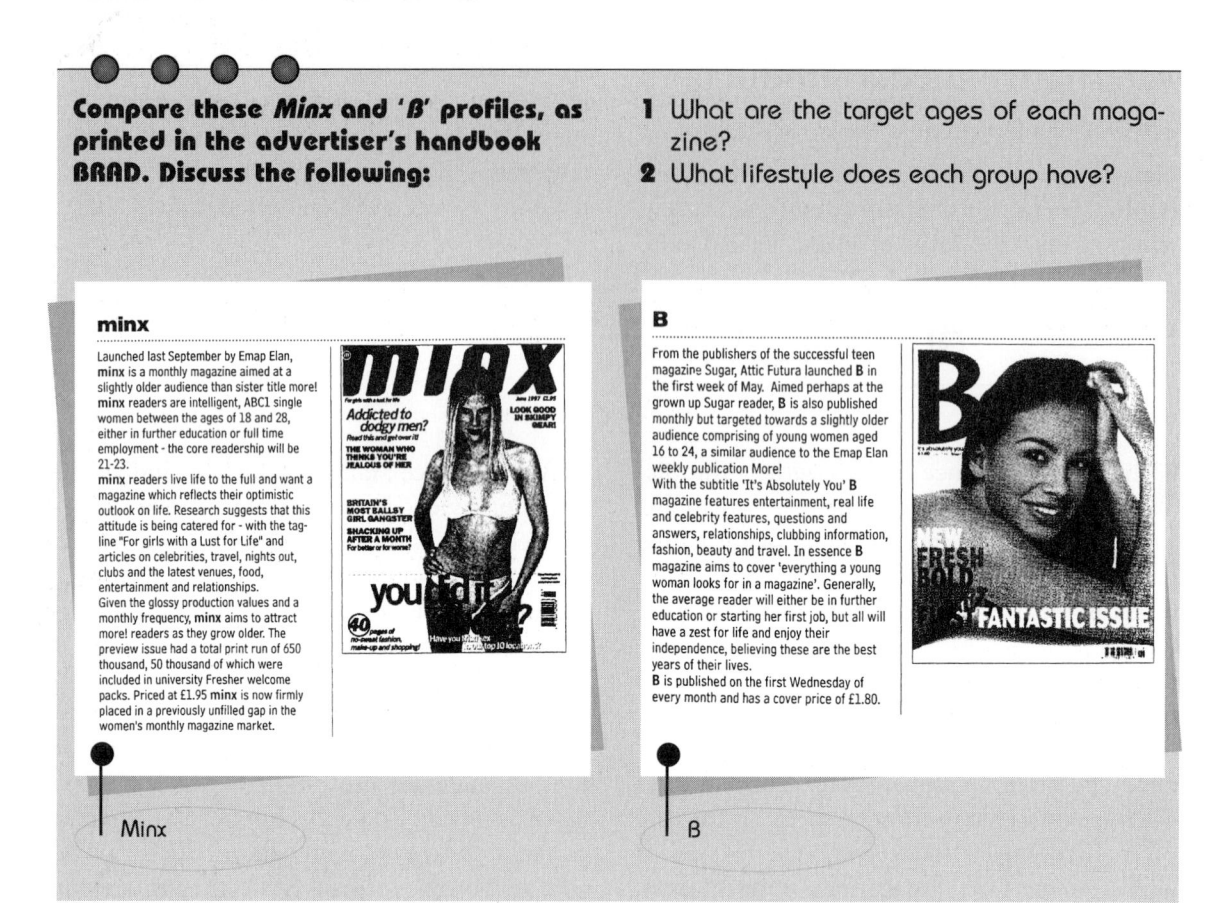

Other media products can be defined as alternative, such as independent music labels which can only be found in specialist shops, sold by mail order, on the Internet or in street markets. They do not use the conventional methods of promotion adopted by other media, such as posters or magazine advertisements. These products exist through word of mouth and playing concerts. Alternative products also serve a small section of the total market, a niche (see page 44).

Definitions

The definition of an audience depends on who defines it.

- Industry: circulation and readership figures and target readership.
- Industry: constructed audience.
- Government: demographics.
- Advertisers: segmentations (lifestyle and aspirations).
- Social scientists: values.
- Social scientists: passive/active.
- Social scientists: identity.

Circulation and readership

What is most important to owners and producers of media products is whether they sell or not. The audience is first and foremost a buyer and a consumer and the financial wellbeing of

National newspaper circulation

	Dec 1998	Nov 1998	% change	Jul 98–Dec 98	Jul 97–Dec 97	% change
Dailies						
Sun	3,537,760	3,658,704	-3.31	3,675,286	3,779,605	-2.76
The Mirror	2,214,981	2,322,684	-4.64	2,338,049	2,324,109	0.60
Daily Record	662,999	672,737	-1.45	676,411	685,039	-1.26
Daily Star	618,534	632,454	-2.20	646,314	712,182	-9.25
Daily Mail	2,318,287	2,310,025	0.36	2,350,364	2,237,949	5.02
The Express	1,068,844	1,097,895	-2.65	1,118,700	1,202,291	-6.95
Daily Telegraph	1,039,840	1,041,447	-0.15	1,054,418	1,098,440	-4.01
Guardian	390,514	394,655	-1.05	391,919	403,999	-2.99
Times	723,094	748,197	-3.36	751,862	792,151	-5.09
Independent	218,389	221,229	-1.28	221,398	260,223	-14.92
The Scotsman	77,643	80,221	-3.21	79,686	n/a	
Financial Times	385,574	369,808	4.26	366,969	328,793	11.61
Sundays						
News of the World	4,062,561	4,196,149	-3.18	4,225,599	4,425,708	-4.52
Sunday Mirror	1,870,043	2,015,652	-7.22	1,988,579	2,276,089	-12.63
People	1,670,347	1,659,089	0.68	1,717,277	1,895,121	-9.38
Mail on Sunday	2,281,506	2,321,976	-1.74	2,312,329	2,219,430	4.19
Express on Sunday	973,846	1,003,064	-2.91	1,027,049	1,140,328	-9.93
Sunday Times	1,305,589	1,364,276	-4.30	1,349,925	1,343,324	0.49
Sunday Telegraph	809,923	816,604	-0.82	829,032	887,204	-6.56
Scotland on Sunday	122,404	126,800	-3.47	125,124	n/a	
Sunday Business	47,632	50,697	-6.05	n/a	n/a	
Observer	398,778	395,205	0.90	398,983	439,573	-9.23
Independent on Sunday	249,846	255,196	-2.10	253,907	287,543	-11.70

Figure 3.5 National Newspaper Circulation
Source: ABC

most newspapers and magazines depends on how many people read the product.

Study the list of newspapers in Figure 3.5.
1 Which daily newspaper has done the best since November 1998?
2 Which newspaper (daily or Sunday) has the sold the most newspapers?
3 Which newspapers have sold the least copies?

BRAD

The *British Rates and Data Handbook* (BRAD) is used by advertisers to decide which journals and magazines to put their advertisers in. Circulation figures published in *BRAD* show how many readers buy a particular magazine, and the readership figure gives an estimate of how many people read it. The reason for the extra number for readership is that if a magazine is placed in a household, dentist or waiting room, more people will read it. The target readership in the case of a magazine like *Just Seventeen* is 'girls between the ages 11–19 who are fashion conscious, sussed in outlook and style leaders within their peer groups'. This type of definition of target readership is created by the magazine to encourage advertisers to place their advertisements in it.

Constructed audience

In order to make an audience feel part of a like-minded community a magazine may adopt a style of clothing and make-up, or use an advertisement which creates a particular image for its readers. For example, the 'Rachel haircut' in the American situation comedy *Friends* programme became popular for a time. Subsequently, many magazines published images of women wearing the 'Rachel' hairstyle. Readers then identified with a hairstyle they already had themselves or that they recognised as being fashionable.

Advertisers on television then started to use the 'Rachel' hairstyle to promote their product. Again, by using familiar images which audiences already identify with the individual is in turn constructed by the fashionable images of the moment. The producers can therefore be said not only to have targeted their audience but also to have actively constructed them.

DEFINING AUDIENCES

Demographics

The Government has defined the population into what are commonly known as demographic groups.

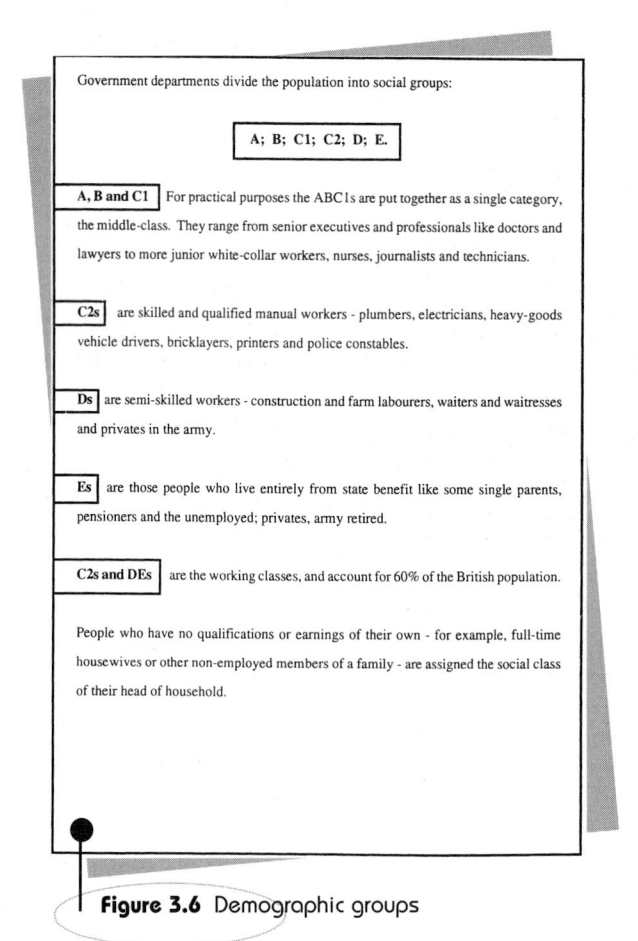

Government departments divide the population into social groups:

A; B; C1; C2; D; E.

A, B and C1 For practical purposes the ABC1s are put together as a single category, the middle-class. They range from senior executives and professionals like doctors and lawyers to more junior white-collar workers, nurses, journalists and technicians.

C2s are skilled and qualified manual workers - plumbers, electricians, heavy-goods vehicle drivers, bricklayers, printers and police constables.

Ds are semi-skilled workers - construction and farm labourers, waiters and waitresses and privates in the army.

Es are those people who live entirely from state benefit like some single parents, pensioners and the unemployed; privates, army retired.

C2s and DEs are the working classes, and account for 60% of the British population.

People who have no qualifications or earnings of their own - for example, full-time housewives or other non-employed members of a family - are assigned the social class of their head of household.

Figure 3.6 Demographic groups

The definitions in Figure 3.6 are used to define what type of tax or social benefit people are entitled to. Advertisers and media producers also look at the demographics published in *BRAD*, for their own research, to define what types of people might buy their product.

From the article below study how new ideas for labelling people are invented all the time.
Do you think you fit into any of the categories mentioned?

So, are you a Mouse Potato or a Cybersnob?

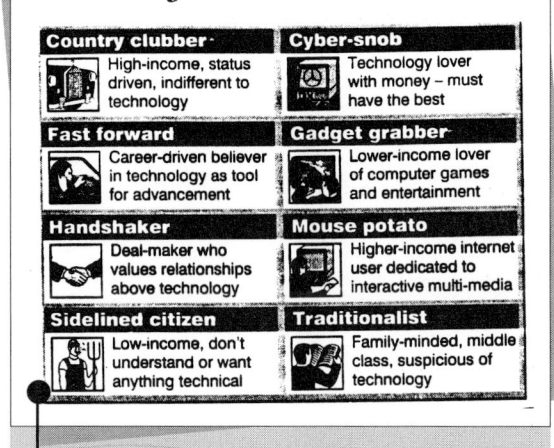

Country clubber - High-income, status driven, indifferent to technology

Cyber-snob - Technology lover with money – must have the best

Fast forward - Career-driven believer in technology as tool for advancement

Gadget grabber - Lower-income lover of computer games and entertainment

Handshaker - Deal-maker who values relationships above technology

Mouse potato - Higher-income internet user dedicated to interactive multi-media

Sidelined citizen - Low-income, don't understand or want anything technical

Traditionalist - Family-minded, middle class, suspicious of technology

New definitions: fact or fiction?
Source: © *Independent on Sunday*, 2 February 1997

Segmentation

Advertisers use their own categories of people in addition to the categories of demographic groups. These groupings can vary enormously but one model is the one which divides people into seven segments: the succeeder, aspirers, carers, achievers, radicals, traditionals and the underachiever. These descriptions are thought to provide information about a person's attitudes and psychological character. By splitting people into these groups advertisers attempt to estimate whether their audiences are likely to spend money on their products. For example, if your family spends a great deal on holidays every year it will be worth a company trying to target you when selling holidays. They can do this by researching which type of magazine you are likely to buy.

Social values

Another way of defining the audience has come from social scientists who want to provide information to their clients. These are usually commercial clients who want to target their media entertainment products to sell. In addition to class labels, there are also people's attitudes to consider. Possible attitudes include:

▶ Traditionalist – keep things the way they are.
▶ Materialist – have something now; pay later.
▶ Hedonist – to play now.
▶ Post materialist – to be something later.
▶ Post modernist – to have, to be, and to play.

Active or passive audiences

The traditional view of the audience is one of the 'couch potato', where television supposedly switches off the brain and ruins the art of conversation. Most recent studies have shown that viewers can be described as active in their engagement with television. Many people use the remote control and actively search out the channels they want to watch. People do not, as a rule, spend an evening sat in front of the television; they partake in other activities such as games and conversation. For many people having conversations about television is a very important part of their lives. Discussing ideas or keeping up-to-date on the latest soap opera constitutes a form of activity.

Uses and gratifications

One existing media theory concerns how people use the media for different reasons:

- As a diversion from everyday life.
- To gain information about the outside world.
- To compare themselves with other people.
- Companionship.

If you look back at your answers to the questionnaire in the introduction you will see how much and what media you particularly liked. Audiences use the media for different purposes; to satisfy needs and wants. Sometimes watching television can serve as an escape from thinking about work. Occasionally watching television is about informing oneself about ideas and facts on a particular subject.

Audience identity

Another way of categorising audiences is by grouping according to the following criteria:

- Gender
- Age
- Race
- Family
- Class

A further set of categories are:

- Education
- Religion
- Region
- Political belief
- Urban or rural background

Amongst academics the idea exists that audiences have varying responses to what they watch. They either accept, negotiate, oppose or reject messages and values which are conveyed to them by television programmes. For example, if the programme is racist or sexist the viewer may dislike it and thus reject it.

GCSE MEDIA STUDIES

Extension Tasks

1 Examination Specimen Question Topics (you should check to see what current topics are).

These tasks are not actual previous examination questions. The questions are the sole work of the author and are devised to match the style, mark allocation and format of the relevant questions from AQA and OCR. They are designed for examination practice. The Tasks are designed to follow the examination paper timings and mark allocations. It is essential that candidates check the specified topics set for the year of their examination, by the examination board. For previous examination questions, contact the exam board direct.

OCR (MEG). Paper 1: Section 2 (1hr): Explain with reference to at least two soap operas their attraction for audiences.
(25 marks)

2 Specimen question for AQA (SEG). Paper 2 controlled test (4 hrs).

a What are the typical features of soap operas? Discuss content and structure, characters and themes.

b Why do you think soaps appeal to large audiences?
(40 marks)

3 Study the following:

a A job advertisement for a publicist for *EastEnders*.

BBC Broadcast

Publicist - EastEnders

Marketing & Communications

Salary c.£24,000. Elstree, Herts.

EastEnders is television's number one drama serial. Do you have the experience and ability to implement a publicity strategy to make sure it stays that way? BBC Drama Publicity is seeking a second energetic, motivated and highly creative Publicist to promote the BAFTA-award-winning EastEnders to the print, broadcast and online media in a highly competitive market place. Probably with a journalistic background or three years' publicity experience, you will need strong media contacts and proven success in news management. You will be able to demonstrate creativity, determination, discretion, tact and good organisational skills, including the ability to handle conflicting priorities and a strong sense of humour! This is no nine-to-five job, but is a demanding and rewarding post which puts you in the front-line of programme publicity. You should also possess the ability to deal swiftly and sensitively with difficult issues and to build solid relationships with 40 regular artists, production teams and senior programme executives.
(Ref. 30429/G)

---

b A job advertisement for a picture editor for *LOOKS*.

---

emap élan publishes
LOOKS
ELLE
Red
New Woman
ELLE Decoration
J17
more!
minx
Bliss
Mother & Baby
Pregnancy & Birth
Parents
Period Living
Slimming
Here's Health
Top Santé

emap élan is committed to developing people. We are part of emap plc and offer opportunities for career development across consumer magazines, radio, TV and business communications in the UK and abroad.

LOOKS PICTURE EDITOR

Want to join the fastest-growing magazine in the young women's market?

We need an ace picture editor who can lay their hands on the most glamorous photos at the most reasonable prices! This is a fantastic, high-profile job on the glossiest, coolest celebrity style mag on the planet. Here's the deal — you'll have:

- At least 2 years' experience in the Picture Dept of a newspaper or magazine (staff or freelance)
- The gift of the gab to get LOOKS the best photos without blowing the budget
- The know-how to source specific celeb pix (eg Cameron in *that* Prada coat holding *that* box bag)
- Tons of agency & photographer contacts
- Enough charm to sweet-talk the scariest American agents... and get what you want
- Great organisational skills (you *never* lose trannies)
- A flexible attitude and a rather loud voice

Sounds like you? Send your CV plus your opinion of the photos in the current issue to: Eleni Kyriacou, Editor, LOOKS, Endeavour House, 189 Shaftesbury Ave, London WC2H 3JG. Or e-mail eleni.kyriacou@ecm.emap.com Closing Date: Monday 13th January. All applications are treated in the strictest confidence.

emap élan
A fresh approach to women's magazines

---

c Identify what knowledge and skills are sought from applicants for each of the two job advertisements **a** and **b**.
(10 marks)

4 A soap opera character is going to be written out (killed off) by the producers of one of the following programmes: *Emmerdale Farm*, *Coronation Street*, *Home and Away*, *Family Affair*, *EastEnders*, *Brookside*, *Hollyoaks*, *Heartbreak High*. You are responsible for marketing and publicity relations with the press, television and radio, and for the online media campaign. **Select** one of the soaps listed.

Either

Invent and design a front page of a listings magazine like the *Radio Times* or *TV Times*, (one side of A4) announcing the imminent departure of the soap character, this week.

(35 marks)

PRODUCERS AND AUDIENCES

Or

Produce a ten image storyboard of a TV advertisement, announcing the departure of a soap character.

(35 marks)

5 Write a 100 word memo to the Executive Producer of your soap explaining:

▶ Which media you are going to use for your campaign and why.

▶ What your main images mean.
▶ The purpose behind any wording or slogans you have used.
▶ Who and what you are going to promote? Where and for how long, and how much are you going to spend?

(15 marks)

Examination Skills

Knowledge and Understanding

Knowledge of press releases and their format, structure and style are essential to answer these questions. A knowledge of soap forms and conventions is also important: how do characters get introduced into a series and how do others get phased out? What types of media publicity would be appropriate to let the public know what is going to happen? The composition of the press release should follow the structure of the example given.

A good analysis of the two job advertisements in Question 3 will demonstrate an awareness of certain skills of promoting and organising under pressure and with other people. The memo in Question 5 should contain understanding of scheduling, cross media publicity and the importance of simple and perhaps controversial means of attracting publicity, for example the manner of their departure or death.

Textual Analysis

Examiners want to see evidence in Question 2 of knowledge of storylines and the way soap narrative is structured, types and stereotypes of the main characters and technical effects.

Practical Work

In the examination, practical activities include: creating storyboards, radio jingles, front pages for magazines and letters summarising key points. The skills required involve the ability to sequence ideas visually and aurally; and to select and to summarise and present information in report or letter form.

4 Messages and Values

WHAT IS THE MEANING AND WHY?

In this chapter you will study the concepts of representation, stereotypes, ideology and realism. How do media texts convey ideas, values and messages about places, people and events? What are the typical ideas and values of the media texts we consume? How do we judge if a media text, like a soap, is realistic, accurate or effective? What judgements might other people make? On whose behalf is the text speaking? How, for example, are images of the British nation created and received abroad? You will also explore how messages can be obvious or hidden in media texts through the production or analysis of specific media texts.

KW

Messages ▪ values ▪ representation ▪ selection and construction ▪ ideology ▪ types ▪ archetype ▪ stereotype ▪ bias

TW

Slogan ▪ reconstruction ▪ edit ▪ crop ▪ photo-opportunity ▪ series ▪ serial

WHAT ARE WE LOOKING AT?

A teacher went into a class and showed the children a poster of the Spice Girls and asked the class what it was they were looking at. Some of the class said they were brilliant; others said they made them feel sick; others said nothing at all. The teacher then asked them again what it was they were looking at and someone again said: 'The Spice Girls'. Grinning slyly, the teacher said: 'I asked you what you were looking at? You are all wrong – it's a poster of the Spice Girls!'.

Unless the viewer is very young, most people learn very quickly that, for example, the figures in the children's programme, *Teletubbies*, are part of a television screen image and cannot actually be touched or hugged. The real material used to create the television image is filmed, edited, mixed with sound and format-

MESSAGES AND VALUES

ted. Then it is transmitted into the home via electronic cables or airwaves.

There are three main points to consider before evaluating the meaning of media texts:

1. Media texts can only refer to real subjects whether they exist in reality (for example, news) or as fiction (for example, soaps). They are representations or recreations simulating reality.
2. All media texts are the products of several production stages involving different technical processes: selection of material, recording, editing and presentation.
3. People respond to media texts differently with regards professional quality, accuracy, truthfulness, realism or its artistic merit.

REPRESENTATION

It may seem obvious, however, media products can only show an audience a second-hand version of the real subject. A photograph of you as a baby is only an image of you at a particular time. Representation is the term given to describe the final image which has been recorded and then processed to depict a real or fictional subject, in a media form.

Video cameras or photography are not allowed in the British law courts. Television and newspapers use the hand drawn colour illustrations of a professional artist who recreates some of the static scenes in the courtroom.

The drawings often show the defendants in the dock, so that people who are not present can see a representation of how they look in court. If you were asked to draw a picture of what the Spice Girls looked like in 25 years time you would have to create a representation of them as older people, using both technical drawing skills and imagination.

In a similar way, modern technology can convert the original scene into a new format and shape. For example, photographs can be chemically or digitally processed and cropped (cut down to size or shape). The images are then fitted into the design and layout of a page with text above, below or even on the image, before printing on a newspaper or magazine page.

SELECTION AND CONSTRUCTION

The images we see and listen to in a documentary or soap is a selection of what was originally recorded as prerecorded television is edited. The final product is literally a re-presentation of the original subject. The process of filming, recording and editing film or news bulletins involves the selection and reconstruction of the original material. This process means that real life is literally re-presented in another shape, to fit news media technology and programme format.

Crimewatch UK

Crimewatch UK is a public service television information programme that reconstructs crimes in the form of a drama. It aims to alert the public to actual crimes that have occurred. The programme makers hope the public will come forward if they have witnessed or know something about crimes shown on the programme. *Crimewatch UK* includes reconstructions of crimes, and uses actors to recreate the event. The programme does not show all the details of the violence or the methods used in the crime. The reason why these aspects are not shown is to ensure that the programme is not too sensational and to avoid giving ideas on how to commit certain illegal crimes or violent actions. The reconstructions usually contain the actual word 'reconstruction' so that viewers do not believe they are watching a police drama series such as *The Bill*.

IS THE MEDIA TEXT ACCURATE, TRUTHFUL AND/OR REAL?

In May 1998, 13 Arts students convinced the press into thinking they spent their grant on a holiday in Spain, and showed the press an exhibition of their frolics on the Costa Del Sol at Leeds airport. The show was called *Going Places*, borrowing the name of the travel agency. Although pretending to be doing an outrageous art project, in fact they had fooled the press into thinking that the students had been to Spain. The photographs of them swimming, supposedly in the Mediterranean, had all been taken in a swimming pool in suburban Leeds.

When the press accused the Arts students of wasting public money they revealed they had been no further than Leeds. The next wave of press then wanted photographs of them in the sea at Scarborough to simulate the holiday hoax.

Figure 4.1 The faked photo snap representing a sterotypical image of a holiday in Spain
Source: *The Guardian*, 27 May 1998

MESSAGES AND VALUES

Discuss and make notes on the following:

1. What are the clues, or signifiers, that make the image in Figure 4.1 appear to be:
   a a typical holiday photograph?
   b in Spain?
2. Comment on the lighting, given that this is inside a swimming pool and not in the open Spanish air.
3. Produce a rough sketch of a typical family high street studio portrait photograph. List all the elements of colour, lighting, facial expressions and body postures you would expect to see.
4. Produce a rough sketch of an untypical family portrait, entitled 'the family as it really is'. Again, list all the elements of background, props, lighting, body posture, facial expression you would expect to see.
5. Study any photographs of you taken at home. Which ones would you be most happy and least happy to show to other people. Explain your reasons.

A photo-opportunity is where the press photographer sets up the photograph in a place or at certain key moments. This event or 'publicity stunt' involved two types of representation. The first was the original construction of the holiday by the students. The second was the vague reconstruction of a holiday seaside event to give the newspapers some sea backgrounds and a line up of the remaining hoaxers.

Figure 4.2 The hoaxers pose as paddling art students in the sea, on Scarborough's beach
Source: Dobsons Agency, Scarborough

STEREOTYPES

Stereotypes are fixed and customary ideas that we grow to accept as being normal. Consider stereotyped views of teachers. Female teachers are sometimes thought of as wearing glasses, as do librarians. Male teachers are often thought to wear corduroy trousers and Marks and Spencer jackets. Other people's views of media studies students and teachers may also be stereotyped, however, one should ask the question: do they all look the same?

Archetypes

Archetypes are fairy tale or universal types. Vladimir Propp, a Russian anthropologist, noted that, in any fairy tale, there were certain features of action and character types which appeared in all of the fairy stories he studied. An example of a film is *Star Wars*, where archetypal characters and a fantasy story line combine high action adventure with dialogue.

GCSE MEDIA STUDIES

Typical archetypes include the old wizard, the hero, the tempter and the princess.

The image of the Going Places Spanish holiday photograph is very familiar as they depict stereotypical images of students and holidays in a Mediterranean hotel pool. You may have seen such images before in holiday brochures, magazines or newspapers.

SOAP OPERAS

Discuss and write down your responses to the following questions:

1. How are people, places, events and ideas represented in soap operas?
2. Which soap is the most realistic? Give reasons for your answer.
3. Which soap is the most unrealistic? Give reasons for your answer.
4. Compare your answers with those of other people. Did you find other people's answers different and/or persuasive?

Realism in soaps

Realism in soaps works on the basis that:

- The story line is told in the order of events of a normal day, i.e. there are no flashbacks or flashforwards.
- The place looks like a real location. Sets are built to look like markets, streets, shops, etc.
- The community of people appears to be like ones that exist in real life, for example pubs, shops and cafés.
- The events which occur are based on domestic reality and focus on key life events, for example, relationships, conflicts, births, marriages and deaths.
- The real world events, such as Christmas, Easter or Valentine's day are worked into the script so that the soap community appears to live a life parallel to that of its audience.
- Several soaps, such as *Brookside*, deal with contemporary issues over several episodes. For example, AIDS, incest and battered women relate to issues present in the real world.

Critics of soaps say that the realism appears only on the surface. They claim that the world of the soap never precisely matches the real world for the following reasons:

- The range of age groups is unlikely to always meet in the same place, for example the same pub in *EastEnders*.
- The characters change their personalities too suddenly to fit the story line properly.

MESSAGES AND VALUES

Task 8

Invent the name of the company who has produced it.

MESSAGES AND VALUES

It is possible to examine three spheres within which media products operate: Government, propaganda or public information or commercial and alternative.

Propaganda

Figure 4.3 Government propaganda or public information is used to persuade people
Source: The Advertising Archives

In the second world war (1939–1945) meat products were in short supply. The Government encouraged people to grow their own vegetables and posters were displayed in prominent places. Figure 4.3 shows a typical British working class male looking happy about growing vegetables.

Propaganda campaigns are direct pronouncements by the Government to their 'people', telling them to do something. In Singapore, the Government often has public behaviour propaganda, for example, to not spit or to be courteous to customers. In Britain, the Government uses the Central Office of Information (COI) to convey their message. 'Don't drink and drive' campaigns, tax return reminders and television licence evasion warnings are some examples of Government information promotions. In these campaigns, the message is usually very direct and clear.

The state and ideology

If you look closely at the picture in Figure 4.4, you will see that it is a picture of a street scene and a large poster in the background.

In the poster there is picture of a child reaching out to the man to the left of centre. There is a female and a male adult on the right-hand side who are holding the child up. There is writing in Chinese and in English – it states that 'Family Planning is a Basic National Policy of China'.

Figure 4.4 Billboard for one parent families in China
Source: Louise Gubb/The Image Works

Below the poster people are looking at the wall displays and one man in the foreground is also carrying a child in a wicker basket.

The message of the image is that you should trust the doctor to look after you on behalf of the state. If you do this then everybody will be happy, judging from the smiles on all their faces.

In China, there has been a policy since the 1970s that couples can only have one child per family. As the population of China has increased phenomenally these controls were introduced. The poster is part of a campaign to drive the message home. The idea for the design for the poster came from an artist, but the idea of a national Family Planning Policy came from the Chinese Government.

State control of messages and values is easy to identify, however, in the western hemisphere most messages about products are commercial. The aim of advertising in the western world is to sell something for money.

Bias

A person who brings you a product is also a person who has a point of view. Every media product that is broadcast and distributed has been produced by someone, for some purpose. Therefore, audiences should always look to see if there is a personal viewpoint expressed by the director, the script writers or journalists. Alternatively, it is worth seeing if there is an owner who would like certain information left out or kept in.

Often we only need to know who is the main force behind the advertisement. If it is Cadbury's or Coca Cola, for example, we know that the message is to buy their product. These messages are obvious because the products are well-known and have a long history of advertising and promotion. However, all media products also convey ideas about society, some of which the makers are aware of, others which are not consciously expressed.

Even the news, which is supposed to be neutral, can be said to be biased in favour of the majority view of the people in the country. Those people who choose not to live in houses or wear clothes or speak like the BBC news presenters may feel their point of view is not represented. Alternative groups such as Undercurrents, produce their news on video and distribute by mail order. The typical content of their videos, is of protests and demonstrations about the environment, animal rights and pollution. This kind of presentation could be seen to be biased towards the makers' viewpoint.

Alternative values

Non-commercial products and non-governmental organisations with little money have a low chance of success of reaching a mass audience because they have no access to exhibition or points of interaction with the public. Free publicity can be gained by performing 'stunts'. Campaigning agencies such as Greenpeace and

MESSAGES AND VALUES

Amnesty International put their money into specific projects. Greenpeace has a history of daring stunts such as climbing Big Ben or beseiging whaling ships to gain free publicity about 'green' issues on the news. Amnesty International uses strong messages in their photographs to shock people into awareness of abuse of human rights, cruelty and political imprisonment issues.

Added value

In advertisements it is usually obvious what you are being sold. The aim is to persuade the consumer to buy the product. The slogan or catchphrase will be visible or pronounced loudly by the presenter or narrator.

The images of the product are presented to give an idea of what the real product is, but also shown is a lifestyle or a benefit – an 'added value'. If you buy X you will also get Y. Alternatively, if you buy X you will save money. Financial gain is the main message of this aspect of advertising.

Social value

Values about society also are packaged into advertisements, soaps, game shows and news, in fact any type of programme or medium. For example, the 1998 Heinz soup advertisements show a lorry driver returning home to his meal after a cold and long day, and suggest that a soup eater will have a secure home and a warm, family life. These are what are known as values, what society thinks is worth having. Values convey society's ideas about a range of important aspects of everyday life: identity, gender, age, race, family, class, material wealth and politics.

The messages in television advertisements are often spoken by an unseen voice, by a presenter or written on the screen. In televised government health warnings the voice is often direct in telling the viewer what to do, for example, 'Don't Drink and Drive'. These words are usually also printed on the screen or the poster to add impact.

Ideology

Through studying its media it is possible in any country to understand the way its people think about the family, religion, education and political beliefs. The values of the business woman in the city of London will be different from those of the business woman in the Jordanian city of Amman. The main difference is likely to concern religion. In Jordan, the main religion is Islamic in comparison to Church of England or Catholic in the UK, for example. This means that the way in which the citizens of both countries make or consume the media will be different. Even if the advertisement is for Coca Cola and the basic messages are the same, the reading of the image used may be different.

Ideology and advertising

Another example is the hair product Wash and Go. This product combines conditioner and shampoo in one bottle. The American advertisements depicted happy and busy working women going for exercise workouts at the gym, and then using the product. The setting of the television advertisement in a changing room, was indicated by lockers behind the women, thereby depicting the changing room as a typical place for social activities which relate to having to wash your hair. The women in the advertisement were seen with the product and the 'story' works by showing that other women observe that the happy-go-lucky women are using this product and leaving early because they have taken less time to wash their hair.

When the advertisement was shown in Russia, the advertisement did not have the same happy, sporting associations for those who watched it. In Russia, a room with lockers in the background was associated with communal workplaces, prisons and cramped, squalid settings. The idea of a happy, sports loving, working city woman with a few minutes to spend cleaning her hair in a lunch break did not convey well in Russia.

Association

The reading of images depends on the individual's background and the associations the audience has with the image before they look at it. As with the students who responded to the Spice Girls poster by saying whether they liked them or not, everyone makes judgements. These judgements are the audience's opinions and are a question of taste and personal values.

Whatever the content or the ownership of the product, audiences are potentially able to make of it what they will.

'On behalf of'

It is a common phrase to hear someone in films or in television programmes involving lawyers or business people, say that they are representing someone else. Similarly, the production of media products is often carried out 'on behalf of' someone else by advertising companies or corporate film and video companies. This does not mean that the message is neutral or without values. The important factor to establish is whose message is being presented and why, and to whom.

Successful awareness campaigns depend on having the finance to repeat the advertisement frequently with a simple but identifiable message. In many cases the aim is not to interest the consumer, for example, in the film industry the promotional aim is to raise awareness of the product's existence.

NATIONAL IDENTITY

What is the image of Britain abroad? In 1996, according to the Americans, British Pop and all things British were considered cool (see Figure 4.5).

However, by July 1988, after the World Cup which included media reports of British citizens involved in violent fights outside football matches, the British image was seen to be declining (see Figure 4.6).

Britishness

Study the images in Figure 4.7 published by the French daily newspaper Liberation of what British people appear to look like to the cartoonist, Willem.

| MESSAGES AND VALUES |

Figure 4.5 The rise of the British image abroad in 1996

Source: *Newsweek*

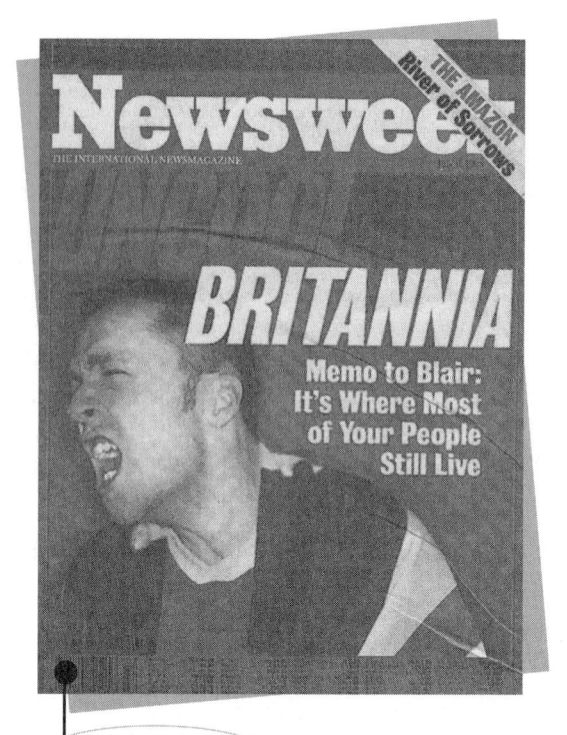

Figure 4.6 The decline of the British image abroad, in 1998

Source: *Newsweek*

Figure 4.7 Britain as others see us – is this a true/fair representation?

Source: © *Guardian Review*, 2 January 1999/Willem

GCSE MEDIA STUDIES

Discuss the following:

1. What images of Britain are suggested by the depiction of the characters in figure 4.7?
2. What elements do you think are true?
3. Are there any positive or negative images?
4. What images of British people are missing?
5. Do you feel you are represented in these images of Britain?

MESSAGES AND VALUES SIMULATION

Specimen examination question: AQA (SEG)

These Tasks are not actual examination questions. The questions are the sole work of the author and are devised to match the style, mark allocation and format of the relevant question papers from AQA and OCR. They are designed for examination practice. The Tasks are designed to follow the examination paper timings and mark allocations. It is essential that candidates check the specified topics set for the year of their examination, by the examination board. For previous examination papers contact the examination board direct.

Paper 2 controlled text (4hrs)

You are an advertising company and you have been asked to draw up a rough idea of a promotion by the Central Office of Information (COI). Your target is the European family audience; demographic groups ABC1 and C2. The time the advertisement will be broadcast in European countries is 6pm–9pm. You will have to pitch your idea to the COI to win the contract. The pitch should consist of a short, written presentation and the production of a storyboard.

The brief: Produce a television advertisement encouraging Europeans to either: buy British fruit and vegetables or buy British beef. Either advertisement should include images of a range of different types of British people. Ensure that you cover the range of social groups by: gender, race, class, age and disability.

Task 1

Explain the representations of social groups in one or more magazines or television advertisements that you have studied.

(40 marks)

Task 2

Read the brief at the beginning of this exercise.

a Draw up to ten frames for your storyboard of the promotion.

(20 marks)

b Annotate the storyboard with sound, including voice-over and soundtrack, camera angles and movement (see Chapter Two: Languages and Categories).

(10 marks)

MESSAGES AND VALUES

Task 3

Write a commentary on the storyboard created in Task 2 explaining what messages you have tried to convey.

(15 marks)

Task 4

Explain in a letter to the COI what other marketing strategies and values you have decided to use and promote.

(15 marks)

Extension Tasks

1. **Collect** three or four magazine advertisements which include male models and three or four that include female models. These should be adverts for products such as food, cars, clothes and perfumes. **Compare and contrast** how men and women are represented in terms of:

   ▶ Denotation and connotations.
   ▶ Images of men and women – types and stereotypes.
   ▶ Lifestyle and aspirations.
   ▶ Presentation of content, slogan and catchphrases.
   ▶ Difference and conformity to the 'norm'.
   ▶ Target audience (see Chapter 3, audience demographics).

2. **Analyse** the messages of radio advertisements on local radio. What form and structure do the advertisements take? What do the advertisements tell us about families, the state, religion and work? Who are the advertisements targeted at? How do these advertisements construct the audience?

3. a **Produce** a jingle for an advertisement for a new takeaway pizza service, also available on the Internet. The advertisement should include details of how to order by phone or via the Internet. The idea behind the advertisement is that the pizza image on the computer screen allows the purchaser to select from the range of toppings by clicking on the mouse and sending the order by E-mail.

   b You should also **consider** the following: audience demographics, representation and sound-bite slogan, and music soundtrack. See if you can **identify** images of America (or another country).

4. **Create** a paper collage of magazine and newspaper images of America. Annotate (write notes next to the images) and **analyse** their connotations. What are the images of? Is there a repetition of the same sort of image? Who has produced these images? **Collect** a number of advertisements from television, newspaper, magazines or Internet to compare.

5. **Redesign** a classic book cover for a youth audience. William Sutcliffe's book, *Are You Experienced?* (Penguin Books, 1998) sold 10 times more when its book cover was redesigned. The new cover included an image of a female belly button, a psychedelic colour scheme and a buckle in the shape of a cannabis plant.

   Other examples of 'redesigned' media products include: *Great Expectations* (recently released as a new version of the film in 1998), *Vanity Fair* and *William Shakespeare's Romeo and Juliet* (1996). **Explain** in your commentary the ideas behind your representations, audience targeting and format and layout decisions.

6. **Produce** a poster, press release and a television campaign (storyboard) for your own 'Don't Drink and Drive' campaign. The target audience is males in the 40–55 yrs age group. Research has shown that this age group is the most likely to ignore these types of campaigns. How will you research where to place your advertisements and posters? What images will be most effective?

7 Produce an advertising campaign to launch a new drink for the 16–25 year old market. **Design** an advertisement for a magazine. Which magazines will the advert appear in? What mix of media will you use to maximise your campaign and where will it be seen and heard? What is the lifestyle associated with the drink and what else is the consumer of the drink likely to do for leisure and work? **Devise** a bite-sized phrase or slogan, for example, 'Go to work on an egg', which was used for years to promote egg eating.

Examination Skills

Knowledge and Understanding

There should be an ability to apply conceptual and technical terms such as representations and serial. There should be a strong understanding of the links between producers and audiences, messages and values and audiences and producers.

In making media texts, including storyboards or scripts, there should be an understanding of audiences and producers, codes and signifiers of meaning. Commentaries should be informed by a knowledge of form and content of mainstream and alternative texts. The understanding of the terms values and ideology will inform the best commentaries.

Knowledge of the use of storyboard conventions: wide variety of shot sizes, camera angles and movements, soundtrack and lighting.

Textual Analysis

Students should be able to denote, connotate and explain the broader ideologies by interpreting a media product, using technical and key words terminology. The importance of categorisation, genre and representation should also be recognised as these concepts are linked together.

Students should exhibit an awareness of social institutions and values by reference and links to key social groups or institutions (i.e. Church, Government, work/education and family) and how media texts convey ideas about each of these.

The representation of British people by other European countries in their advertisements is often of a bowler-hatted commuter or a fist-waving football supporter. English behaviour, in other European country's news media and cartoons, is still represented as either terribly polite and charming, or thuggish and brutal. The upper class image is not surprising, since films like *Four Weddings and a Funeral* contain stereotypical images of upper class English society, and of pretty postcard images of village greens and churches. These images and stereotypes of Englishness are perhaps why the film sold so well around the world.

Practical Work

Constructing a new product or re-working an old product involves the demonstration of an understanding of concepts of representation, audiences and producers. Close attention to visual and aural forms of representation is necessary. Layout and design skills are less important than a broad understanding of the format and typical content of the following: press releases, storyboards, radio jingles, TV news bulletins, print-based advertising, popular television formats, photography, music video, films and trailers, and posters.

5 Music industry

JINGLE BELLS, JINGLE ALL THE WAY

This chapter covers the music industry, its promotion of the product, the role of the music press, radio playlists, television music shows and videos, and the criteria for making a hit single at Christmas.

KW

Mainstream ■ **youth culture** ■ **street credibility** ■ **genre** ■ **indies** ■ **image** ■ **major** ■ **unique selling point** ■ **segmentation** ■ **synergy**

TW

Chart ■ play lists ■ point of sale ■ dance ■ rap ■ techno ■ drum 'n' bass ■ garage ■ artists and repertoire

WHAT IS MAINSTREAM POPULAR MUSIC?

Is it Radio 2 or Radio 1; Kiss FM or Virgin, television's *Top of the Pops* or magazines like *Smash Hits* or *New Musical Express*? Is it today's popular bedroom-produced techno music or club-based dance/rap music?

When people refer to 'mainstream pop music' they usually mean one of the following:

- The modern, chart music that is played on Sunday's 'Official Top 40' chart show on BBC Radio 1.
- Television's *Top of the Pops (TOTP)* on BBC1.
- The Pepsi chart show on Channel 5.

The charts are mainly youth oriented, for the age group 10–25 years. *TOTP* is broadcast at 7.30 on Friday evenings, so many over 25 year olds also watch the programme. It could be argued that Radio 2 is more of a popular music channel as it appeals to a wider age range of people. Their programming targets people who grew up during times when the popular music of the day was different: 1930s and 1940s big band, 1950s jazz music and rock and roll, pop's great explosion in the 1960s and 1970s, and new romantic and punk in the 1980s are all examples of music broadcast by Radio 2.

Mainstream chart-based popular music is the music also heard on local radio stations

UK Top 40 Singles

This Week	Last Week	Weeks in Chart	Title/Artist/Label
1	-	1	MARIA Blondie Beyond/RCA
2	1	2	YOU DON'T KNOW ME Armand Van Helden featuring Duane Harden ffrr
3	-	1	BOY YOU KNOCK ME OUT Tatyana Ali featuring Will Smith MJJ/Epic
4	2	3	PRETTY FLY (FOR A WHITE GUY) The Offspring Columbia
5	-	1	ENJOY YOURSELF A+ Universal
6	3	13	HEARTBEAT/TRAGEDY Steps Jive
7	5	10	WHEN YOU'RE GONE Bryan Adams featuring Melanie C A&M/Mercury
8	-	1	CAN'T GET ENOUGH Soulsearcher Defected
9	7	3	WESTSIDE TQ Epic
10	4	2	THESE ARE THE TIMES Dru Hill

Figure 5.1 Top 10 Singles, February 1999
Source: *Music Week*

such as Radio 1 and on television, in clubs and in dance venues. Music that is first played on the Sunday charts show on the radio is then often used in other venues throughout the week.

YOUTH CULTURE

Youth culture as a marketable idea began with the growth of the popular music industry during the 1950s, when rock and roll was born. Electrified blues and swing music were combined, and the background of today's popular music came into being. Youth culture developed as a reaction by teenagers against their parents. Images of youth enjoying music separately from parents became commonplace. Rebellion in films was focused on icons such as James Dean, star of *Rebel Without A Cause* (1954). Rebellion and youth culture were packaged together and sold back to its own youth audience. Teenagers could buy related consumable goods, such as drinks, cars, records, concerts and films. Various rock and roll stars, especially Americans, were created in the process: Elvis Presley, and Bill Haley and the Comets being just two examples.

Street credibility

Yesterday's 1960s rebels, for example The Rolling Stones, have become today's superstars and are now enjoying renewed street credibility. To be considered non-mainstream the artist or band has to have an attitude that is not concerned with selling products. The term street credibility applies when the artist does not seek to promote image above content. The fans respect the artist or band for the music, despite the promotional excess they may have thrust onto them. In gaining street credibility the artist is therefore often difficult to categorise in terms of the genre of their music. The content of the music tends to avoid mainstream categories of music.

'Indies'

Bands who sign up to indie labels (for example, Beggars Banquet or Mushroom Indie) can be more concerned with content than image. They are also currently more likely to be heard in record shops, independent radio stations, clubs, concerts and on the Internet. A few selected mainstream DJs may plug indie bands, however they are restricted by the policy of the mainstream stations to play what is in the week's popular chart listings.

Indie bands usually have to work with small distributors and labels to get their product sold. Other methods of selling records include:

- word of mouth
- through mail order

1 **Write** notes under the heading 'popular music genre'. How many genres of music do you know? What genres do you like? Are they mainstream or at the alternative end of music culture? Create a large scale wall 'map' of music culture showing music labels and their companies and how they relate to various genres and bands.

2 **Analyse** the covers of two compact discs (CDs) by the same artist or band, using denotation and connotation techniques of analysis (see Chapter 2). Use the headings and prompts below to discuss your CD covers and music.

a **Image**. Look at the visual imagery and the graphics used in the packaging of the music product. You might compare two CD covers by the same artist to show how they have common themes or how they have developed a new image or style. What ideas do the images denote and connotate (see definitions in Chapter 2)? Are there any key signifiers? Is the band included in the image and if so, how are they represented? If they are not included in the cover image, why not? What graphics and typefaces have been used? Do they convey a style or image?

b **Musical style**. What type of music does your artist/band play? Is the artist or band mainstream or at the alternative end of music styles? What image and attitude do the band's members appear to have from the way they look? Note their dress, body language and facial expressions.

c **Audience**. Who is the audience aimed at? Note the age and gender?

d **Institutions**. What is the label and the parent company? For example, Sony is the parent company for Creation record label. Who is the distributor?

IMAGE

Promoting a band

To promote a single, with a few notable exceptions, you need an image. If you are interested in selling your record to more than just your friends and local people, then the idea of your music and the band have to be portable and travel widely. This can only be achieved by

Record Company Structure

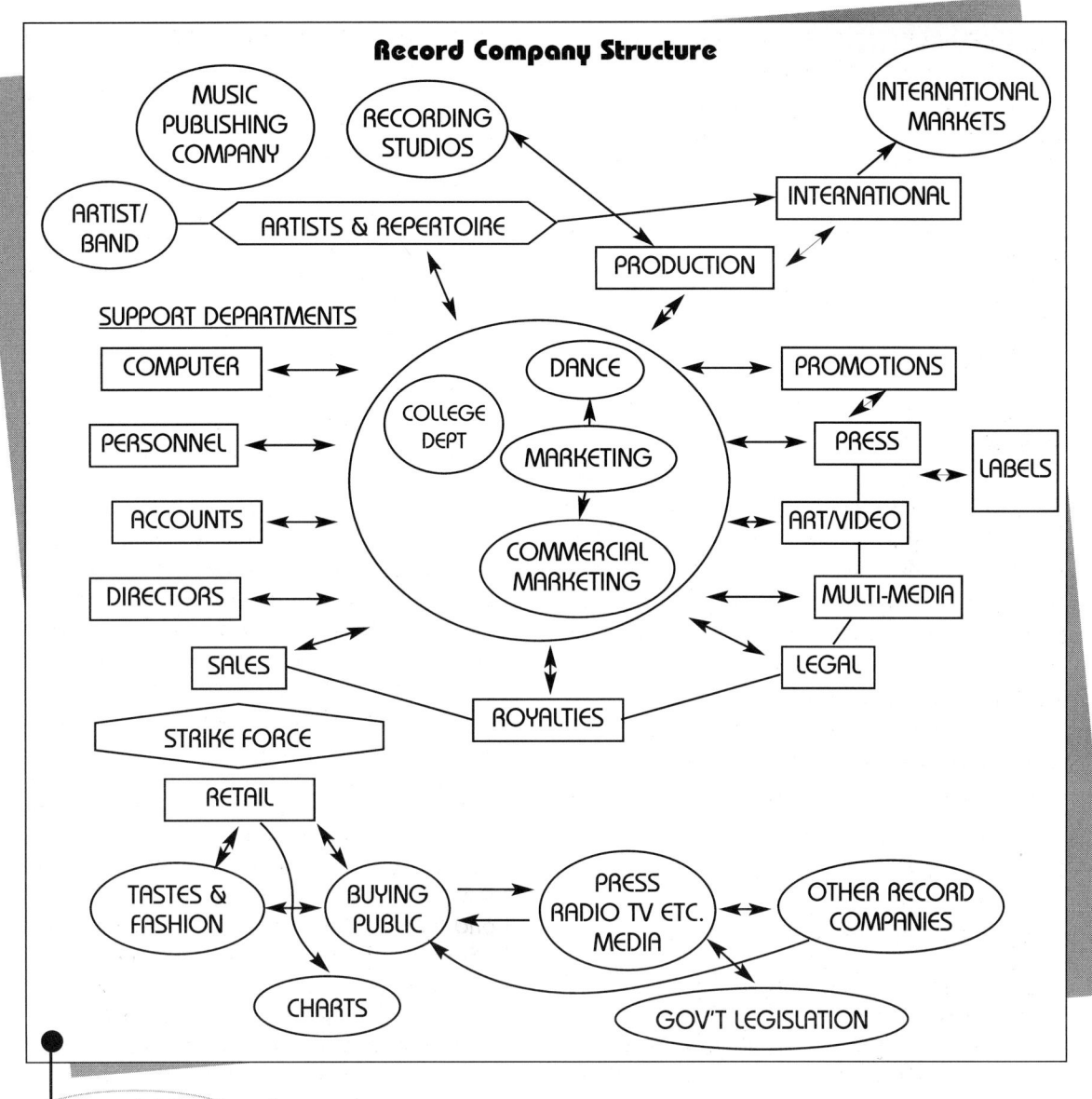

Figure 5.2 Structure of a record company

projecting the image you wish to present. The scale on which you can do this depends on your budget.

Major companies

The major record companies can afford to spend a great deal of money on promotion and they have staff employed to fulfil various roles in different departments. An example of a record company structure is given in Figure 5.2.

Two examples of promotional activity within a company are the Artist and Repertoire, and Strike Force departments.

MUSIC INDUSTRY

Artist and repertoire

The artist and repertoire (A&R) department searches out, develops and nurtures a company's talent. To develop a band's image they make sure the band wear the appropriate clothes and sometimes modify the musical arrangements to make them sound more professional. The A&R department will look after their safety at concerts and handle press interviews. A&R also act as talent scouts looking for new bands and fresh talent for the market.

Strike force

The strike force department promotes sales of records, tapes, and compact discs. They will visit music shops to make sure the music is prominently displayed. They will arrange special offers, special artist appearances and highly visible shop displays, for example using stands and cardboard cut outs of the record or the band. This is called point of sale marketing; meaning at the place where the customer makes the actual purchase.

Seagram — MCA, Island, Polygram, Mercury, Geffen, Polydor, Mowtown, Decca, A&M — 34%

Time Warner — Warner, Electra, Atlantic (WEA), Reprise — 10%

Bertlesmann — RCA, Arista — 5%, 12%

EMI — EMI, Parlophone, Chrysalis, Virgin — 12%

Sony — Columbia, Work, Legacy, Epic, Classical, Nashville, 550 Music, Legacy, Creation (49%) — 27%

Independents — One Little Indian, Beggars Banquet, Maverick, Mute (some examples of independent labels)

Bold Type = Major record companies Plain type = Record labels

Figure 5.3 Major record companies and labels

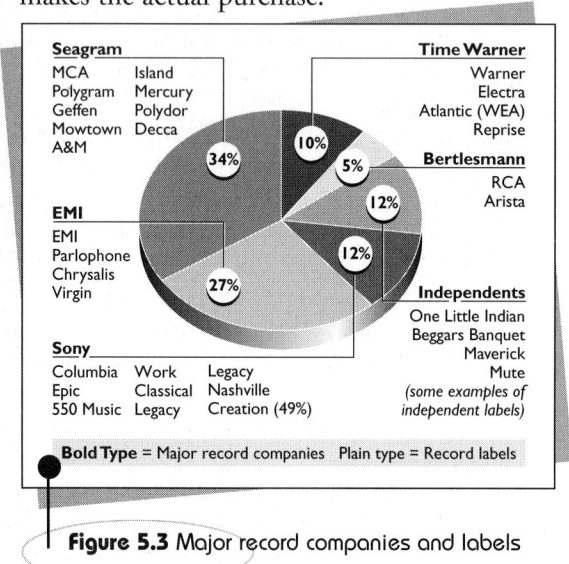

Other sources

Indie labels often have to rely on word of mouth, radio or the music press to give them strong record sales. Small indies, where only a small office runs the label, are particularly weak financially and have to use a major company to distribute their products. The bigger indies have a stronger reputation as they are associated with certain types of artists. However, even they will collapse if their major artist either decides to quit the music business or becomes unsuccessful. For example, Factory Records closed when New Order folded in the early 1990s.

Following is a profile of an indie record label (as promoted by itself).

'Mushroom Records has been established in the UK for 4 years and started in Australia 25 years ago. It has grown from strength to strength over the last couple of years, largely due to the success of its roster and the concept of total artist control that allows the artists to create innovative and mind blowing music. Mushroom Records are at the cutting edge of the new wave of modern music that has now become a common part of everyday life.

The company has a diverse and well catered for rosta. Garbage are now an established band with a platinum selling debut album. In April 1997, The Wildhearts, who are an act in their own league, signed to Mushroom Records. Their frontman Ginger said, "We signed to Mushroom Records because it is the undisputed coolest label in Britain, their philosophy is music before money ... that way the money always rolls in and the music always rocks out". The renowned Ween are another of Mushroom's signings. The label's roster also includes more mainstream artists such as Peter André (platinum debut album) and Deni Hines.'

Source: Adapted from Mushroom Records in The Knowledge Label Profile (Where Alternative Music is)

Advantages of signing to independent labels:

- Contract is often 50/50% share.
- More artistic freedom.
- More care and attention to band's wishes.
- More street credibility.

Advantages of signing to a major label:

- An advance payment is often given, and a royalty (which is a percentage of every CD or record sold).
- Promotion will be much more widespread and effective, with a greater amount of money and personnel behind the campaign.
- Greater investment in production and distribution costs.
- Better international market possibilities.

THE MUSIC INDUSTRY

Music industry statistics

- The British music industry is worth £2.5 billion a year, of which £1.25 billion is generated abroad.
- The industry employs 115,000 people. (Source: IFPI (International Federation of Phonographic Industry)).
- Piracy costs an estimated £6.25 billion a year in sales and lost royalties. Most of the piracy involves illegal duplication of tapes and takes place in Russia, Thailand, China and the Far East.
- In 1998, singles sold 80 million compared to sales of 210 million CD albums. The value of retail trade in albums was £1500 million compared to £250 million for singles.
- Current structure of the singles market (1999) is: CD accounts for 78%, cassettes 15%, 12" account for 6% and 7" less than 1%.

The average cost of a CD is £13.99 and can be broken down into the following:

- Songwriter publisher   0.68p
- Artist's royalty   £1.61p
- Manufacturing   0.65p
- Distribution   0.72p
- Retailer's margin   £4.67p
- VAT   £2.08p
- Profit pre-interest/tax   0.65p
- Miscellaneous overheads   £1.32p
- Other artists/repertoire costs £1.61p

Survey and quantity analysis

1. Conduct a survey of a class or at least a sample of 20 people in the same age range (half girls and half boys).
   a Find out how many bought a single last year.
   b How many bought an album of the same artist?
2. Create bar charts showing:
   a The breakdown of boys' and girls' consumption
   b Answers to how many bought an album as well as the single.
3. Comment on the figures you have collected:
   a Is there a link between any of the figures?
   b What is a typical pattern of consumption for boys and for girls?
   c Does purchase of singles lead to purchase of albums by the same artist?

MUSIC INDUSTRY

Radio

Listen to Virgin, Heart FM, and Radio 1.

> A music critic once complained that there is crude sexual stereotyping involved in the way in which radio programmes are constructed. Discuss this statement. Do you agree?

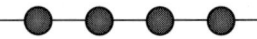

1 Listen to two or three of each radio channel's advertisements and note down who you think they are targeted at.
2 Would you say the advertisers are more interested in one section of the population than another? Discuss.
3 Research your local radio station(s). Analyse the music content and define its audience. Does the advertising reflect any age or gender group? If so, how does it do this?

In the *Independent on Sunday* on 25 January 1998, Matthew Sweet accused various radio stations of either being 'lads' stations full of sexism and Mike and the Mechanics, or 'cosy chats' for girls and Celine Dion (see Figure 5.4). He claimed that Virgin FM has advertisements for breakfast bars, cough sweets and cars, whilst Heart FM has advertisements for fitness centres, healthy breakfast cereals and 'Ladies Nights' in clubs.

FOR GIRLS
Capital gold MW 1548: proper "choons" from the Sixties, Seventies and Eighties for retired rock chicks who aren't too proud to get down to Leonard Skynner as they hoover. Listeners: thirtysomethings who never had that much taste in music in the first place
Heart FM 106.2: lots of solo songstresses, lots of chart, plus keynote golden oldies from Katrina and the Waves and the Eagles. Non-crunchy and Gallagher-free. Listeners: office girls; teenagers; sub-urbanites
Melody FM 105.4: slushy love songs, showtunes, the Carpenters. Radio 2 with ads, only less challenging. Listeners: new-borns and the hard of thinking

FOR BOYS
Virgin FM 105.8: Britpop, Mike and the Mechanics, Aerosmith, Steve Winwood, plus irritating indie pop from the Lightning Seeds et al. Listeners: New lads and old bores
Jazz FM 102.2: Otis Carmichael, er, Fats Backgammon, that sort of thing. Frankly, it's a mystery to you and me. Listeners: polo-neck wearing, chess-playing, purist jazz bores who tune in to complain about commercialisation and jazz-funk fusion
XFM 104.9: Very alternative, very cutting edge, very indie, very hard work. The John Peel show for the chemical generation. Purveyor of fodder to the review pages of the *NME* and *Melody Maker*. Listeners: erstwhile fans of the Cure; disaffected youth; depressives

Figure 5.4 Are all radio music channels either for boys or girls?
Source: © *Independent on Sunday*, 25 January 1998

Recipe for success

Following is a 'recipe' for marketing a typical 'boy band'.

1 Auditions (on basis of looks and sex appeal).
2 Training the band to dance, with a professional dance teacher.
3 Clothes and makeover – the 'look'.
4 Songs written by professionals.
5 Music produced by professionals.
6 Sound test on group.
7 Studio recording of songs (with or without band).
8 Tour booked.
9 Single released in advance of the tour.
10 Promotion – TV chat shows, interviews with music and leisure press, daily nationals, local radio, local press, local school performances. Plus, press release, CD covers, telephone campaign, record, trailers.
11 Tour.
12 Reviews.
13 Record new album.

If the initial campaign begins to create interest, then a single in the Top 40 must be the first target. This gives the band a passport to massive television exposure. Once successful, the main television programmes to promote the single range from chart shows, to chat shows, to children's entertainment programmes.

Chart shows

Top of the Pops

BBC1 Fridays, 7.30pm (and repeated Saturdays):

- *TOTP* is targeted at 10 to 45 year olds.
- *TOTP Magazine* has a circulation of 500,000 and its target audience is 10–12 year olds.

Pepsi Chart Show

Channel 5 Thursdays, 8.00–8.30pm:

- Targets 10 to 25 year olds.

Entertainment programmes

TFI Friday

Channel 4, Fridays at 6.00pm and 11.00pm:

- Targets 12 to 45 year olds.

Ozone

BBC2, Wednesdays:

- Music programme with news and a youth oriented slant
- Targets 10 to 18 year olds.

General entertainment

- *Big Breakfast*, Channel 4, weekdays 7.00–9.00am family programme.
- *Live and Kicking*, BBC1, Saturdays, 9.15–12.00 noon, 8 to 15 years age group.
- *National Lottery Live*, BBC1, Saturday nights 7.50–8.10pm family programme.
- *Late Night with Jools Holland*, BBC2, Saturdays 11.00pm, 18 to 55 years age group (a more specialist music programme).

Music video TV channels

The Box, VH1 and MTV are all channels dedicated to nonstop music, including videos of the bands. Videos of bands help sell them when they cannot perform in person.

When bands like The Rolling Stones were on tour it was too tiring to return to London to mime their records on *Top of the Pops*. Instead, they filmed some footage of themselves at the bottom of Beachy Head and used it play over over the soundtrack. In the 1970s, the Queen video of *Bohemian Rhapsody* became known for its technical inventiveness, similarly with Peter Gabriel's animated 'Sledghammer' video.

When MTV started broadcasting continuous music videos in 1982, they created a new life for many bands who were able to picture themselves in many countries. Some bands, who had no fans in their own country, were able to build up followers abroad.

Music videos

Music videos tend to fall into three categories: performance, narrative and abstract. The most common type of video is where the band is seen on stage, and their live performance has been edited. The narrative style of video is where the band perform with their instruments, but also appear informally, sometimes even acting some of the lyrics. If the video contains a solo artist then the individual may be the centre of the storyline, for example Madonna or Michael Jackson. The third type of video is where the band only appears minimally and the entire sequence is an abstract interpretation of the lyrics.

MUSIC INDUSTRY

Textual analysis: select two music videos by one artist and answer the following:
1. Identify what type of video it is according to the categories described previously.
2. Explain how the video communicates its ideas visually. Does the video focus on the artist or on the song? What image(s) does the video seek to portray?
3. Consider also where is the video set? Does the setting relate to the lyrics?
4. How does the editing and camerawork link in with the rhythm and pace of the music? Is this effective?

> 'Each record is chosen on musical merit and they are judged individually, not according to who the artists are. These decisions have nothing to do with the band or, as has been suggested, an artist's age. However, as part of Radio 1's obligation to provide a distinctive service, the network does support new artists and new music, and it is a contemporary music station.'
>
> Source: BBC Information

Research the popular music output of Radio 1 and discuss:

Do your think the play list tends to favour one type of artist or age group?

Radio play lists

Play lists are the lists of singles that radio stations draw up, to repeat throughout the week. The 'P' list contains the top 8–10 records; the 'A' list is the next twenty and the 'B' list is the next twenty singles after that. The influential 'Top Forty' Sunday afternoon show on Radio 1 plays them all in ascending order. During the week DJs on Radio 1 ensure that the 'P' list has more plays than the 'A' list, which in turn has more plays than those on the 'B' list.

RADIO 1 play list

Of approximately 250 singles released each week, only around 55 are play listed on Radio 1. 60% of the network's output is play list material, mainly during the daytime. Following is a statement about Radio 1's selection methods:

Who buys singles?

The percentage of people who bought a single last year can be broken down according to sex (Adapted from *BPI Annual Report*, 1998):

- Men – 37%
- Women – 41%
- Everyone – 40%

According to social group:

AB – 37%
C1 – 39%
C2 – 44%
DE – 38%

DJ, MC and club music

Much music is created in clubs and the role of the disc jockey (DJ) has changed dramatically in the last ten years. With music created by remixing old records and manipulating vinyl records, the DJ becomes an artist in their own right. Dance music has also allowed the audience to concentrate more on group participation than on the spectacle of the performer on stage. With the rise in so many different types of music, the music industry is finding it hard to sell a single type of music to the whole audience.

Segmentation

With so many different genres the music industry is now like an orange with many segments that are attached together but do not connect. This defines the term 'segmentation'.

THE MUSIC PRESS

The music press are often useful for increasing interest in a band but in many of the biggest promotional campaigns the press has not made much difference. *Smash Hits* has probably made the biggest impact in recent years in increasing interest through its large scale posters of artists that can be pinned up on the wall. *Q*, *Select*, *NME* and *Melody Maker* offer more in-depth interviews and reports. For the specialist genres, such as heavy metal fans, there are magazines such as *Kerrang* or *Hot Metal*.

The campaign for relaunching Meatloaf in 1993 avoided using any music press. Instead they reached their audience of 25–45 year olds through the national dailies and Sunday newspapers. News of bands tours, interviews and background to the bands provide details that fans can obtain exclusively from the magazines. However, with the rise of the fanzine, the Internet and teletext, more information can be obtained by other means. This poses the question: does the music industry need music press or does the music press need the music industry?

The look

The front covers of music magazines do provide additional publicity coverage for bands. News retailers effectively provide space for the faces of bands to be seen by the public. Photographs of the artists tend to involve portrait shots with the artist looking straight out at the viewer. The images are usually well lit and the straplines (the words in bite size sentences) summarise the point of the article inside the magazine.

Award ceremonies

The major award ceremonies are the high points in a promoter's year. At these events all the world's media meet and the opportunity for free publicity is great. If an artist/band is nominated for an award then more attention is granted and sales are generated. Some major awards are:

- Brit Awards UK (early February)
- Grammy Awards USA (late February)
- Mercury Awards UK (September)

MUSIC INDUSTRY

Study these profiles of two different music magazines. They appear in BRAD (British Rates for Advertising Data). The data about editorial profile and target readership is presenting the magazines' view of themselves. What current artists/bands do you think each would cover?

1 Mojo
Est: 1993
Publisher: EMAP
Frequency: Monthly
Price: single copy £2.75
Editorial profile: Monthly specialist music title. In-depth coverage of legendary musicians past and present.
Regular features: Music (blues, classical, country, general, jazz).
Circulation: 212,000 (July–December 1999)
Readership: 256,000 (6.0 readers per copy)
  Female readership: 67,000
  Male readership: 189,000
Target Readership: 25 to 44 year old ABC men with a core of 30 to 40 year olds. Upmarket, urban, stylish and passionate about music.

2 Smash Hits
Est: 1978
Publisher: EMAP
Frequency: Fortnightly
Price: single copy 90p
Editorial profile: Sharp, humorous in language of its own, asks the stars questions no other magazine could get away with. Editorial covers stars and music from Ash to Celine Dion.
Regular features: Music, general style & fashion, entertainment, cinema and film technology.
Circulation: 295,061 July–December 1999
Readership: 843,000 (2–3 readers per copy)
  Female readership: 639,000
  Male readership: 203,000
Target readership: 11 to 19 year old boys and girls who are cool, sassy and aspirational.

Mojo – projecting the artist's image
Source: © Mojo/Alpha Pictures

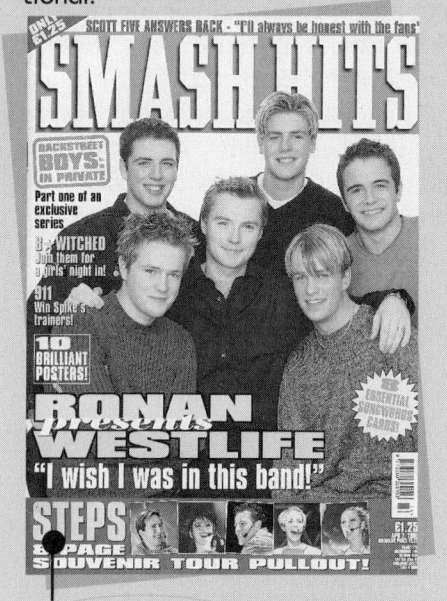

Smash Hits: the front cover of a popular magazine is great free publicity
Source: © Emap Metro Ltd.

Robbie is crowned king of the Brits

BY HIS own standards, it was a disappointing result. Robbie Williams, nominated for six Brit awards, walked away with just three statues at the annual celebration of pop music last night.

But with two nominations in two categories, the 25-year-old former teenage heartthrob could only win a maximum of four awards.

The night's other big winners were more of a surprise: the Manic Street Preachers followed their success at the Brits two years ago with surprise victories in the best British album and best British group categories.

The Australian singer and former soap star Natalie Imbruglia won Brits for best international newcomer and best international female solo artist. In the latter category she beat off competion from established stars such as Madonna, Alanis Morissette and Sheryl Crow, and acclaimed solo newcomer Lauryn Hill. Norman Cook, aka Fatboy Slim,

And the winners are

Best British Group Manic Street Preachers
MasterCard Best British Album This Is My Truth Tell Me Yours, Manic Street Preachers
Best British Newcomer Belle & Sebastian
Best British Dance Act Fatboy Slim
Best Soundtrack/Cast Recording Titanic
Best International Group The Corrs
Best International Newcomer Natalie Imbruglia
Best International Male Solo Artist Beck
Best International Female Solo Artist Natalie Imbruglia
Best British Male Solo Artist Robbie Williams
Best British Female Solo Artist Des'ree
Best British Single Angels, Robbie Williams
Best British Video Millennium, Robbie Williams
Outstanding Contribution To British Music Eurythmics

capped an entertaining week. On Monday his engagement to Radio 1 DJ Zoe Ball was announced and last night he won the Brit for best dance act, in the face of stiff competition from the likes of Massive Attack, Jamiroquai and All Saints.

Williams's success caps a triumphant year following his exuberant performance at last year's cermony dueting with Tom Jones. As well as nominations in the Best British album and best British male artist categories, he had two nominations in the video and best single categories.

The outstanding achievement award was presented to the reunited Eurythmics, who gained the honour of having won more Brits than any other act. Between them Annie Lennox and Dave Stewart already have 10 trophies. Last night the pair dedicated their set to "the families of Stephen Lawrence and Michael Menson" - a reference to the two young black men allegedly killed by racists.

Figure 5.5 The Brit Awards is a prime marketing tool for artists or bands
Source: © The Guardian, 17 February 1999

MUSIC SALES

Hit singles at Christmas

In a typical year top chart singles can sell between 60–100,000 copies. At Christmas, the figures can be ten times as much as this.

Over Christmas 1996, The Spice Girls' '2 Become 1' single sold 495,000 copies. Yet the January 1997 hit, 'White Town' by Jyoti Mishira, sold only 26,000 copies to achieve top of the chart status. Over Christmas 1984, Band

MUSIC INDUSTRY

Aid sold 800,000 copies of Do they Know it's Christmas.

The Christmas market is the most difficult of all. According to Selina Webb, editor of *Music Week*:

> 'Normally, a record company would send out a club mix a few weeks before release, and get radio plays, and have a good idea of how a record would do. But not even the most confident of companies would dare predict what will go to the top at Christmas. People who buy records now don't do so at other times of the year'.
>
> Source: *Music Week*, 22 November 1997

Jonathan King's techniques for chart topping success at Christmas (record producer and publisher of *The Tip Sheet*) are:

1. Release the single on the Monday before the final Christmas chart, as the first week of sales is all important.
2. Find a link with a worthy cause, or a television programme like *EastEnders*, or a band with a huge fan base, like the Spice Girls.
3. Make sure Woolworths is targeted as they are the biggest base for family shoppers.
4. Provide incentives to retailers to sell more copies:
   - Give aways (for example, ten free copies for each one sold).
   - Sell 30 copies and get three albums free.
   - Lower price.

Some of these practices are on the edge of legality. It is important to remember that record companies are *not* allowed to do the following:

1. Supply dealers with records by another artist free of charge or upon specially favourable terms.
2. Cause records to be bought as anything other than genuine consumer purchases.
3. Interfere with sales recording equipment.
4. Offer money or other benefit(s) to a dealer.
5. Use a non-related or excessive gift to encourage record sales.

The number of records sold in the first week will determine its popularity and the sales figures after that week.

Synergy

Celine Dion's single, 'My Heart Will Go On' was reputed to have sold over 1 million records worldwide. The printed music sold over 200,000 copies. As the song is the main soundtrack theme for the film *Titanic* (1997), the music has had a massive public promotion. This cross-media form of advertising is called 'synergy'. Another example of synergy was when the film *Philadephia* (1993) boosted sales of the hit single of the same name, by Bruce Springsteen.

The official UK singles chart

The Chart Information Network (CIN) compiles the main singles chart used by the BBC, *Music Week*, and others. CIN uses sales returns sent electronically from more than 4,500 shops, including specialist chains such as HMV and Virgin. There are also more general shops such as Woolworths and WH Smith and supermarkets such as Asda and Tesco who contribute figures. Independent outlets such as Tower Records and Andy also make up 1,300 of the contributing shops. Each week a sample is taken from 80% of these shops and weighed to 100%, based upon criteria including store turnover.

The electronic process for producing the singles chart:

1 Two types of computer at the cash desk collect sales data: Epson and Electronic Point of Sale (Epos) units. The Epson terminals are used less, since they require a sale to be recorded separately from the cash transaction and so can distort true sales figures. With Epos, money must change hands for a sale to be recorded. With both systems, barcodes are recorded and any sales data stored electronically.
2 Each night from 11.00am to 4.00am a central national computer telephones each shop, allowing data to be downloaded automatically.
3 Security checks are carried out to identify any sales cheating.
4 Chart positions are announced every Sunday at 1.30pm. Each title is awarded a final sales position, based on total sales and calculated by computer. The BBC has first broadcasting rights and the UK Top 40 is played on Radio 1. This is just 18 hours after the last sale has been logged.

Singles to albums to profit

The expense of promoting a single to become a hit is a largely offset by enticing the audience to buy the artist's album, which is where the real money is made.

Press releases

A press release should be designed to fit onto one side of A4 paper so that it can be faxed and easily read. Typically, press releases include the following:
▶ Logos and addresses of the production label and the distribution company.
▶ Introductory paragraph stating the main news, for example, 'On release in two weekends' time, the new single from D'siree is destined to become the chart hit …'. A single sentence outlining the song's themes and qualities may be introduced at this point.
▶ The second paragraph will probably be shorter and provide more information about the cast, the USP or the artist's previous history of performing or songwriting records.
▶ The third paragraph will talk about other aspects of the single, such as the production team, other musicians and the technical crew.
▶ The fourth and final paragraph will enthuse about the single's qualities and invite the press to obtain further information about concerts or a video. A quote from the producer, a reviewer or another authoritative voice will also liven up the text.
▶ A contact name, fax and/or telephone number and E-mail number are also essential.

Figure 5.6 CD cover artwork, *Silver X*, by Nansi Mellor: original photograph of fictional artists duo, combined with computer graphics

MUSIC INDUSTRY

Unique Selling Point (USP)

The unique selling point of an artist describes most important feature of a single's promotion.

USP: possible selling points

1 It could be the sexiness of the boy or girl band, in which case the looks of the band would be featured most prominently.
2 It could be how loud the music is, so the band would be featured playing their instruments very loudly, with very specific straplines to accompany the image.
3 It could be the rebelliousness of the artist.
4 It could be the mysterious, romantic nature of the songwriting, therefore the images of the artist or landscapes would be in soft focus.

Discuss

You are a photographer and you have to convey the USP given to you in your brief, by the agent for the artist or band. How will you compose, light and background your shots?

PROMOTIONAL CAMPAIGN

Plan a promotion campaign to support one of the following artists or bands for the Christmas Number One spot in the charts. Choose from:

1 A new, manufactured two boy and two girl band – one asian, one afro-caribbean, one white and one Kurd.
2 A French indie drum n' bass band playing 'Jingle Bells' in French.
3 An *EastEnders* star's debut song.
4 Linton Kwezi Johnson singing 'I Love my Turkey (Don't Eat Him)'.
5 Your choice.

Read the relevant sections of this chapter and study the information to decide what is the best plan for your campaign.
Note: You will have to create song titles, some words and names for your artists.

Task 1

Outline your step-by-step campaign to reach the Number One *Top of the Pops* spot at Christmas.

(20 marks)

Task 2

In your campaign, list the unique selling points of your artist.

(5 marks)

Task 3

In two columns, list possible weaknesses and strengths of the artist or the campaign.

(10 marks)

Task 4

Produce a press release to send to press, television and publicity agents.

(15 marks)

Extension Tasks

1 Analyse two or three videos by a manufactured artist or band who is concerned with their star appeal. Consider:
a Star performance.
b How the lyrics link to the images.
c How the music links to images, camerawork or editing speed, and rhythm.
d What is your verdict on the effectiveness of the video? Explain your reasons.

Compare these videos with an artist or band which does seem to be manufactured. Use the same questions as before.

2 Produce packaging for a band of your own invention. Choose following formats:

▶ A CD cover, back and front.
▶ Featured on the cover of a magazine (include straplines, etc.).

You will need to create an image to sell the music. What kind of signifiers can you use for this? You will need to take a photograph and find people to appear in it. Draw a sketch first. Include details of your artist or band's facial expression(s), gesture(s), body posture and dress. Include also a background, a foreground and props. Take photographs, scan the images into a computer and add text and graphics.

3 Produce a press release for the band to coincide with a new song release or tour. Write a commentary of 300 to 500 words explaining your intentions behind the main messages, the unique selling point, and the audience and institutions (invented).

4 Analyse the lyrics of a band or artist, with a view to its suitability for a video in which the artist does not appear. Turn the lyrics into a storyboard, showing where lyrics match the images and sound. Write a commentary on how you would expect the images to convey the artist's ideas and sell the product at the same time. Imagine that the video might appear on MTV.

5 Produce a one minute radio jingle for an evening dedicated to one music genre, for example, hip-hop, jungle or soul. Use excerpts from songs, mix with a voiceover, interviews and comments to promote this unique evening. Select an appropriate radio channel and identify the audience. Write a commentary on the intentions, audience, sponsors and institutions involved.

Examination Skills

Knowledge and Understanding

In essay questions about the music industry, it is useful to have a working knowledge of majors and independents. Be aware of how they are organised, of their promotion campaigns and their relationship to other media, for example videos. There should be emphasis on the idea of an image as the heart of the construction of the mainstream and independent band – the unique selling point. Focus also on the different ends of the music business – mainstream as products for businesses, and music with fun or messages attached for the independent end of the spectrum.

Textual Analysis

You will have to be able to analyse how meaning is constructed in images of bands and associated ideas that carry the band's style and attitude (CD covers, videos, press releases, posters). Videos convey ideas about lyrics, stars, and band's performances. Distinguish between the various types of videos, for example, band performs; band plays a part in the narrative of the video; band does not appear and the video is an abstract visual interpretation of the lyrics. Commentaries on practical work should show an ability to stand back from the process and analyse images in terms of signifiers and meaning. This can be difficult if the band is completely the work of the student's imagination, but the aim is to explain how the content of the images convey meanings via association or suggestion.

For example, an analysis of a magazine cover might be:

The solo artist is wearing glasses and clothes which connect them to a street level of credibility. The hip-hop genre of music is associated with rapping words and beat-based music. The artist is photographed against the wall, suggesting the idea of the street-based sounds. The gesture of their foot raised in the air indicates a level of street 'cool' and savvy. It is possible to see this gesture as mixing the idea of kung fu arts and dance. The closeness of the foot in the foreground gives depth and drama to the image as the viewer's eye is drawn back into the picture past the lettering.

Practical Work

Production of images for CD or magazine front covers require an understanding of the following: typical forms and conventions, use of graphics and layout to improve the image and the style; use of cropping, composition using foreground and background, signifiers of expression, body posture and gesture and props as signifiers. Awareness of the difference between manufactured bands and independent bands is also important. How audience (positioning of images) and institutions (label, studio and distributors) are built into the identity of the product is a further area to study. Radio jingles use excerpts from songs and mix with voiceover, interviews and plugs for purchase of records. Skill in combining these elements effectively should be evident.

6 Film industry and promotion

MAY THE FORCE BE WITH YOU!

In this chapter you will study how films are started, made, promoted and sold. How are films developed through the production process before, during and after filming? Who are the main people involved in making a film successful? Who decides certificate ratings for a film? How are other media products used to brand and promote the film in the market?

KW

Genre ■ *mise-en-scène* ■ narrative ■ enigma ■ major ■ independent ■ Art house ■ distributor ■ exhibitor ■ promotion ■ marketing ■ advertising

TW

Electronic press kit (EPK) ■ trailer ■ poster ■ credit block ■ tag (or catch) line ■ teaser ■ unique selling point (USP) ■ press release ■ below the line and above the line costs

Review

Reread the sections on film languages in Chapter Two: Languages and Categories to review the terms 'film genre' and 'narrative'. These terms also relate to the way a film is promoted and what audiences expect of a film.

WHAT IS THE FILM INDUSTRY?

Study the following list of the Top 10 films in the UK and the USA.

1. Which of these films have you seen and why did you, or did you not, go to see them?
2. For which of these films did you see the publicity or merchandise?
3. Judging by the titles of the films, identify the genre of each one.
4. What age group (audience) do you think went to see the first five films in the US Top 10 list?
5. Compare the top box office British ratings with the US box office ratings. Why do you think there is such a difference?

FILM INDUSTRY AND PROMOTION

Top 10 UK		Weeks	Screens July 31-Aug 2	Gross July 31-Aug 2
1	(-) Lost In Space Dir: Stephen Hopkins	new	403	£3.13m
2	(-) Dr Dolittle Dir: Betty Thomas	new	379	£3.05m
3	(1) Godzilla Dir: Roland Emmerich	3	461	£1.10m
4	(2) The Wedding Singer Dir: Frank Coraci	9	201	£240,000
5	(3) Six Days, Seven Nights Dir: Ivan Reitman	5	172	£185,000
6	(4) Grease Dir: Randal Kleiser	5	199	£150,000
7	(5) Barney's Great Adventure Dir: Steven Gomer	6	290	£140,000
8	(-) The Castle Dir: Rob Sitch	new	152	£116,000
9	(7) The Little Mermaid Dir: Ron Clements, John Musker	6	317	£116,000
10	(9) The Magic Sword: Quest For Camelot Dir: Frederik du Chau	2	261	£87,800

Top 10 US		Weeks	Screens July 31-Aug 2	Gross July 31-Aug 2
1	(1) Saving Private Ryan Dir: Steven Spielberg	2	2,111	$23.6m
2	(-) The Parent Trap Dir: Nancy Meyers	new	2,247	$11.4m
3	(4) There's Something About Mary Dir: Bobby and Peter Farrelly	3	2,145	$10.9m
4	(-) The Negotiator Dir: F Gary Gray	new	2,436	$10.2m
5	(-) Ever After Dir: Andy Tennant	new	1,767	$8.39m
6	(2) The Mask Of Zorro Dir: Martin Campbell	3	1,701	$8.51m
7	(3) Lethal Weapon 4 Dir: Richard Donner	4	2,602	$7.71m
8	(5) Armageddon Dir: Michael Bay	5	2,491	$7.52m
9	(6) Dr Dolittle Dir: Betty Thomas	6	2,184	$4.56m
10	(8) Mafia! Dir: Jim Abrahams	2	1,944	$3.67m

Figure 6.1
Source: © *The Guardian*, 7 August 1998

Film is a business

All of the films in both the Top 10 lists, with the exception of *The Castle* (Australian), were produced by American companies. The film industry is dominated by Hollywood business. Its main aim is to make money. Hollywood studios employ people with skills in finance, technology, creative arts and science, and America has become the world's most successful country in selling its films at home and abroad. Some films are made by independent companies and if they enter into the mainstream cinemas, they are often helped by major distributors.

The cycle of production

The life of a film's creative production can be divided into three main stages:

▶ **Pre-production** is the period when the film is conceived, written into a treatment and screenplay, and when the financial investment, director, cast, technicians, props and locations are planned and found.
▶ **Production** is the filming process itself.

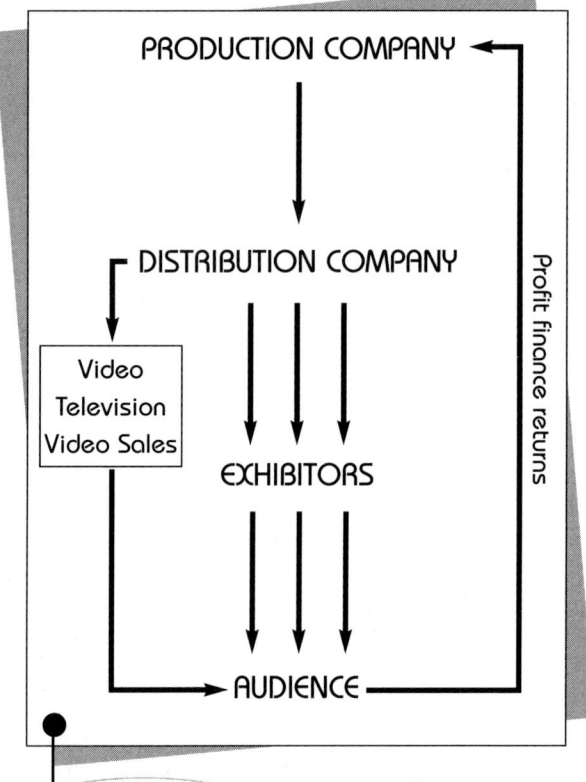

Figure 6.2 Diagram showing the cycle of production

▶ **Post production** is the editing process, where sound and image, special effects and titles are added.

The cycle of money

The total life of a film is much longer than the production process alone. It involves the machinery of an industry that is designed to make money:

▶ **Pre-production sales** covers the financial investment that is often raised by the sales department, offering the film package to distributors and exhibitors even before the film is made.

▶ **Production** is the process of writing and making the film itself.

▶ **Distribution** is the selling, publicising, marketing and print replication.

▶ **Exhibition** is when the film is seen by the public in cinema theatres.

▶ **'Sell-through' and TV transmission rights** is a subsequent stage of exhibition and distribution of the film through video hire, video sales, television broadcasting and, for example, aeroplane.

FILM MAKING

The pitch of the idea

To make a film you need money. If a producer already has enough money or is an established big name in the industry, then they can go ahead with production. They may however, use an independent production company to actually shoot the film. If the producer is actually an independent company, they will need to convince banks, investors or distributors to lend them money.

Almost inevitably a production team will pitch their creative idea to several potential investors. This means presenting ideas clearly and enthusiastically both verbally and on paper. The hopeful film makers deliver an explanation of their film ideas as sharply and clearly as they can to producers and sponsors.

A good example of a dramatic pitch occurs in a scene in the film *The Player* (1992), a film about Hollywood by Robert Altman. An English scriptwriter, played by Richard E. Grant, approaches Tim Robbins who plays Griffin, the producer, in a chance meeting beside a pool in a Los Angeles hotel.

Imagine the first scene, outside a US penitentiary. It is during the night and there is a demonstration calling for the electrocution of a 19-year-old black man who is on death row. He is guilty. There is a candlelight vigil; the lights twinkle like Japanese lanterns in the rain. It is silent as a black limousine glides up outside the gates and out gets the District Attorney, who is greeted by the prison director's wife. They shake hands and they go in through the gates.

This is the beginning of the pitch for a

FILM INDUSTRY AND PROMOTION

whole film; it is visual and it is dramatic. To succeed in pitching a film in real life, you will probably have to tell your story hundreds of times. You need to be very persistent, patient and energetic. You also need to 'sell' your idea to the people who will make copies of your film and send it the cinemas and distributors. These people will need to be confident that they can pass your film on to the exhibitors, the cinema owners (who want all their seats occupied by the customers) and the audience.

Your film will become what is known as a 'property' and will be made into a 'package'. Like any other product, the Hollywood 'factory' has to be packaged and presented in order to reach the widest markets. The film script may attract stars, directors, musicians and special effects companies. They will become part of the whole 'package' that the public will see in the publicity before and during the film's cinema release.

Ideas for a film

Firstly, you have to decide what genre of film you want to make. You must have clear ideas about the *mise-en-scène*, narrative and character. It is also important to outline the setting in as much detail as possible.

Mise-en-scène

Mise-en-scène is the placing into the setting of all the elements to be filmed: props, lighting, character behaviour, make-up, sets and anything else that is in the frame of the camera lens at the time of filming. For instance, one might expect the *mise-en-scène* of an adaptation of Charles Dickens' novel *Great Expectations* to include authentic period costume and Victorian buildings, gas lamps and horse-drawn carriages. A typical Dracula horror film might include graveyards, mists, moonlight and lightening-filled night skies.

> A more recent film version of *Great Expectations* (1998) had a modern setting, and starred Ethan Hawke, Gwyneth Paltrow, Anne Bancroft and Robert De Niro. The contemporary settings included New York and Florida.
> **Discuss in pairs**: why do you think the setting has been updated to American and modern times?

Setting and genre

Setting is the major element in establishing what the genre of a film is. It would be confusing to set a science fiction film in the wild west of nineteenth century America. Or would it? *Back to the Future Part 3* did exactly that, with time travel. Science fantasy movies can 'travel' across historical periods.

In pairs, discuss, invent and draw (in rough) the opening shot of one of the following types of films:

a American high school comedy (indicate the type of comedy (for example, slapstick, screwball, farce).

b Agatha Christie murder mystery (indicate the 1930s period).

c Science fiction horror (note: this is a horror film, not a monster movie, like *Godzilla*. What is the difference between a thriller and a horror film?).

You can use one shot only but you may have to draw more than one frame. This could involve a moving camera, zooming or tracking, panning or tilting (see Chapter Two for explanation of camera terms). Explain all the visual elements of the *mise-en-scène*, including the music, sounds or special effects. What signifies an American setting, a thirties period drama or a horror?

Present your opening shot to the rest of the class. Try to also outline the rest of the film's narrative. This will take the form of a pitch: who will buy your idea and is it convincing? Does your class audience think it conveys the genre you chose successfully?

Film marketing

Having successfully persuaded a sponsor to accept your idea, the complete script must be written. This can sometimes take between two and ten years. Before filming can start, the script is used to attract stars and directors to work on it. The script is also used to sell the film to potential distributors, exhibitors and buyers. Marketing a film always starts early on in the process.

Selling the film

It would seem logical to suggest that a film must be made before it can be sold. In fact, many films are sold before they are made. A film production company has to find money to pay the actors and actresses, the camera crew, hire the costumes and locations and pay the director and lab. technicians.

If it is not a big company with financial reserves, it can borrow the money from a financier or alternatively can promise a share of the profits to the distributors or the exhibitors. A distributor such as Miramax will see the opportunity to invest in a film that they like the sound of. They will provide money to the production company in advance on the basis that they can share any of the profits or have exclusive rights to its distribution. Direct support can be provided in the form of promoting the film, as well as distributing and exhibiting the film.

Marketing campaign

If a film maker is successful in obtaining money, a studio to produce it, a distributor and exhibition outlets, then it will still need to promote the film. A promotion campaign aims to persuade the audience to go and see it. Without this campaign a film maker cannot compete with all the other hundreds of films also trying to reach the audience. Films live or die according to the success of their promotional campaigns.

Once the film is almost finished the marketing campaign swings into action. Marketing a film falls into two categories: advertising and publicity. Advertising is paid for, and consists of press, TV and radio advertising, in addition to posters and trailers.

Publicity is not paid for directly, although it is created by the publicity department and includes reviews, articles and interviews in the media, plus special gala screenings.

Promotions

What does a typical promotional campaign consist of?

- Teasers
- Posters and radio
- Trade press screening
- TV and video trailers
- Merchandising
- Tie-ins
- Special events – galas and stunts

There are several media products that are used to promote a film: Electronic Press Kits (EPK), trailers, advertisements, news publicity and advertising merchandise such as T-shirts, games and toys.

FILM INDUSTRY AND PROMOTION

Figure 6.3 Promotion: *The Mask* and Burger King
Source: © Burger King Corporation, 1998

Teaser trailers in cinema	November
Teaser posters in cinema	November
Teaser posters in cinema	February
Trade press exhibitor screening (alerts exhibitors to content of film)	February
New trailers in cinema	March
Cardboard cut out 'standees'	March
Publish book of the film	March
Banners for foyers	April
Release single of the film	May
New trailers	May
Actors and actresses, director start to appear on TV and radio chat shows	June–August
Press invited to preview film	July
Billboards	July
Television teaser trailers	July
Press advertisements	July
Photographs of filming, specially selected for certain media papers and magazines	July
Gala evening in London's West End to premiere the film, plus stars and celebrities	July
General release	August

Figure 6.4 Typical promotional campaign and strategies

Following is a typical promotional campaign for a summer blockbuster (a Hollywood action film with a major star). As an example, this schedule is based on a film released on 1 August, during children's summer holidays.

Further publicity is continued during the screening of the film around the UK (August to September).

> Discuss and write an explanation of the impact each of the strategies in Figure 6.4 has on the publicity for the film (see example given for trade press screening).

Tie-ins

Tie-ins are related products that are often connected to characters or figures in films, such as *Star Wars* toys or *Men In Black* guns. Many non-film companies like to join the film's publicity trails to sell specifically tailored products. For example, *The Lost World: Jurassic Park* (1997) tie-ins were:

- Marks and Spencer – in the form of clothes and food, for example, Dinosaur products such as chocolate, crisps and cakes, steaks and gums.

- Burger King carried the logo of the film on their trays and bags.
- Kellogs, KP and Tetley also produced related pack promotions.
- Toys were produced by Hasbro.
- The novel of the film by Michael Crichton had already been published by Random House and a movie tie-in version was published by Arrow Books Ltd.
- Music soundtrack by John Williams was also sold on CD.
- The making of the movie books.
- Junior versions in the form of board games, comic books, or video games.

Cross media links

Films today, especially those from Hollywood, attract a great deal of attention because they are extremely well publicised through trailers and posters. The marketing and promotion departments of film companies produce a plentiful supply of images and extracts of the films, before they are released, so that they can be endlessly seen and talked about across television, newspapers, radio, videos and magazines. This type of promotion also includes trailers and posters in the cinema itself. Films are often linked to other media, for example, when *Titanic* (1997) was first released in 1997, the music soundtrack single by Celine Dion went straight to the top of the UK music industry charts.

Teasers

The teaser campaign is usually a poster or a trailer which comes out before the film is released and which states: 'Coming soon' or 'at your local cinema' on a particular date. The information is very basic and tells you little about the film itself. It is designed to whet your appetite and tease you into thinking, 'I wonder what this film is about?' The teaser for *Independence Day* (1996) involved using the initials ID4, which created a sense of mystery. Independence Day itself falls on 4 July, when America celebrates its anniversary of political independence. Hence the date was used in much of the teaser campaign to convey the desired message.

The teaser campaign for the independently produced *Transpotting* 1996 involved pictures of the main characters on posters placed around the London underground and bus shelters, with only their name and a little orange block of colour – the plot of the film was never given away but the word of mouth campaign which went with the film made it into a cult movie when upon release. The soundtrack of contemporary Brit-Pop music was another selling point.

Press release

A press release is a news summary about an event or a new launch. In the film industry, a press release is often included as part of the Electronic Press Kit (EPK). This pack includes photographs (stills) of the film as it was being made, stills from the final film, trailer clips of the film, cast and credit lists and a press release.

Press releases are aimed at film review journalists and cinema owners who need information in order to write about the films or to show them. A press release ideally comes with a video or CD of the film that gives the reviewer plenty of information with which to write about or to hire the film.

Marketing an independent film

Celia is an Australian film made in 1989, which is about the psychological development of a young girl (Rebecca Smart) who suffers a number of traumatic experiences that lead to a fatal killing. The UK film poster suggested it

FILM INDUSTRY AND PROMOTION

might be a horror film, using the shadow of a creature's claws cast on the background.

The film was shown in independent cinemas, often known as Art House cinemas, and was popular with those people who went to see it. However its poster publicity did not give a true sense of the psychological drama of the film; it certainly was not a horror film, even though the poster gave that impression. The marketing agent promoting *Celia* confessed to finding it difficult to market this complex though gripping film.

One main reason why independent films do not become box office successes so frequently is because they are not aiming to appeal to everyone. The second reason is that they are competing with the massive marketing and publicity machine of the Hollywood industry. They are competing with the 'blockbuster', the film that will fill all the seats in all the main cinemas in America in its first and second weekends of screening.

Compare the low impact of *Brassed Off* (1996) with the phenomenal success world wide of *The Full Monty* (1997). Although *The Full Monty* was not intended to be a blockbuster, it was supported by Twentieth Century Searchlight as its distributor, thus making its American release much more assured. Both films were about the effects of unemployment and the attempts to salvage some respect in the face of indignity.

Posters

There are three types of film poster:
1 The teaser poster – this poster contains basic information to whet the appetite of the film audience. It may not indicate much about the plot.
2 The main poster – this contains the main information about the production personnel and distributors.

Figure 6.5 *Men in Black* promotional poster
Source: © BFI

3 The poster with the short, one line reviews, often to accompany the video release.

Discuss:
What are the typical elements of a film's main poster? How many elements can you can think of? Discuss information, images and layout.

Key elements of a poster:

▶ Images of the key settings and the main characters are usually incorporated into the film poster. They are literally blended without concern for real perspective or size relationships between people and setting.
▶ Most posters are horizontal or landscape in shape, however, if they go onto a bus shelter or magazine page they are vertical or portrait in shape.
▶ The catch or tag line indicates the action, genre or attitude within the film. For example, 'Protecting the earth from the scum of the universe' was the tag line for *Men in Black*. 'A chilling, bold, mesmerising, futuristic detective thriller' was the tag line for *Blade Runner* (1982)

GCSE MEDIA STUDIES

- The title – typeface and graphics indicate the style.
- The billing block includes credits and information. The credit block gives details of the main people in the cast, making and distribution of the film.
- Certificate – for example, PG, 12, 15 18.

POSTER ANALYSIS

Compare posters from two films that feature Leonardo DiCaprio in them: *Titanic* and *Romeo and Juliet*.

Task 1

a Denotate and connotate the two posters in Figures 6.7 and 6.8 (see Chapter Two).
(10 marks)

b Which poster do you think is more effective and interestingly designed? Explain your answers. **(5 marks)**

c What *mise-en-scènes* are suggested in these posters? **(10 marks)**

Task 2

What type of personalities are illustrated by the images of the characters in each poster?
(5 marks)

Figure 6.7 *Romeo and Juliet* poster
Source: © BFI

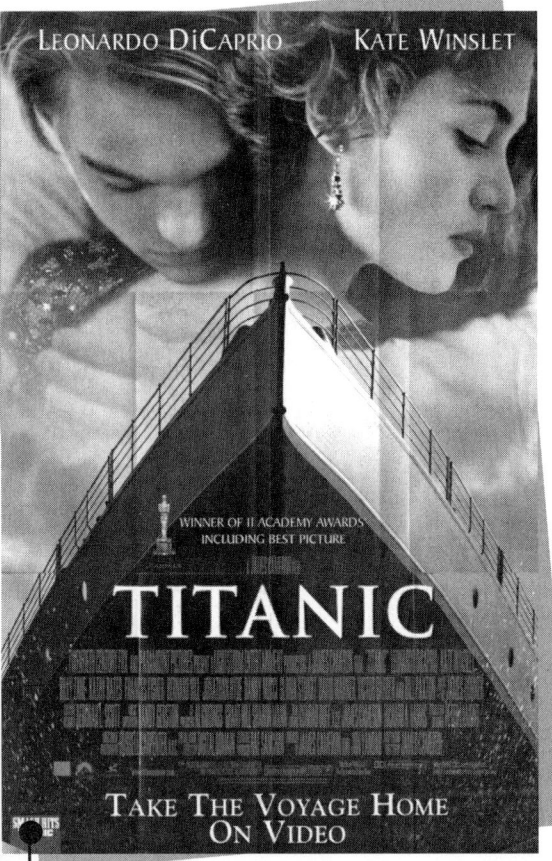

Figure 6.8 *Titanic* poster
Source: © 1998 Twentieth Century Fox Entertainment, Inc.

FILM INDUSTRY AND PROMOTION

Task 3

What would you say the posters' makers wanted to emphasise as the unique selling point (USP) in each poster? For example, is it the plot, the themes, the setting or the characters?

(10 marks)

Task 4

Both films have plots and endings that many people know already through history or previous versions. Why do you think the posters might make audiences want to go and see these films?

(10 marks)

FILM PEOPLE

Stars

Actors and actresses are turned into celebrities; their faces and fame are often used to sell a film. Will Smith, Leonardo DiCaprio, Kate Winslet, Demi Moore and Sandra Bullock are some good examples. Films often command massive budgets and films like *Titanic* can recoup enormous profits when helped by big name stars' names and image.

Figure 6.9 Will Smith: stars can make a movie a success

Source: Associated Press

Budgeting for stars

There is also the issue of how many stars, if any, will feature in a movie, and who will be selected, according to the budget. Hollywood actors and actresses are given 'star ratings' by film magazines such as *Variety*, *Entertainment Weekly*, *Hollywood Reporter* and *Premiere*. These ratings can help film makers assess which stars they can afford to hire, and are divided into 'A*', 'A' and 'B' lists according to:

- Current salary
- Previous film successes
- Loyal audience following
- Behaviour on set
- Oscar winning capability

The lists which follow have been compiled from a number of sources (for example, *Variety*, *Hollywood Reporter* and *Premiere*) and are rated by audience popular choice. It should be noted that the composite list is the work of the author's and is not intended as a definitive or an objective statement of status or bankability.

'A*' list

Guaranteed foreign sale, regardless of the other elements the film contains. Examples include: Tom Cruise, Harrison Ford, Mel Gibson, Arnold Swarzenegger, Tom Hanks, Brad Pitt, Jim Carrey, John Travolta, Jodie Foster.

GCSE MEDIA STUDIES

Figure 6.10 Harrison Ford   Source: © BFI

Figure 6.11 Bruce Willis
Source: © Ronald Grant Archive

Figure 6.12 Demi Moore
Source: © Ronald Grant Archive

'A' list

Could be hired if the director and budget are right:

Michael Douglas	Drew Barrymore
Sylvester Stallone	Samuel L. Jackson
Jack Nicholson	Demi Moore
Julia Roberts	

'B' list

Other factors in the production may prove to be more important.

Matt Damon	Gene Hackman
Kim Basinger	Michael Keaton
Liam Neeson	Wesley Snipes
Sigourney Weaver	

FILM INDUSTRY AND PROMOTION

Money matters

Average A* actors receive around $15 to 20 million for their roles in films. Therefore, it is possible that a quarter of a $100 million film budget could be spent on one star. A report in 1998 stated that 'A'-list actresses finally seem to be catching up with their male counterparts. Julia Roberts' salary for her role opposite Richard Gere in Paramount's *The Runaway Bride* (1999) was reported to have been more than $20 million. Jodie Foster reportedly received more than $15 million for Twentieth Century Fox 2000's *Anna and the King* (1999).

Directors

Even director's names can sell genres, such as John Carpenter and horror, Steven Spielberg and fantasy and historical drama, Quentin Tarantino and crime. Once a film has become successful, like Spielberg's *ET* (1982), then a studio can use its success and name to aid the promotion of another film. Of course, if a studio becomes as successful as Steven Spielberg, it can then afford to form its own production company. However, even Spielberg's production company has worked with a major studio, Paramount, to ensure greater distribution of films. The $80 million cost of *Deep Impact* (1998) was shared by the two companies and had to make $140 million to produce profits.

Biggest audience

The successful promotion of a Hollywood film depends on making it attractive for the audience to want to go and see it. It is important for the film to be easily categorised to reach the widest potential and global markets. If an audience can easily identify a film's genre, stars or its directors, then it will be more assured about what it is going to watch. The audience will be then more likely to risk spending money to go and see it.

Distributors

Distributors have to produce many copies of films to reach the widest possible audience, and they must reach the audience very quickly in first run theatres, usually in urban centres. The first weekend is crucial in gaining public interest and allowing word of mouth to promote the film.

How do distributors and audiences identify a film genre?

Posters, trailers on television or video hire copies, and cinemas are the main places where films are promoted. Labelling posters with words 'the ultimate horror spoof' is one way of telling the audience what genre they can expect to see. Films with easily recognisable genre categories such as science fiction, crime, westerns and musicals make it easier for the public to define what they are watching and whether or not to go to the cinema.

Study the list of distributors below. How many do you recognise? Can you name any four films that they have distributed? Where would you find out information on the distributors of a film?

1. Universal International Pictures (UIP)
2. Buena Vista
3. Twentieth Century Fox
4. Warner Bros.
5. Columbia Tri-Star
6. Entertainment
7. Polygram
8. Guild
9. Film Four
10. Rank
11. First Independent
12. Artificial Eye
13. Electric

Unique selling point

The unique selling point (USP) is the key element of the film which the promotions department want to push. It could be the stars, the special effects, the unusual storyline, or any combination of these elements. The USP is often fairly obvious, as it is stated in the slogan, the tag line or the voice-over commentary on a trailer.

> **Discuss**
>
> What is the USP of a film promotion you have seen recently?

CINEMA

In the early period of cinema between the late 1890s and early 1900s, the idea of setting up a special building as a cinema didn't catch on for a while, until it became profitable. When it did, the Americans were the fastest and most effective at making money from it. Although the French had perhaps done the most to take the leading role in developing technical inventions (the travelling shows of the Lumiere Brothers toured and amazed citizens of the major cities of the world), the Americans were the first to really turn the whole process into a business.

The early days

Cinema as a real presence on high streets began when the first new buildings made for screening were erected. In Britain there were cinemas around in the early 1900s and by the 1920s, lavish and grand theme-based cinemas were constructed in America, often adding to the glamour and attention paid to the moving pictures, their stars and studios.

By the 1930s Hollywood had managed to establish itself as the major global economic force in the film industry. It had the advantage of great financial support from East Coast American bankers, and plentiful sunlight on the west coast of America to film all day in any season. Hollywood also attracted a high number of creative artists, actors and actresses, writers and production crew who were interested in making a serious living from films. Film was not only the new twentieth century art form, but was now big business.

In the 1890s and early twentieth century, films were very short and several films of different kinds might be shown in the same viewing. There were two reasons for this. Previously, in Europe, music hall entertainment consisted of several performers, such as comedians, trapeze artists and dancers each of whom would all do a short act before the next performer. The second reason was that initially films only held a novelty value and simple dramas or scenes from real life were shown to introduce the newcomer to moving pictures.

The rise of the multiplex

By the sixties, cinema going fell into decline due to factors such as the advent of television. However, by the 1980s numbers visiting cinemas began to rise, as people sought new places to spend their leisure time.

FILM INDUSTRY AND PROMOTION

Today, cinema goers can see mainstream films at multiplexes, where several films are shown in different cinemas throughout the building. The costs of keeping the building running are paid for by showing several of the most well publicised films for as long as they remain popular. As many as 500 prints are produced for the first screenings in the USA; as opposed to perhaps only 250 for the most popular films in the UK.

Where and how you view films is today more varied. Video hire and sale are both relatively new formats and can be watched at home. Films are shown on television, cable and satellite; it is possible to see films on aeroplanes, in pubs and private clubs films. New technology such as Digital Versatile Disc (DVD) also extend the range of domestic formats now available.

Certification

Films have to be submitted to the British Board of Film Certification (BBFC). This is a service that the film industry has created for its own members, for classification into U, PG, 12, 15 and 18 categories. This means that audiences can be assured of the type of material they can expect to see. Certification can also give street credibility to a film, and if the film gains an 18 certificate the distributors can entice the older teenager to watch it, in the knowledge that violence, sex or bad language may be included. Distributors' main target audience is the age group of 15 to 18 years, and if this audience can be reached then the chances of a box office success will be more likely. The widest possible audience is for a PG rated film.

CASE STUDY: SCIENCE FICTION

In Chapter two, the word 'genre' was introduced. The important art of selling films to the public depends on explaining the genre of the films simply and clearly. One theory is that the public need to be told what to expect, although this can annoy many people who enjoy sophisticated mixes of genres.

Many science fiction films originally come from novels. Jules Verne's *2000 Leagues under the Sea* (1954), H.G. Welles's *Things to Come* (1936) are examples of filmed versions of novels.

When we read a science fiction novel we experience emotions and ideas differently than when we sit down to watch a science fiction film.

We might think more about the special effects in a film. We might think about when and how the monster will jump out and scare the victim in a thriller film. In a crime thriller, we might try to work out which of the suspects

Figure 6.13 *Things to Come*

Source: © BFI

> Science fiction films have a distinctive set of elements. Write down, on your own and then discuss in pairs, what these elements are under the following headings:
> 1 *Mise-en-scène*
> 2 Situations
> 3 Characters: good and bad
> 4 Plot lines
> 5 Narrative structure
> 6 Iconography (for example, typical icons of a western are cowboy hats, saloon bars and tumble-weed strewn deserts)

in the police line-up committed the crime. In a novel we are left to our imaginations, through the written descriptions of the creature from outer space. In the film we are shown the actual shape and figure of the evil alien, through music, sound effects, various shots, special effects, props and creative make-up and costumes. If the make-up or special modelling is shown to be superficial, audiences will feel let down by the lack of ingenuity and sophistication. Such is the demand for realistic and specialised effects, or so many people in Hollywood think.

Mise-en-scène

Examples of setting in science fiction include:

- Space
- Another planet
- Earth
- Time travel
- Spaceship
- A futuristic place that exists only as a concept in the mind (for example hell or paradise)

Mise-en-scène also includes costumes, camera movement and framing, lighting and acting.

Situations

These could include:

- Earth is threatened by an alien force.
- A space mission goes wrong.
- Earth has already been destroyed or taken over – only a few heroes or heroines survive.
- Machines rule a future world – what role is there here for humans?
- A futuristic world of a mix of planets and space travellers co-existing in space. Who or what is the dominant force?
- Everyday life is turned upside by a freak of nature, such as an excess of ants or spiders.

Characters

These tend to follow the types and stereotypes of any dramas. The qualities of reasoning versus intuition are explored best in *Star Trek*, between the logical alien Dr Spock and the emotional, intuitive Captain Kirk. Evil characters are usually physically repellent and often given reptilian features to make them appear sinister, for example in *Alien*. In many films, such as *Invasion of the Body Snatchers* (1956) and *Men in Black* (1997), the aliens inhabit the bodies of human beings to disguise themselves.

Plot and narrative structure

The science fiction writer Ray Bradbury once said:

FILM INDUSTRY AND PROMOTION

> 'The thing about science fiction is that it is not about tomorrow, it is about today.' The setting may be technologically beyond us (although often it is not) but the stories we, science fiction writers, are telling are the issues of today.'

In Michael Crichton's *Jurassic Park* (1992) we are taken into the world of biological science: of genetics and the control of DNA. The science fiction film is often based on ideas deriving from real scientific discovery: to extend the natural life span, cloning birth outside the womb, perfect genetic planning, biological warfare and robotic intelligence.

Much of a plot is based on the 'what if?' factor. The narrative structure tends to fit the normality, to displacement, to normality pattern. A tranquil setting is attacked by an unidentified force, chaos ensues – the antidote for which the defenders must find if they are to survive – and finally order is restored.

Themes are often contemporary, for example, the role of the action women or computer guided robotic intelligence. Sigourney Weaver in the *Aliens* film series plays a female heroine who is the supreme fighter, and she is more capable than any man of handling the monster. Is it possible for a robot to have a memory or even be more human than humans, for example in the films *2001: A Space Odyssey* (1968) and *Blade Runner* (1982)?

Iconography

This can include:
- Alien creature
- Paranormal evidence (flying objects, invisible movement)
- Spaceship (complex control panels)
- Space (galaxies)
- Sophisticated weaponry (lasers)
- Technology (scanners and computers)

Where do ideas for science fiction films come from?

Books

Science fiction films are often based on novels. *Jurassic Park* (1992) and *The Lost World* (1997) are based on novels by Michael Crichton. *The War of the Worlds* (1953), *The Invisible Man* (1933), *Things to Come* (1936), and *The Invisible Thief* (1909, based on *The Invisible Man*) were first written as novels by H.G. Wells. *2001: A Space Odyssey* (1968) was based on a short story by Arthur C. Clarke.

Previous films, radio or comics

Star Wars (1977) was originally going to be a remake of the 1930s *Flash Gordon* serials, but was stopped due to copyright problems. In this case there were references to the Holy Grail, the Bible, *The Adventures of Robin Hood* (1938), *The Wizard of Oz* (1939) and the western genre. *Judge Dredd* (1995) was based on the comic of the same name by 2000 AD comics.

Television

Some science fiction films began as TV series, such as the cult series *The X-Files* and *Star Trek*, the latter of which has had numerous film versions made of it. Interestingly, the popularity of the science genre in television serials has continued with *Babylon 5*, *Space Precinct* and the satirical comedy sci-fi series *Red Dwarf*. Comics are also a source for films such as *Judge Dredd* (1995).

> Science fiction saw a revival in 1977 with the massive success of Star Wars. In the 90s, a whole series of Aliens and Star Trek films have been successful.
>
> **Discuss:**
> 1 Why is science fiction so popular?
> 2 Why do you think TV programmes like the X-Files hold so much interest?

1 Read the short descriptions of the following films and make notes under two headings: theme and *mise-en-scène*. What are the main themes and *mise-en-scène*?

a *Things To Come* (1936) – the creation of a one world state after a devastating world war.
b *The War of the Worlds* (1953) – alien invasion from Mars. How does Earth respond?
c *I Married An Alien From Outer Space* (1958) – aliens take over human beings' bodies. Expectant fathers at a maternity hospital save the day. Comedy.
d *2001: A Space Odyssey* (1968) – the evolution of man has been subject to strange forces which have waited until mankind has the reached the point at which space flight is possible – a serious space journey.
e *Star Wars* (1977) – the intergalactic wars are raging and Princess Leia Organa is being pursued by an Imperial Star Destroyer. Will Darth Vader wipe out the last of the good Jedi Knights who have kept the world a safe place as warrior-guardians? Good does triumph over evil, but only until the sequels.
f *Blade Runner* (1984) – space cop Harrison Ford has been sent back to earth to track down a group of killer robots who have hidden themselves in the bodies of earthlings.
g *Independence Day* (1996) – the world watches as spaceships hover over the earth's major cities. These extra-terrestrials have only one aim, which is to destroy the world as we know it, on the fourth of July – America's independence celebration day.
h *Star Trek – First Contact* (1998) – the crew of the Starship Enterprise fight to prevent a time-travelling plot that will change the world forever.

2 Imagine, you are to select six films from 1936–1984 and they are to be released today as a new classic sci-fi video six pack box collection. What would be the box set's unique selling point: what catch lines could you write for each film's mini poster?

FILM COSTS

How much do films cost?

Typical costs include the following:

- Development of script and contracts for rights
- Producer's unit
- Direction
- Cast
- Travel and living costs
- Production staff
- Set and staff
- Wardrobe, make-up and hairdressing
- Special effects
- Camera department
- Second unit
- Transport and locations
- Film editing
- Music and sound
- Main and end titles

FILM INDUSTRY AND PROMOTION

Above the line and below the line costs include: fees for the producer, director, or actors and technicians. These costs are generally known before the production.

Below the line costs include: film stock expenditure, equipment hire, hotel and catering costs, scenery, costumes and location hire. These costs can vary. The cost of feeding and accommodating a crew can rise if the weather is bad and rain stops filming. If this requires more filming to be done these costs can become very expensive.

Star Wars (1977)

Stars Wars (1977) was one of the most expensive films ever made. *Star Wars* cost $11 million to make, which was $1 million more than the original agreed budget. It then took a further $16 million to release and promote it. A breakdown of the film's costs follows:

Cost	$
Development money	10,000
Final script	50,000
Cast including the director	750,000
Other salaries	2,100,000
Music	100,000
Film and processing	200,000
Costumes	300,000
Stage rents (studios)	300,000
Insurance	200,000
Set construction/lighting	1,600,000
Special effects/models	3,900,000
Transport and location costs	700,000
Interest on loans, etc.	800,000
TOTAL	**11,000,000**

Figure 6.14 Breakdown of costs for *Star Wars*
Source: Adapted from *Screen International*, January 1978

Today, an average large scale film costs $100 million to make. *Waterworld* (1995) and *Titanic* (1997) cost over $200 million. Although *Waterworld* was considered one of the most expensive box office flops, after five years it made profits through video sales. It is important, therefore, to look at films' expenditure and profits over a period of time. *Citizen Kane* (1941) was given poor reviews because it appeared to criticise the real life newspaper tycoon Randolph Hearst, but over the years it has been voted the top of the viewers', critics' and film makers' polls.

In May 1998 a record $50 million (£31 million) was taken in USA cinemas. These days Hollywood films need to receive over $100 million each to become hits. The $80 million production costs of *Deep Impact* (1998) were shared by Steven Spielberg's DreamWorks and Paramount. The film had to clear $140 million in order to produce profits. *Deep Impact* grossed $40 million in its first weekend, which shows that it is possible to make substantial profits if the marketing is successful. In order to make *Lethal Weapon 4*, with Mel Gibson in 1998, Warner Bros. spent $180 million. They had to spend 40% of the budget on the stars alone.

Men in Black (1997)

Men in Black was a comedy that sent up some of the conventions used in traditional science fiction films.

Synopsis

New York Police Department cop Will Smith is recruited to join Tommy Lee Jones on the super secret team that monitors thousands of aliens who already populate the earth, without most people knowing it. One violent alien turns up and it is then a race against time to find the prize the alien is looking for, before the earth is blown up. Based on a comic by Lowell Cunningham.

Production notes

Men in Black took two years to make from the time the pre-production was started to the film's release. The second year was spent in post-production, where special effects were produced by the company Industrial Light and Magic.

FILM INDUSTRY SIMULATION GAME

Working in a team, form a film production company and give it a name.

Your production company would like to make a science fiction film but you need finance to make it. You will need to approach a sponsor or studio to gain backing for your amazing idea for a film. Note that you will also need to decide on the breakdown of the estimated budget expenditure according to the information you have been given in this chapter.

Task 1

Decide on the following:
a The genre.
 (2 marks)
b The narrative (200 words max).
 (8 marks)
c The characters (brief outline of main cast) and the settings (consider budget).
 (10 marks)
d The stars (give reasons for casting) and the director (explain your choice).
 (10 marks)
e Merchandise and spin-offs (specify potential consumers and audiences).
 (5 marks)
f The promotional campaign (what, where and when).
 (10 marks)

g Budget (consider what proportions will be for casting, promotions and special effects).
 (5 marks)

Task 2

The sponsoring distribution company you have approached also owns: a whisky and fizzy drinks company, a clothes store and fashion design house, a major rock band they want to play on the soundtrack and a publishing company that publishes newspapers, magazines and books.

a Discuss whether your production company will co-operate with the sponsoring distribution company's wishes. The sponsoring company has its own stars, locations, tie-ins and product placement (i.e. their clearly branded whisky and fizzy drinks must appear in the opening sequence of the film). You may or may not want to co-operate with their demands for content and casting, however you must remember that you will need their money to back your film. There is talk of the sponsoring company wanting to make a sequel called *Women in Black*, however this may only be a rumour. Explain the reasons for your decision.
 (5 marks)

b Choose a suitable director from those you know to be established or new directors who show promise. Some examples of established directors of science fiction are: Steven Spielberg (*ET, Close Encounters*), George Lucas (*Star Wars*), Paul Verhoeven (*Robocop, Total Recall, The Starship Troopers*) and Barry Sonnenfield (*Men in Black*).
Explain the reasons for making your choice.
(5 marks)

c You may wish to opt for co-production, and work with another more experienced production company to gain respectability. This will of course mean sharing the profits of the film. Discuss this in your group and make notes on your choice. Examples of experienced production companies include: Amblin Entertainments produced *Men in Black*, Lucas Films produced *Star Wars* and Coumbia Tristar produced *Starship Troopers*.
(5 marks)

Task 3

Present your pitch to the sponsoring company in order to persuade them that your film will be a huge box office hit. Present all the items in the checklist, including the general budget predictions. The sponsoring company will then need to ask questions and make a judgement based on what they hear, and what they discuss as a team panel.

EXAMINATION FORMAT

The format of the sample question paper which follows relates specifically to the OCR (formerly MEG) syllabus Section A. Film and Section B. Film Promotion and also fits the Welsh syllabus. Please refer to AQA's previous examination papers for precise layout and format. The Film Simulation Game which precedes this section could be used as a preparation for the board's simulation style of question.

SPECIMEN EXAMINATION QUESTION

OCR Paper 1: Section A (Textual Analysis)

These Tasks are not actual examination questions. The questions are the sole work of the author and are devised to match the style, mark allocation and format of the relevant question papers from AQA and OCR. They are designed for examination practice. The Tasks are designed to follow the examination paper timings and mark allocations. It is essential that candidates check the specified topics set for the year of their examination, by the examination board. For previous examination papers contact the examination board direct.

Select an extract from a popular mainstream film. The beginning or the end of a film are suitable extracts because they compress narrative, themes and characterisation.
Textual analysis
(Total 50 marks)

Spend one hour on this section, viewing the video and taking notes, and 30 minutes answering the questions.

1 Unseen audio-visual text: viewing the extract.

You will have 30 minutes viewing time of the video extract. First you will be able to read the questions. Then the extract will be replayed. You will then have the opportunity to view it again before answering the questions. Notes may be made during the second viewing.

Watch the six minute closing sequence of *Men in Black* and answer a) to e):

a i Describe the elements which create suspense.

(6 marks)

ii Give two examples of how suspense is created by each of these:
- the use of the camera
- the soundtrack
- special effects

(10 marks)

b What kind of audiences would you expect this film to appeal to? Give brief reasons for your answer.

(4 marks)

c What visual and soundtrack clues are we given to indicate what this film's genre is?

(6 marks)

d Create a storyboard of at least 10 frames for the opening sequence sequel to Men in Black, entitled Women in Black. Use the blank storyboard sheets provided.

(14 marks)

e Explain your storyboard and discuss *mise-en-scène*, lighting, music and soundtrack, casting and director.

(10 marks)

Section B

Essay: Film promotion

(Total 25 marks)

Choose one or more films that you have studied. Describe and analyse the effectiveness of how it was promoted, including the following information: audience, type of film, promotional strategies, and where and when the film was seen.

Extension Tasks

1 Choose a new film that is about to be released. Collect the teaser and the main trailers to this film. Local newspapers often have press packs left over when they have finished with them so this may be worth exploring. Write a case study of the campaign, detailing whether or not you think it was successful. If you think it was unsuccessful, explain why.

2 Which UK film had the most successful world box office sales figures in 1998? **Write notes** to account for its success. Did this film also have the top UK sales figures? Use the *Guardian Media Guide* or the *BFI Film and Television Annual Yearly Report* to help your research.

3 Identify two images from the opening sequence of another film that you think would be suitable to use as publicity stills for the film. **Describe** the images and **explain** briefly why you have chosen them. Where would you place them and what written text (for example tag lines) would you add to them?

4 Research one month's figures for UK cinema attendance and profit from box office returns. What percentage of films are from the USA, compared to UK productions? What percentage of films were non-UK and non-USA?

5 Research the latest film festival that attracted a world film screening, for example

FILM INDUSTRY AND PROMOTION

Cannes, Moscow, Hong Kong, Berlin, Burkino Faso, New York, Sundance or London. Find out which films were given awards and which countries produced them. Find out what categories of films were awarded prizes or accolades. Do you consider it likely that you would want to watch them? Do you think these films are likely to be seen in the UK and if so where (for example, at the major cinemas or at Art House cinemas)?

6 Research a current breakdown of costs and receipts for a multi-million dollar film in the USA. Compare figures to those of a multi-million pound film in the UK. *Screen International* and *Moving Pictures* are useful magazines to use for this research. What genres of films tend to be the biggest sellers?

Examination Skills

Knowledge and Understanding

Explain, supporting with examples, key terms such as: *mise-en-scène*, genre, camera shot, camera movement, size, angle and framing, lighting, editing, soundtrack, special effect, direction and acting. Students who can demonstrate an understanding of the conceptual aspects of the course – languages and categories, audience, agency, messages and values (ideology) and signifiers – will score highest marks, the clearer the answer the better. Successful completion of an essay question demands an awareness of targeted audiences (gender, age, race national), and all the elements described in the section on promoting a film (see pages 87–89) – tie-ins, teasers, posters, tag lines and merchandise.

Textual Analysis

For coursework and the OCR and AQA Examination simulation questions textual analysis skills are required. The ability to denotate and connotate the sounds and moving images is essential.

> Suspense is created by short, sharp edits, which cut between the action and the reaction shots of the main characters. The action is mixed with special effects, which are designed to show the massiveness of the menacing alien overshadowing the diminutive special agents. The effects soundtrack consists of loud and violent crashing sounds to convey the drama of the fight.

Practical Work

Write a review of a film you have seen for your local paper. Explain why it is or is not suitable for the classification given.

7 Television and radio news

WHAT'S THE STORY?

What is newsworthy? In this chapter you will find out about the how, why, who and what of news broadcasting. Studying news involves considering where news comes from, and the way news is processed and presented. There are questions to be asked, concerning who makes news, for whom it is made and why certain items are selected. The reasons why some items are not selected for broadcasting or printing should also be investigated.

KW
Selection ▪ construction ▪ format ▪ news values ▪ gatekeepers ▪ sources ▪ agencies ▪ broadcast ▪ network ▪ mode of address

TW
Bulletin ▪ human interest story ▪ lead story ▪ running order ▪ scheduling ▪ teasers ▪ title sequence ▪ voice over commentary

FEATURES OF NEWS

To create and maintain an audience, TV and radio news must be broadcast at regular intervals or at fixed times each day, such as 'on the hour every hour'. Some TV channels have 24 hour news channels only, however other channels have just a small amount of time allocated for news, often in the form of bulletins. If broadcast news is to be believed, then it has to prove to its audience that it is accurate and reliable.

The news also has to be presented in a shape that is recognisably typical of the forms and conventions of news programmes that the listener or viewer are familiar with. For example, the music that is heard at the start of a news bulletin on the radio or the television tends to have a rhythm and beat that conveys a sense of urgency and immediacy. It is a style of music that audiences associate with news programmes.

Even the names of the programmes should give an indication of their content. Examples of television news programmes are:

TELEVISION AND RADIO NEWS

- The News at Ten
- The Nine o'clock News
- Channel 5 News
- GMTV
- Newsround

Agenda setting

News television and radio news stations select and produce news. They cannot report on absolutely everything that happens. They must select what they consider to be the most interesting and relevant news items for their audiences. This is called agenda setting. An agenda is a list of items drawn up for a committee to discuss. Only items on the agenda are discussed, therefore if there is something happening which is not on this list then it is not discussed. In the section on news values agenda criteria are detailed.

Print or broadcast media?

The majority of audiences today prefer to watch the news on television.

> **Discuss why you think that television is the favourite medium for watching news?**

WHAT IS MEDIA NEWS?

Discuss the question in this heading. Make notes on your definition.

Discuss the following definitions of news. Which definition do you think is nearest to your own definition discussed previously. Which definition from the list below seems to you to be the most accurate?

1 News is about information and updating events.

(Student)

2 News by itself is not entertainment; it is information about current events, but it does have to be made into interesting stories for the viewer.

(News programme director)

3 Good news stories are based on other peoples' misery. Media news depends mainly on negative happenings – otherwise we wouldn't have anything to talk about.

(Trainee journalist)

4 Media news leaves out stories about political issues, womens' sports and third world countries, unless they can be reported in a bad light.

(Oxfam charity worker)

5 News is about people; people stories interest viewers most.

(TV presenter)

6 Television news needs visuals and interviews with eye witness accounts to make it seem real.

(News programme editor)

7 All news is pre-packaged by publicity managers and spin doctors*.

(TV critic)

8 News is just becoming like a goldfish gossip bowl: the lives and wrong-doings of celebrities and the famous are what people want to ogle at.

(TV news executive producer)

Your news versus *the* news

Personal news is what you tell to a friend or someone in the family. When you tell friends about your news, what type of event do you discuss? For example, do you discuss what happened to you at the weekend and how do you tell them what you have done? Is it a momentous, strange or funny happening? Is it simply plain chit-chat about the usual activities? What would you have to do to get into the TV or radio news?

Sources

How do you usually find out about the news? Where do you find out about world, national or local news stories? Select from the list of sources below:

- television
- newspaper headlines
- radio
- a friend or someone at home
- schoolteacher
- any other ways?

1 Conduct a survey of your group, or four people of your own age group. Ask each member to describe the main way they find out about what is in the news, by giving them a choice of the sources listed previously. What is the most common answer and what is the least used source?

2 Now ask four people over the age of twenty years the same question. Then compare the responses of each age group. Are they the same or different? Write down why you think they are the same or different.

Which medium?

In the last 30 years more people use the television as their main source of news than any other medium.

Discuss the following:

1 Why do you think TV news is less appealing to young people, as research has shown?

2 How does watching television differ from reading the newspaper? List two ideas.

3 What is the difference between the television news and the radio news? Aside from the fact that one medium is visual and the other is sound based, list another difference.

---

*Spin doctors are people paid to feed journalists with press releases and carefully presented briefings. They present the ideas that the organisation they work for would like the public to hear.

TELEVISION AND RADIO NEWS

NEWS PROGRAMMING

Technology

Broadcast news, in television and radio, is what an organisation like the BBC transmits to a mass audience. Consider how the transmission of broadcast news to the mass audience has changed over the last hundred years.

Figure 7.1 Travelling caravan, showing news reels in the early twentieth century pre-television

Source: BFI

Pre-production

Where do news organisations find their stories and how do they process the information? Although we may feel TV news programmes are immediate and recent, a considerable amount is achieved in the pre-production preparation before the broadcast.

Newsrooms are constantly sent press releases and letters telling them when events are going to happen. Court cases are often scheduled weeks in advance and anniversaries, for example, are always known and planned out well in advance. Hospitals and police stations provide a steady supply of stories and the journalist has simply to check the day books of either of these places to gain information. Many journalists will scour local newspapers for stories and they will also have contacts who will supply them with potential stories.

NEWS SOURCES
JOURNALISTS & CORRESPONDENTS
LETTERS
TELEPHONE MESSAGES
PRESS RELEASES
POLICE, COURTS, HOSPITALS
HOUSE OF COMMONS LOBBY SYSTEM
NEWS AGENCIES
THE PRESS ASSOCIATION
REUTERS
INTERNATIONAL TV NEWS SOURCES – CABLE NEWS NETWORK, US AGENCIES
INTERNET

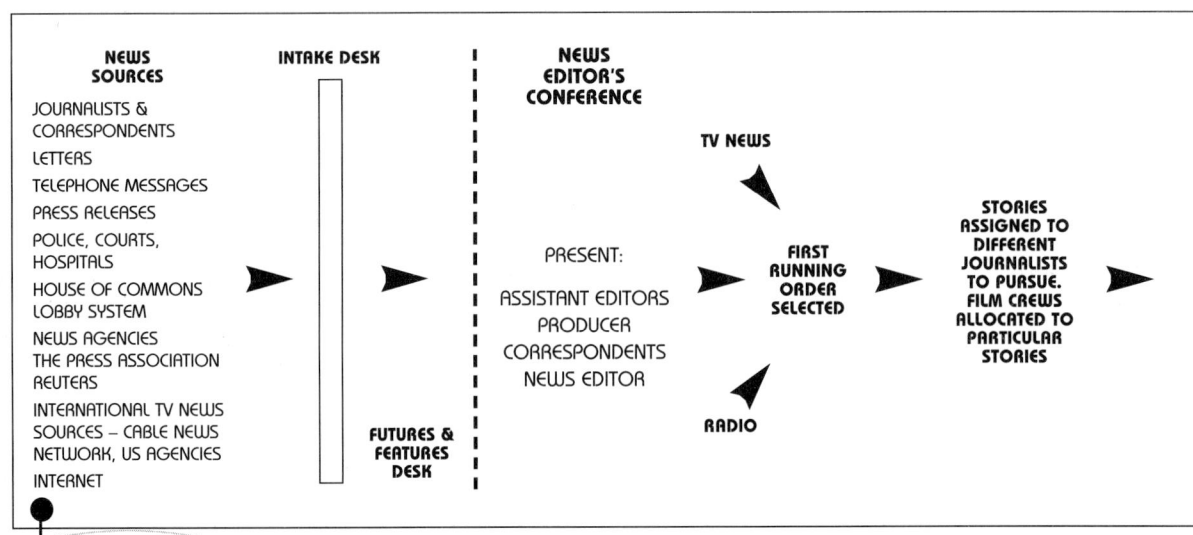

▶ **INTAKE DESK** ▶ **FUTURES & FEATURES DESK** ▶

NEWS EDITOR'S CONFERENCE
PRESENT:
ASSISTANT EDITORS
PRODUCER
CORRESPONDENTS
NEWS EDITOR

▶ TV NEWS
FIRST RUNNING ORDER SELECTED
RADIO ▶

STORIES ASSIGNED TO DIFFERENT JOURNALISTS TO PURSUE. FILM CREWS ALLOCATED TO PARTICULAR STORIES ▶

Figure 7.2 Diagram of bi-media news flow and processors (continued on page 109)

The Lobby System

At national level there is the Lobby System in the House of Commons, which allows MPs and government officials to talk to a select group of journalists, often called political correspondents. All this information goes into the forward diary and this is looked at each day to see if it can be used or if it is too old to pursue.

Some items become features because they do not depend on being immediate and can take two or three days to research and produce. They can then be included into the latter part of a news programme.

Sources and intake

There is a constant flow of information into the newsroom and some of it comes from commercial stations such as Euronews and The Press Association via their Newswire. There are also international news agencies that provide news information and ready-made moving images, plus stories packages, Cable News, Reuters, US News and World Transatlantic News. Satellite and the Internet provide fast link-ups 24 hours a day.

New developments

Locating and producing TV and radio news in big organisations such as the BBC is linked together in what is called a bi-media process. This saves on staff and cuts down on costs in terms of space and technology.

Gatekeeping

The people who decide what news is selected to go into production are the editors. The editor, the producer and journalists who decide are called 'gatekeepers' in Media Studies terms. They define what is newsworthy and what is important for the public to hear. The criteria they use for deciding what is newsworthy depends on news values. These are discussed a little later in this book.

On the morning of an evening programme the most senior staff meet and they create a provisional running order. The running order

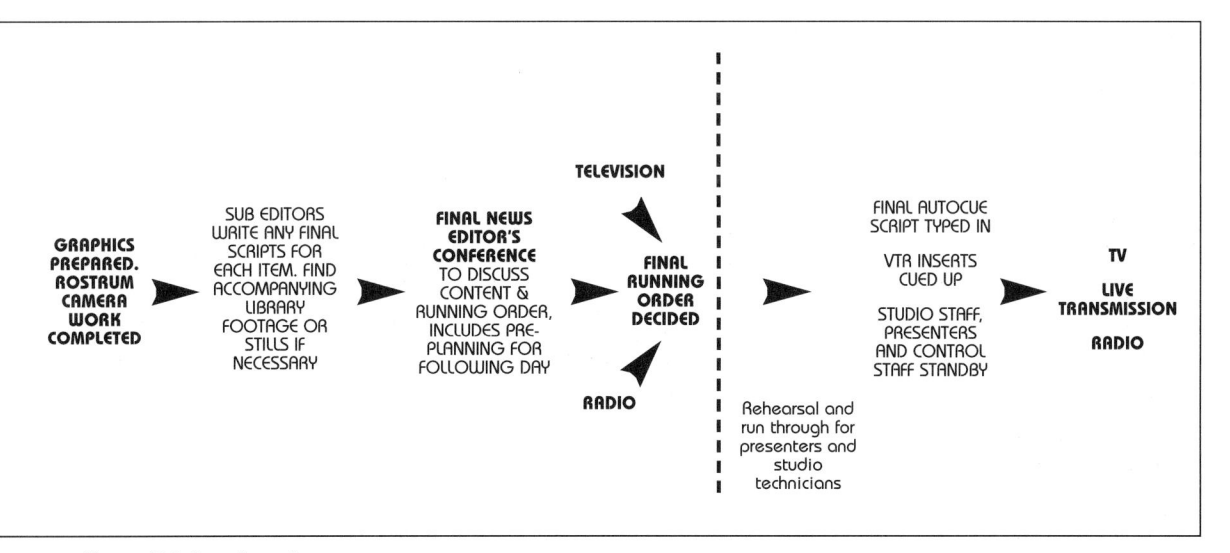

GRAPHICS PREPARED. ROSTRUM CAMERA WORK COMPLETED → SUB EDITORS WRITE ANY FINAL SCRIPTS FOR EACH ITEM. FIND ACCOMPANYING LIBRARY FOOTAGE OR STILLS IF NECESSARY → FINAL NEWS EDITOR'S CONFERENCE TO DISCUSS CONTENT & RUNNING ORDER, INCLUDES PRE-PLANNING FOR FOLLOWING DAY → TELEVISION / RADIO → FINAL RUNNING ORDER DECIDED → Rehearsal and run through for presenters and studio technicians → FINAL AUTOCUE SCRIPT TYPED IN / VTR INSERTS CUED UP / STUDIO STAFF, PRESENTERS AND CONTROL STAFF STANDBY → TV LIVE TRANSMISSION RADIO

Figure 7.2 (continued)

TELEVISION AND RADIO NEWS

is the sequence of items in the order in which they will be presented on the programme. Stories that need to be developed are assigned to different people and these are produced during the day. In the afternoon, another meeting takes place and the final running order is decided. If a story of a fire the previous night is no longer as important as a new story that has broken about a man dying in a police cell, then the fire story may be relegated to further down the running order. If a story cannot be produced for lack of material, then a pre-prepared feature can be shown to fill the space.

Production

Subeditors

Subeditors write most of the stories, process the information and write links between stories to make it all join together smoothly. They are usually given a precise amount of time to work with. They may have to find library film or photographs if the item requires additional visual footage.

Presenters

Presenters practice their lines and links between items and prepare themselves for the live programme at the appointed hour.

Tell me a story

Storytelling is at the heart of news – it is not simply the information, but the way in which the story is told that interests the listener.

Decide from the list below which news items are type (a), (b) or (c):
a regional TV stories
b national TV news stories
c stories that could be either national or regional
1 Prime minister's helicopter lands on school playing fields.
2 Five MPs lock themselves in cages outside Westminster buildings in demonstration about animal rights.
3 Route for town bypass agreed.
4 International conference for tall people (over 6' 4") held today in London.
5 The Queen visits South Africa.

Select one of the above stories. Invent and write an interesting script for a radio presenter to read out. You must use no more than 60 words.

Scheduling

When is news on?

The news is available on the television or radio at regular times each day. Programme planners try to ensure that their news feels fresh and up-to-date throughout the hours of their schedule. Some channels simply have short bulletins and other channels devote whole programmes to serious news analysis. For example, on Channel 4's early morning programme, *The Big Breakfast*, there are regular bulletins, however at 7.00 pm Channel 4 also has 50 minutes of reports and analysis.

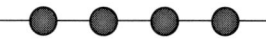

Discuss, research, analyse and write in pairs. Study the listings page for radio and television on one week day and analyse each of the channels belonging to the BBC, ITV and Channel 4.

1 What are the published times of the radio news? On which channel are they broadcast? Is the news on at times that are not written in the listings?
2 Which TV channel broadcasts the most number of hours of news? What does this tell us about the type of channel it is? What types of people do you think watch it?
3 It is possible to watch news on some television channels 24 hours a day (BBC and CNN, for example)?
a Why do some news programme makers think it is necessary to have continuous news?
b Do you think you would be interested in a 24 hours a day news channel? Explain your reasons.
c Are all TV news programmes the same? How do they look different? Remember, it's not what you say but the way that you say it!

Watch and compare three or four breakfast news programmes, for example, *The Big Breakfast*, GMTV, Channel 5 News or BBC News.

Make notes on at least two of these programmes describing and analysing the following:

1 Programme title and time of day (and minutes).
2 Mode of address.
3 Presenters: number, age, gender, race and accent.
4 Sets and furniture.
5 Pace and tone of delivery.
6 Music and colours.
7 Type of content.
8 Title sequence and graphics.

Format

> 'Our local television news is part of what we call a magazine show. Like a magazine it has serious stuff at the front, some more personal items in the middle and sport and lighter entertainment at the end.'
> TV News Editor

There are five types of news programmes:

1 bulletins
2 news updates
3 magazines (e.g. *GMTV*)
4 serious news programmes with analysis
5 newsflashes

The format, or shape, of the regional evening news or evening news programme tends to follow a pattern that has become conventional in many news programmes:

▶ hard news
▶ brief round up of serious news (shorts)
▶ heart-tugger story
▶ lighter features
▶ sport
▶ funny (known as 'skateboarding duck') story
▶ 'bye bye and 'see you tomorrow' link

This format tends to make news programmes more like magazine programmes, with some information but with the emphasis on entertainment and relaxing the audience at the end of the day.

From the list below identify which stories fit into the categories listed above:

1 Man arrested for stealing pillow cases oversleeps and misses his court case.
2 Bomb goes off in Manchester town centre.
3 Little girl learns to walk again.
4 President of USA drinks a pint in Birmingham at World Summit Talks.
5 New England manager of women's cricket team appointed.

TELEVISION AND RADIO NEWS

Selection and newsworthiness

Consider what types of stories are selected for broadcast – how do any of them become news suitable to print or broadcast? Millions of events happen every day all over the world and a fraction of these end up being printed in newspapers or broadcast on television and radio.

NEWS VALUES

There are several theories about why events turn into news stories. These theories are sometimes referred to as 'news values'.

Is the event important or big enough to be 'newsworthy'?

The greater the size of the event, the more likely it is that it will find itself in the media. A story about a man growing the largest tomato in London is less newsworthy than one about a freak tornado sweeping the south east of England. A bomb going off in Number Ten Downing Street is likely to be far more newsworthy.

Is the news negative?

Generally 'bad news is good news' for television, radio and print. If someone dies in a car accident it is more likely to appear in the news than someone passing away in their sleep. Bad news is arguably more obvious and complete than positive events. Positive events are less easy to dramatise, whereas with bad news stories it is easier to make a story out of human conflict or misery.

Has it happened recently?

Is the news fresh enough by the time the story is broadcast? Yesterday's fire at the swimming pool is not as recent as today's unexplained death of a man in the police cell. If the story is also an 'exclusive', that is, one which no other news station has managed to obtain then the story will be unique.

Is the meaning clear?

The simpler the meaning of the event, the more likely it is to be reported. The headline 'Man dies in police cell' makes more immediate and direct sense than 'Report into proposed road bypass recommends three possible options'.

Is the news relevant to us?

There are many events that happen in the world that we might think we should know about. In reality, we do not want to know or we simply cannot find out about all the events in the world for the following reasons:

- Not every event is reported to the media.
- Not every event is selected by the editors and journalists.
- Most national news channels tend to focus on their own country's stories, sometimes almost exclusively.
- It is unlikely that we, the audience, would be able to find the time to find out about every country's news.
- Most people do not have access to all types of media technology, such as satellite,

Internet and radio, required to find out about global news.
- ▶ Whatever is selected to be 'in the news' depends on several people: the editors, the journalists and the news agencies. These people decide, on our behalf, what the news should be. They may have a limited set of ideas they think we ought to know about.

Headlines such as 'Britain dies in plane crash over Turkey' tends to be favoured by news editors to '500 killed in Afghanistan earthquake'. Much as we may disagree in principle, the relevance to news nearer to home is often favoured above the scale of the event.

Is news expected?

When an election is announced, we can predict that there will be pre-election and election news coverage. This is also true if there is a fixed calendar date for a sporting event such as Wimbledon. We can expect that there will be interviews, debates, information and news accounts leading up to the event. In the case of the O.J. Simpson trial, for example, where the court case lasted a year, it was known that each day there would be some drama, therefore the courtroom scenes were televised. Simpson was already a national US celebrity and sportsman when it was alleged he killed his wife – this story attracted national and international interest. The proceedings could be likened to a daily soap opera.

Is news unexpected?

If an event is out of the ordinary, then news editors may want to emphasise this fact. They can focus on certain aspects of a story in order to make the story appear more dramatic. A fire is an unexpected event and the story may be dramatised to draw attention to the firefighters' heroism and to make the dangers they faced appear more perilous: 'Family rescued in towering flats inferno'. The more bizarre aspects of a case can also be emphasised: 'Dog bites man' may not be news, but 'Man bites dog' is a classic example. In recent years, tabloid newspapers have competed to see who could create the most outrageous headings, based on the flimsiest of evidence. 'Freddy Starr ate my hamster!' is another classic example.

Is it already in the news?

News such as a murder trial or a royal family scandal tends to carry on over several days, even for weeks. A news item might even be introduced as, for example, 'the latest in the continuing storm over the political scandal'.

Does the news item fit into the overall balance of the programme?

Most television news tends to contain a mix of what is known as 'hard' and 'soft' news. News programmes often sequence their items, starting with serious news at the top of the running order and moving on to lighter items, finally ending on a more humorous or cheery note. Television news generally follows the following sequence: hard news items, bulletins, heart tuggers, soft news (including sport), light and witty shorts, weather '... and finally' a happy story to end.

If there are no light items, then the programme's customary tone and balance can seem inappropriate. This means that the programme will not be filled with too many of the same type of stories, otherwise there will be no variety of topic or change of mood. News editors believe the news programme should not only be about informing people; it should also entertain and relax them.

Is it possible to personalise the news and make it a story about individuals?

News editors believe audiences find it is easier to identify with a person than the company or the institution they work for. It is easier to video people who represent the human face of an institution than to have a reporter explain abstract ideas such as monetary union or European Common Agricultural Policy.

News tends to use individual names rather than groups, for example, 'the Prime Minister announced a new deal for jobs' rather than 'the Government announced a new deal for jobs'. News in which there are clearly defined 'goodies' and 'baddies' makes the topic more easy to convey. News that does not have a human face makes it more difficult to convey. In this situation, radio may have the advantage over television in that ideas are more easy to focus on in a listening-only medium.

Is the news about top powerful world nations?

American and European news often dominates our screens, radio airwaves and papers. If the US, European, Chinese or the Russian Governments are involved in a global dispute, it raises the possibility of world conflicts. If there is a conflict in a small country, it is often not reported until a major powerful nation becomes involved. In contrast, we tend not to hear about successful stories from African or Indian nations – we more often hear about natural disasters in these countries, and the image conveyed is inclined to make them victims.

Is the news about famous or powerful people?

Much of the news is focused on celebrities from the public world of sport, television, film and music industries. There is also a great deal of attention paid to royalty, politicians, gentry and foreign statespeople. There has been much debate as to whether the media focus on the lives of public people has been unhealthy, especially in prying into the private aspects of their relationships.

Is it simply that news editors are satisfying the public's basic instinct to gossip about the lives of the rich and famous? Should there be rules governing press intrusion and harassment of individuals going about their private business? What rights should we allow to people who make their money and status from being famous, to restrict journalists from reporting their activities, especially in public spaces such as restaurants and beaches?

Questioning the news

Another fundamental question we might ask news editors and the public alike is: is news entertainment or information?

Some critics of modern news claim that the news focuses more on violence, sex and celebrities than the serious issues and stories of the day. News of rising unemployment figures can be ignored while soap and music stars' love lives are given prominent positions. On the other hand, some people argue that there is far too much serious talk of politics and parliamentary activity and that they would prefer a lighter approach to news programmes. Other people say they do not watch television news because they prefer newspapers or radio. Some are not interested in the news at all, in particular the 15 to 25 year old age group.

Further factors that television news editors in particular are concerned with before starting production:

▶ Is there any visual footage?

- Are there eyewitnesses to interview?
- Are there any experts to interview?
- Is there any live material to show that the news is happening right now? For example, an explosion or an election result being announced.
- Is the information exclusive to the television channel, i.e. before other television channels and newspapers can reach it?

Who decides on the news?

Several people are involved in the production of news, but only a few make the important decisions about what is actually selected. Can you name the different production jobs involved in the production of the news?

Mode of address

This concerns how a programme addresses its audience. It is usually visible in the style of the presenter's clothes, the way they look at or away from the camera, the tone, pitch and speed of delivery of the words, the sets and background colours and the music etc. For example, the *BBC News* is more serious, measured and formal, whereas *The Big Breakfast News* is brash, fast and friendly.

The Big Breakfast News

Presenters: Johnny Vaughan and Kelly Brook. Phil Gayle presents the news.
Setting: on the television in *The Big Breakfast*'s living room.
Dress code: tie, brightly coloured smart shirt, but no jacket.
Format: bulletins – celebrities and famous people.
Audience: young (5 years of age upwards) and family.
Camera: medium close-up shot, straight on.

GMTV News

Presenters: male and female hosts, with news presenter.
Setting: studio, sofas, coffee tables, venetian blinds, cityscape in the background.
News presenter at desk, neutral background.
Dress code: smart but informal.
Format: magazine with bulletins.
Audience: 30 years of age upwards, home managers, C2D.
Camera: medium shot, straight on.

BBC Breakfast News

Presenters: male and female.
Dress code: smart and formal.
Format: bulletins and in-depth reports.
Audience: business, ABC1.
Camera: long shot to medium shots.

NEWS SIMULATION

You are a member of **FutureWorld**, which has produced various news programmes for cable channels in Europe. You specialise in the 15 to 25 year age group. You have a publicity and promotions department, in addition to a programme making section. Channel 6 is a new channel and is looking to produce a news programme that broadcasts at 7.00–8.00 am. On the next page is the letter containing the brief given to all companies tendering to produce this new programme.

TELEVISION AND RADIO NEWS

CHANNEL 6

FutureWorld
Surrenden Road
Birmingham
BST 600

Channel 6
Box 6
London
W6T TL

20 April 1999

Dear Colleague,

Channel 6 is looking for a news programme that suits and promotes our company's wonderful approach to our audience. You must come up with ideas and a design for a new programme and outline its unique features in response to the tasks that follow this letter.

Our audience is 15 to 30 years of age and are male and female, fun-loving, style conscious Cosmopolitan, Minx, Mojo and NME readers and clubbers who read books, watch movies and party. They like music, fashion, food and culture but are bored with programmes like The Big Breakfast. They find all the other news programmes too middle-of-the-road and just a little too resigned to over 50s suburbia.

We want ideas for a news programme that is:
- issues based
- controversial
- consumer based
- informative, fun and not patronising

Our channel is committed to equal opportunities and we are definitely not interested in sexist or racist approaches. A good understanding of forms and conventions in presentation and programme construction and programme composition is required. We look forward to hearing about your interesting and innovative ideas.

Yours sincerely,
Jean Bateman

Task 1

a Describe and analyse what you think are the key features of television news programmes.

(20 marks)

b Provide a title for your new breakfast television news programme and explain the thinking behind it.

(5 marks)

c Describe your breakfast television presenters and how will they will appeal to the audience. Comment on style, dress, voice and accent.

(10 marks)

d Describe what your breakfast studio sets will look like and explain how the effect will appeal to the audience.

(5 marks)

Task 2

Note: use the storyboard sheets for part **a** and the plain paper for part **b** (see Appendix).

Either

a Draw, design or describe a ten-shot title sequence for the news programme that will suggest the style and identity of the channel and its treatment of the news.

(15 marks)

or

b Design a set for the news programme (floor plan, channel and news logo).

(15 marks)

Task 3

Note: use plain sheets for part **a**.

Your news programme will need an advertising, and promotion campaign to grab the interest of its target audience. Use notes, scripts, sketches, diagrams and graphic designs to provide ideas for a campaign advertising the new news programme in each of the three activities following:

a **Either** i) Design a full page advertisement for a television listings magazine.
or ii) Write a 30 second radio advertisement for local commercial radio.

(15 marks)

GCSE MEDIA STUDIES

b Describe a range of products that could be advertised during the breaks of the programme, which will appeal to the target audience.

(10 marks)

c Suggest other ways in which you might promote your new news programme.

(5 marks)

Task 4

Produce a covering letter to accompany your proposal, explaining how the key features of your TV news programme successfully meets the requirements outlined in the letter from Channel 6.

(15 marks)

Extension Tasks

1. **Select** a story from any television news programme that you think has a chance of being continued in bulletins throughout a day or for several days (for example, sanctions against Iraq or pigs go missing from farm in Oxfordshire). Monitor how long it stays in the news over a day/week/month. From the description of news values explained earlier in this chapter identify how many values the story covers. Why does it remain in the television news for the period it lasts? Why does it finally lose its place in the news programmes?

2. **Study and compare** the national and regional evening news over a period of two or three days. Look to see if there are any stories in your regional news programmes that also appear in the national news. Compare how they differ in the way that they are presented or treated (for example, a royal visit, accident or a criminal incident). Write notes on how the stories are shaped according to the interests of the national or regional point of view. For example, '6 year old Jamie Bean met the Queen today . . .' (regional) or 'the Queen spoke to spectators of all ages . . .' (national).

3. **Adapt** a recording of a news bulletin of about two minutes length, taped off air. Change the script by rewriting the voice overs to suit a different audience. For example, voice overs on ITN's *Evening News* could be re-scripted for a youth comedy programme entitled *Not the ten o'clock news*. Play the news bulletin with the sound turned down in the right places and read out your new script to accompany the images. How does the new script change the meaning of the images and how does it differ from the original script?

4. **Research** the ITC (Independent Television Commission) through your local library or your teacher. Find out what the role of the ITC is. Find out what the ITC says about the way broadcast news should be reported. Why do you think that radio and television have more restrictions on being politically unbiased than newspapers?

5. **Research** the news agencies Reuters, Agence Press and Visnews on the Internet. Find out which TV channels they supply news to.

6. 'And finally . . .' **write and video** a script for a 1 minute 50 second bulletin, to be broadcast at the end of the evening news. The proposed content includes an interview with a local person who has just invented a new device for detecting which lottery cards have winning numbers on them, under the silver scratch panels. Create three sections: the presenter and the introduction, the interview and the footage, and the link back to the studio. The length of time has to be no more or less than 1 minute 50 seconds.

Alternatively, invent your own 'and finally . . .' bulletin that is upbeat, amusing or is an animal-related story.

TELEVISION AND RADIO NEWS

Examination Skills

Knowledge and Understanding

Examiners setting questions on TV news are looking for a broad knowledge of the typical forms and conventions (media languages) used to present news. You will need to be able identify, compare and explain the different ways the news is presented. You need to show an understanding that producers have different ideas about their audiences in terms of their interests, age, gender, race and nationalities. You will therefore need the skills of memory recall, detailed explanation of common features of news presentation, and a strong understanding and knowledge of recent examples of news values.

Textual Analysis

To produce fully detailed and knowledgeable answers you will have to be able to analyse the presentational aspects of news programmes. For example, what are the differences in style between *The Big Breakfast* and ITV's *Evening News*? If you are asked to explain the effects of music, title sequences, colours and studio sets and design you must use language which indicates a strong ability to interpret the producers' intentions and imagine the likely variety of responses from the audiences. For example, a piece of writing might compare two styles of presentation:

> The blue sets of the BBC are much colder in their effect than the bright, youthful green and orange colours of The Big Breakfast. However, despite the attempt to be wacky and informal The Big Breakfast newscaster although jacketless, Phil Gayle, still wears a tie and shirt. These clothes are a typically conventional sign of the traditional BBC image of the newscaster who is supposed to appear authoritative and serious, so that they are perceived as credible sources of information.

Practical Work

In the examination, practical activities include: creating storyboards, writing bulletins, designing posters or submitting a treatment or outline for a new programme or title sequence. The kind of skills required here demand an ability to think of ideas visually, and in terms of sequences of images and sounds that create interesting television. A series of shots consisting of only a presenter in a studio would not be considered very interesting. A set of shots that had a variety of location, reporter, archive footage and studio presenters would be considered to follow usual conventions of variety.

Clearly, the language of news presenters can be sensational, for example, 'alarm at rural increase in drugs' or it can be more factual, for example, 'a government report today suggested that drug use was more evident in non-urban areas'. The skill of the candidate is to use the appropriate tone and language for their type of channel and audience.

Storyboards – these should include the variety of locations that news presentation tends to cover, the news studio, the reporter and the location footage. The storyboard should be clearly and fully detailed, explaining the type of shots and sounds that are on screen at any given moment. There should be a clear sense of how the words of the report add to the pictures, not simply describing pictures but letting them speak for themselves.

8 Newspaper tabloids and broadsheets

WHAT'S THE STORY WORTH?

This chapter covers the forms and conventions, style and content, values and legal aspects of broadsheet and tabloid newspapers.

KW

Forms and conventions ■ denotation and connotation ■ news values ■ agenda ■ selection ■ construction ■ gatekeeper ■ processors ■ mode of address ■ privacy ■ intrusion

TW

Format ■ tabloid ■ broadsheet ■ editorial ■ advertorial ■ house style ■ libel ■ readership and circulation

FORMAT

The format is the shape and layout of a newspaper. There are two main formats of newspapers: tabloid and broadsheet. Daily national newspapers such as *The Times*, *Financial Times*, *Telegraph*, *The Independent* and *The Guardian* are broadsheets. They are large format, A1 in size. The smaller A3 size papers are described as tabloids, such as *The Sun*, *The Mirror* and *The Star*. As a group, these tabloids are otherwise known as the 'red tops', as they have a wide band of red print at the top of the front page.

Newspapers such as the *Daily Mail* and *The Express* are also tabloid in shape but their content is considered to be 'middle brow'. The broadsheets are also sometimes refered to as 'high-brows', 'qualities' or 'heavies'. 'Middle brow' means that the content is mostly serious but is also mixed with lighter items, such as you would find in a magazine. In 1999, the *Daily Mail* has the highest circulation figures (number of papers sold) of the middle brow tabloids and broadsheets, as a result of successfully attracting the bulk of readers in the middle of the market. 'High brow' means that the content is serious and contains a higher proportion of political and economic news.

NEWSPAPER TABLOIDS AND BROADSHEETS

Labels pointing to parts of the front page:
- Pug
- Masthead
- Pug
- Exclusive
- Kicker
- Headline
- Splash
- Strapline
- Caption
- Standfirst
- Byline

Figure 8.1 *The Mirror*: main features of a newspaper front page

Source: *The Mirror*, 26 February 1999

---

309 DAYS TO 2000 AD

The Mirror

Friday February 26 1999

www.mirror.co.uk

THIS PAPER COSTS JUST 20p

I'M SO SORRY

Exclusive: Vanessa Feltz comes to The Mirror and says 'I have wept buckets .. but thanks for exposing my show as fake. You were right'

FULL STORY: SEE PAGES 2 & 3

DISGRACE

Straw slammed as Lawrence report identifies witnesses

By JAMES HARDY

HOME Secretary Jack Straw was slammed last night after an astonishing blunder identified witnesses who named Stephen Lawrence's killers.

Secret names and addresses of up to 40 people were mistakenly revealed in an appendix to the inquiry report.

Witnesses are now living in fear of revenge attacks and some have been given police protection.

Yesterday Mr Straw amazingly DENIED responsibility for the latest mistake — even though he had 10 days to study the report.

He said: "It would have been wholly wrong for myself or anyone else in the Home Office to go through the report checking it."

Last night, a top Scotland Yard officer said: "People's lives have been put at risk. It's the worst breach of trust I've seen."

The bungle heaped further humiliation on the minister, who has already been condemned for trying to gag the press over the inquiry.

Shadow Home Secretary Sir Norman Fowler said: "This is an extraordinary affair." Labour's Clive Efford — MP for Eltham, south London, where 18-year-old Stephen was killed — called it a "catastrophic error".

Yesterday's shambles came after a sick paint attack on the stone memorial to Stephen in the street where he died. Later, shamefaced police were forced to apologise after admitting that a spy camera trained on the spot was a dummy.

Yesterday Mr Straw visited the paint-spattered memorial with Stephen's parents Neville and Doreen Lawrence. He said in despair: "Words fail me."

The Mirror is now offering a further £10,000 reward for information leading to the conviction of those responsible. It comes on top of our £50,000 reward to anyone who can help jail one or all of the five Lawrence murder suspects.

The Lawrences said they will sue police unless the force pays them compensation for the "incompetent and negligent" investigation into the murder of their son.

Their solicitor Imran Khan said: "I will give them seven days. After that, we go to court."

FULL STORY: PAGES 4, 5, 6 & 7

SILENT: Jack Straw and Doreen Lawrence at the desecrated memorial yesterday

Parts of a newspaper

Layout, typical features and technical terms – featured also on Figure 8.1

Masthead

The masthead is the title block or logo identifying the paper at the top of the front page. Sometimes an emblem or motto is also placed within the masthead. The masthead is often set into a block of black or red print or boxed with a border. *The Independent* has an eagle (standing for fearless independence), the *Daily Mail* has an emblem consisting of the words 'Dieu et Mon Droit' (God and My King) underneath the royal crest of a lion, a unicorn and the imperial crown on a shield with St. George's cross. The latter suggests English patriotism.

Pugs

These are at the top left and right-hand corners of the paper and are known as the 'ears' of the page. The price of the paper, the logo or a promotion are positioned there. Pugs are well placed, to catch the reader's eye. They can promote the new price of the paper. On the left-hand side of the paper the pug includes the statement 309 days to the millenium.

Kicker

This is a story designed to stand out from the rest of the page by the use of a different typeface and layout. In Figure 8.1, the aim is to promote their exclusive interview with Vanessa Feltz; the story for which is featured inside the paper. A cut out photograph and a large headline is used.

Exclusive

This means that the story is solely covered by that paper and no-one else. The paper will pay their interviewees to buy an 'exclusive' so that no other paper can get it. The idea is that people will buy the paper because it is the only place to find out about the 'real' story.

Other features of a newspaper include:

Splash – the 'splash' is the main story on the front of the paper. The largest headline indicates which this is. In this case the Stephen Lawrence story for example, the splash reads: 'DISGRACE'.

Headline – this is the main statement, usually with the largest font size, describing the main story. A banner headline is when the headline spans the full width of the page.

Strapline – this introductory headline is usually just below the main headline. In the edition of *The Mirror* shown in Figure 8.1 the strapline is below the headline: 'DISGRACE Straw slammed as Lawrence report identifies witnesses'.

Standfirst – the 'standfirst' is the introductory paragraph before the start of the feature. This is in bold print in the edition of *The Mirror*. 'Home secretary Jack Straw ... Stephen Lawrence's killers'.

Cross-head – subheadings that appear in the text and are centred above the column of text. If they are set to one side then they are called 'sideheads'.

Byline – the name of the reporter, if they are important, is often included in the beginning of the feature, rather than at the end, or not at all. Here the byline reads 'by James Hardy'.

Caption – typed text under photographs explaining the image.

Sidebar – when a main feature has an

NEWSPAPER TABLOIDS AND BROADSHEETS

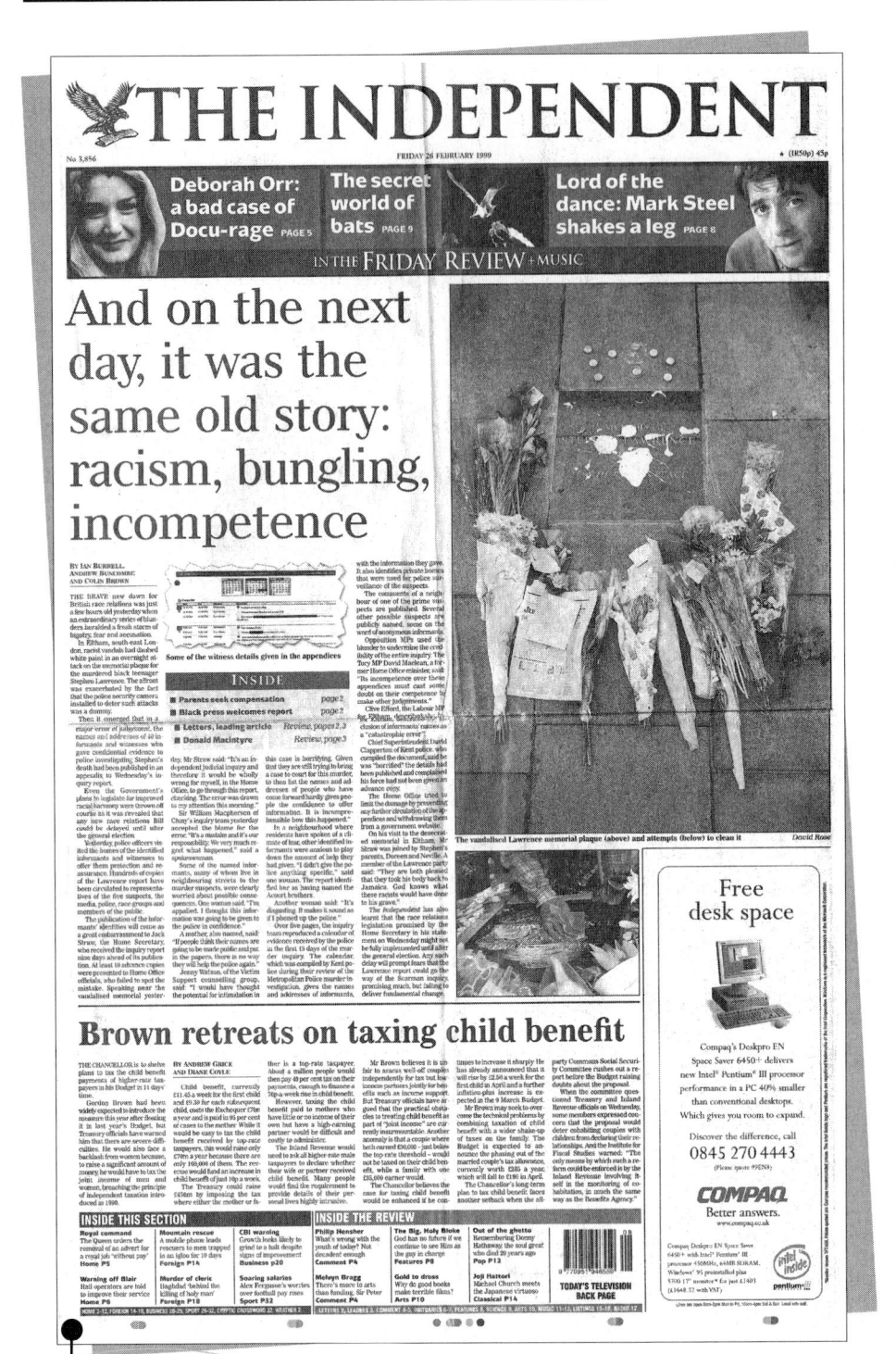

Figure 8.2 *The Independent*: Broadsheets are twice the size in shape of the tabloids

Source: *The Independent*, 26 February 1999

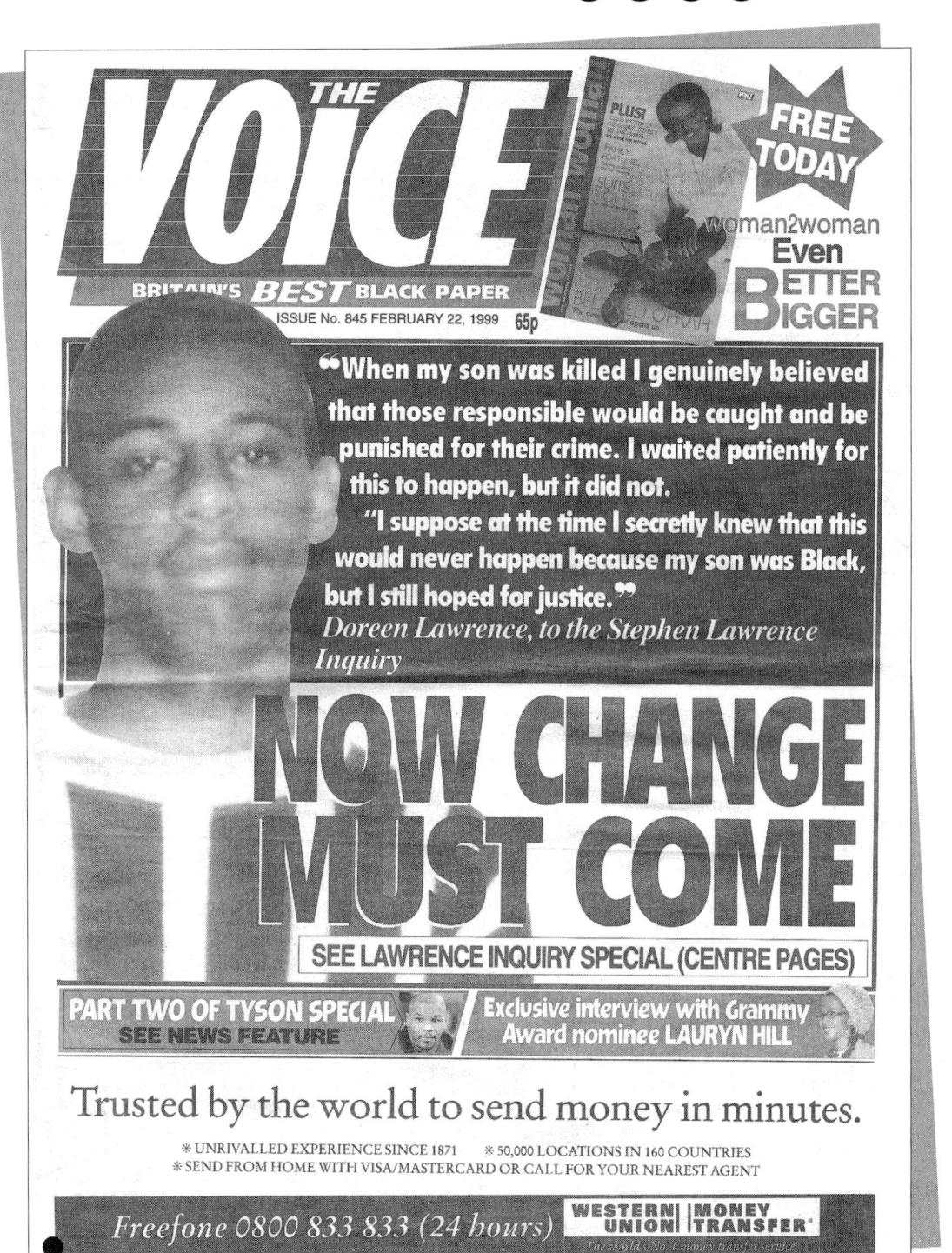

Figure 8.3 *The Voice*: a black tabloid national newspaper

Source: *The Voice*, 22 February 1999

additional box or tinted panel placed in or alongside it, this is called a 'sidebar'. Examples can be seen in Figure 8.2.

Credits – the author of the feature may be given credit in the form of a byline. Photographs may have the name of the person or agency who took the photograph alongside them – this is known as a credit.

The Voice

The Voice (see Figure 8.3) uses white lettering, a sans serif typeface, set on a black block, with a pinstripe effect. The font size is very large and the word slopes to one side, giving the impression of looking forward and being up-to-date.

1 Research other newspapers such as the *Daily Telegraph*, *The Times* or *The Sun*. Analyse and write notes on each of the following:

- style of typeface
- font size
- use of upper and lower case
- layout.

2 Are any of the following typeface or font settings used:

- ordinary
- bold
- italic
- roman
- Arial or Universe
- Serif
- Sans serif

3 What image of the newspaper does the typeface and size convey about itself?

NEWSPAPER LANGUAGE

Study the headlines from *The Mirror* and *The Voice* shown previously in Figures 8.1 and 8.3. Note that these headlines did not appear on the same day.

Both headlines relate to the result of an enquiry into the death of Stephen Lawrence who was allegedly killed by a gang of six white men while waiting for a bus. The enquiry found that the police had been negligent and that the suspected killers had not been properly investigated, allowing them to avoid prosecution.

Discuss the approach and tone of each of the headlines and the message they each convey. How do they reflect the papers that they belong to?

Approach and tone

The approach of *The Mirror*, for example, is to make a single word, bold statement. It uses a very large point size for the lettering. The tone of the word is critical, in the manner of an outcry.

Similarly, *The Independent* uses a critical tone, however it is more cynical in its condemnation of officials. Unlike *The Mirror*, the headline is a long sentence, as the paper is a broadsheet, therefore there is plenty of room for text. With the use of upper and lower case making it more like a strapline, the effect is less sensational than the one word 'DISGRACE' of *The Mirror*.

The Voice is bold in its demand for justice – 'NOW CHANGE MUST COME' – and that the rights of black people should be heard. The strapline is extremely emotional as it is a direct quote from the mother of the murdered teenager. The whole of the front page is dedicated to the strapline and quotations and the headline.

Typeface and type size

The choice of typeface is very important in creating an image of a newspaper. Broadly speaking, tabloids like *The Sun*, *The Star* and *The Mirror* use simple, and large fonts. This typeface, as used in *The Mirror*'s headline 'DISGRACE', is called 'sans serif'. All the letters are in bold and are in upper case format.

The broadsheets tend to use a typeface that is more ornate. This typeface style is described as 'serif', such as can be seen in *The Independent* and the *Daily Mail*. In *The Independent*, both upper and lower case headlines are used.

The typeface of the masthead also differs in each paper, to convey individual styles. *The Mirror* has a simple sans serif typeface, with the 'M' as the largest letter dropped below the rest of the word 'Mirror'. The *Daily Mail* uses what is known as Old English typeface, which suggests a more old-fashioned and traditional image. *The Independent* uses a serif typeface, which resembles the ordinary typeface used throughout the rest of the text.

Photographs

If you study the photographs in *The Mirror* shown on page 122 you will see that the images have been:
▶ snatched
▶ posed
▶ cropped
▶ captioned

The photo snatch

Many sensational photographs are taken without the consent of the people pictured. Even if they do not mind, there is sometimes no time to ask the subjects to stand still and pose. The photographer then has to 'snatch' a photograph as best they can in the time given. Often this means using a telephoto lens, which allows images to be taken from a long distance.

The effect of snatching a photograph often means that the front page contains slightly out of focus or blurry images. This effect is now associated with sensational news images and is sometimes deliberate. The image can be enlarged, to make it look grainy and blurred. The group of photographers who are said to track down celebrities are called paparazzis.

The posed photograph

The Mirror's photograph of Vanessa Feltz is clearly posed (see page 122). She is looking straight at the camera and her expression is one that has been staged purely for the purpose of the newspaper article. She appears to be regretful and apologetic. One arm is resting on the table and the other reaches up to her chin, where she rests her fist. The smart clothes are those that she wears for her role in her chat show. The shadows around her are created by artificial light, and her hair is highlighted by bright top lighting. This give her the glamorous look that the picture is trying to convey.

The photograph has been cut so that just a profile is used on the page. Her profile is positioned on the right-hand side of the page and sits next to the headline and strapline. Ms Feltz's hairline is used to go over to the masthead. This has the effect of making her image appear larger than life, so it stands out from the page. It also draws the eye up to and down from the pug with the (low) price in the masthead.

NEWSPAPER TABLOIDS AND BROADSHEETS

Cropped photos

Even if an image is in focus, it is sometimes not large enough to make out the detail. In the image of Jack Straw, for example, the picture editor would have to cut out any of the bodies of the two figures which distract from the close up of the two people in conversation. This technique of cutting out unwanted material is called cropping (see Chapter Two: Languages and Categories, for more examples of this).

Captions

Captions will be written by a subeditor, whose job it is to bring together the visual layout and the copy (copy is the written text) from the journalists. The purpose of using captions is to fix the meaning (see Chapter Two on anchorage) and add some explanation of what is happening in the picture.

NEWSPAPER PHOTO ANALYSIS

Task 1

Study the image shown previously in *The Mirror* of Jack Straw and Doreen Lawrence.

a How does the caption focus on the meaning of the picture?

(3 marks)

b Cover up the caption and devise two other captions. These should be different, but no less serious, than the original.

(4 marks)

Task 2

Collect two or three tabloids, broadsheets and regional or local newspapers. Study the photographs in these papers, including those inside. Write down the title of the paper and answer the following questions:

a How many photos have been 'snatched'?

(2 marks)

b How many photographs have been posed and constructed with the co-operation of the subjects? Give evidence to support your judgements.

(3 marks)

c What percentage of photographs are posed, compared to those which are 'snatched'?

(2 marks)

d What is the difference between local and national newspapers in the way photographs are constructed?

(4 marks)

Task 3

What does your answer to Task 2, question (c) tell you about:

a the types of news that the papers tend to present?

(4 marks)

b the age, gender, race, class, physical abilities or income of the readers?

(3 marks)

Total = 25 marks

GCSE MEDIA STUDIES

NEWSPAPERS: PAST TO PRESENT

Since the 1980s newspapers have had to compete with television, teletext and radio for their audiences. However, print media still has an advantage over electronic news, as it is portable and can be read in different places and stored more quickly for reference. Instead of competing with other media formats for speed, newspapers have become more like magazines, offering a range of sections and services for different target audiences. The reader usually turns to the page that interests them, therefore it is important that the front page and the inside page tell them exactly where to find what they want. Readers are enticed by the following:

▶ special offers
▶ in-depth features
▶ supplements
▶ pages of letters
▶ gossip columns
▶ sports
▶ television and radio listings
▶ crosswords, horoscopes and cartoons

The decline in newspaper sales

Study the circulation figures for January 1999 for newspapers, published by the Audit Bureau of Circulation, on page 130.

The Sun is the highest selling newspaper with a circulation figure of 3.7 million.
The *Daily Mail* is the highest selling 'middlebrow' paper with a circulation figure of 2.3 million. The overall picture is one of a decline in circulation among the national titles. In January 1997, the daily papers together sold 14,064,089 copies. In January 1999, the total figure had reduced by 500,000. The Sunday titles have reduced by almost a million in two years.

1 Study three newspapers, for example, *The Mirror*, *The Independent*, and *The Voice*.

2 Create a chart with the title down the left side and include the headings: 'Features' and 'Service/Special Offer' on the right. Use the following as a guide:

Title	Features	Service/Special Offer
The Mirror	Inside story on Vanessa Feltz Full story on Lawrence bungle	cheap price (usually 30p) website contact – days until 2000
The Independent		
The Voice		

3 What type of feature or service/special offer does each front cover offer the reader? Discuss what is on the cover as well as what is promised inside.

Welcome to ABC DataBank

National Newspaper Circulation Figures by month for the current year

NATIONAL NEWSPAPERS
MONTHLY AVERAGES FOR 1999

	Jan-99
The Mirror	2,289,373
Daily Record	680,306
Daily Star	539,991
The Star - RoI	90,073
The Sun	3,722,416
The Express	1,103,813
The Daily Mail	2,342,694
The Daily Telegraph	1,040,140
Financial Times	384,679
The Guardian	399,152
The Independent	219,549
The Scotsman	80,867
The Times	746,317
Racing Post	66,894
Evening Standard	446,750
News of the World	4,314,352
Sunday People	1,734,594
Sunday Mirror	2,048,902
Sunday Sport	220,913
Express on Sunday	1,009,683
The Mail on Sunday	2,291,247
Sunday Mail	795,639
Independent on Sunday	252,587
The Observer	419,876
Scotland on Sunday	130,246
Sunday Business	53,320
The Sunday Telegraph	810,587
The Sunday Times	1,371,869
Sport First	84,378

Figure 8.4 Circulation figures for national newspapers
Source: ABC Audit Bureau of Circulation

The fight to retain readers

Newspapers tabloids and broadsheets have fought to retain and to win new readers over the years. *The Mirror* tried to win new audiences by changing its name from *The Daily Mirror*. Its old image was typically aimed at working class men over the age of 40. In 1995 however, the new image was targeted at trendy ABC1s (see Chapter Three on demographic profiles) who live in the cities. By introducing younger music world personalities, such as Tony Parson, and football stars to 'write' features, *The Mirror* hoped to fight back against *The Sun* who reduced the price of their paper to 10p, for long periods of time. It is generally accepted that this is what happened – in News Corp terms, it would be considered weak if such a strategy had not been undertaken. This proved unsuccessful however and so *The Mirror* has now returned to a more familiar approach of ensuring that show business features attract the over 20 year olds as well as those under the age of 30.

Sales boosting tactics

- Reduced price.
- Free gifts.
- Prize-winning competitions.
- Subscription offers.
- Increase in personalisation of stories, for example, the royal family or politicians' private lives.
- More show business stories.
- Changes in layout and format, for example, tabloid newspaper format.
- Supplements offering specialist sections, for example, women's page or financial guide.
- Changing editors more frequently.
- Slimming down the number of people employed.
- Using technology to download news feeds, information and images.

All newspapers have become more competitive about their audience. This has been described as 'dumbing down' if the paper is a broadsheet and 'dumbing up' if the paper is a tabloid. 'Dumbing down' means being less serious and including more sensational or leisure-related items.

NEWSPAPER CONTENT

The content of newspapers differs for the following reasons:

- Cost.
- Expected literacy level of the reader.
- Each paper caters for what they think their particular readership is interested in, for example, sport, politics or culture.
- Readership varies according to social group (see Chapter Three: Producers and Audiences) class, age, gender and race. People make their choices according to their interests, politics, education and class and family tradition.
- Newspaper conventions about what is newsworthy – news values.

Cost

The cost of a newspaper is an important factor in the choice readers make. In 1999, tabloid papers can cost as little as 20p and the broadsheet papers cost about 45p. With price wars dominated largely by NewsCorp, the owners of *The Times* and *The Sun*, the market has been tough for all newspapers.

Since electronic media have tended to take up to 70% of the market for news as a source (*Spectrum Magazine*, ITC, Winter 1996), papers have offered lower prices or occasional discounts to lure the reader to their paper. Free holidays, lottery tickets and free gifts are a few of the techniques used.

Readership

Every newpaper is thought to have some political leanings, some of which change according to the issue of the day. Following are some examples:

- *The Guardian* and *The Independent* – broadly left of centre and liberal politics.

NEWSPAPER TABLOIDS AND BROADSHEETS

- *The Mirror* and *The Daily Record* – traditionally old Labour but now said to be anti-Labour.
- The *Daily Mail, The Telegraph, The Times, The Sun, The Daily Star* and *The Express* – Conservative ranging from centre politics to far right.
- *The Voice* – black community politics.
- *The Daily East* – pro-Pakistan politics.

The politics of a paper is not a concern to everyone, and other factors such as age, specialist interests and price may be the overriding reasons for buying a paper.

Local papers tend to target the older demographic of over 25 year olds, though they can rely on the fact that events in schools, workplaces and the town generally involve everyone at some time. Classified adverts and 'what's on' sections are also important elements of local newspapers. Advertising revenue contributes more to local papers than the nationals, who earn more through sales. The massive increase since 1980 in free sheets (papers given away or posted through the letterbox) showed how advertising is an important part of financing local papers whilst also providing a service for bargain hunters and special interests needs. However, the recent decline in free sheets shows that even this tactic did not last.

News values

In Chapter Seven: Television and Radio News, the concept of news values was introduced. Review the following questions:

1. **a** Is the event big enough for people to find it interesting or 'newsworthy'?
   b Is the news negative? Has it happened recently?
   c Is the meaning clear? Is the news relevant to us?
   d Is it expected? Is it unexpected? Is it already in the news?
   e Does the news fit with other news in the paper?
   f Is it possible to introduce personalities into the story? For example is it Tony Blair's problem, rather than the Government's problem? Is the news about famous or powerful people?
   g Is the news about the UK, USA, Europe, Japan, or Russia?
2. Study the front covers of the papers pictured earlier in this chapter.
   a Draw up a list of types of news item for each paper using the questions above as a guide.
   b How many items are devoted to features that are about negative news or Westminster?
   c How many items are devoted to celebrity and leisure-related stories?
3. Write a summary of your investigations answering the question: is there any difference in the balance of types of stories between the different papers?
4. Study a selection of a day's newspapers and list the main items covered on that day by percentage of space column inches used. You could compare coverage between a tabloid like *The Sun* to a broadsheet such as *The Telegraph*. For example, from the 28th February to the 6th March 1999, the amount of column inches judged the most important by Britain's main 'highbrow' and 'middlebrow' papers (including *The Guardian, The Times, The Daily Telegraph, The Independent, The Sunday Times, The Observer* and the *Daily Mail*) were as follows:

GCSE MEDIA STUDIES

Feature	Number of column inches
Lawrence report	1672
Ugandan murders	1262
The Euro	531
Nigerian elections	366
Care of the elderly	354
Kosovo	321
Monica Lewinsky	248
Prince Charles and beef ban	172

THE PRESS

Freedom of the press

News stories are often written to tell the public that someone is hiding something from them. The media and journalism are one of the four major forces in society, after the state, the church and the family unit. The national press is often the first to expose the wrongdoings of politicians, personalities and companies. The bigger the scandal; the bigger the story. The paper involved can claim a 'scoop', which is the term used to describe the first paper to print the story exclusively. 'Scoops' on allegedly corrupt politicians and adultery among the royal family have helped the newspaper industry to thrive in the last fifteen years.

Journalists can also pay people to talk about their neighbours or adulterous lovers. Some journalists wait near school gates to catch parents, to follow them into the house or even to their sick beds in hospitals to snap photographs. The resulting dilemma is not easy to solve. On the one hand we want our press to expose corruption and wrongdoing. On the other hand we should have a right to privacy and have no fear of harassment and intrusion from greedy journalists.

Voluntary code of conduct

In the UK there has been no strict code of conduct to prevent the press from intruding on private lives, except if the subject is under the age of sixteen. There is however, a code of conduct that is voluntary.

This code is managed by the Press Complaints Commission (PCC). The PCC self-regulate the news industry. This means that although there are no actual laws that can be used, all papers agree to abide by this code. An example of this was when the *Daily Mirror* published pictures of Lady Diana training in the gym, and the paper was fined and suspended from membership for a short time.

NEWSPAPER TABLOIDS AND BROADSHEETS

PRESS CONTROL SIMULATION

NEWSPAPER AND MAGAZINE PUBLISHING IN THE U.K.
CODE OF PRACTICE
(Ratified by the Press Complaints Commission 26th November 1997)

All members of the press have a duty to maintain the highest professional and ethical standards. This Code sets the benchmarks for those standards. It both protects the rights of the individual and upholds the public's right to know.

The Code is the cornerstone of the system of self-regulation to which the industry has made a binding commitment. Editors and publishers must ensure that the Code is observed rigorously not only by their staff but also by anyone who contributes to their publications.

It is essential to the workings of an agreed code that it be honoured not only to the letter but in the full spirit. The Code should not be interpreted so narrowly as to compromise its commitment to respect the rights of the individual, nor so broadly that it prevents publication in the public interest. It is the responsibility of editors to co-operate with the P.C.C. as swiftly as possible in the resolution of complaints.

Any publication which is criticised by the P.C.C. under one of the following clauses must print the adjudication which follows in full and with due prominence.

1. Accuracy
(i) Newspapers and periodicals must take care not to publish inaccurate, misleading or distorted material including pictures.
(ii) Whenever it is recognised that a significant inaccuracy, misleading statement or distorted report has been published, it must be corrected promptly and with due prominence.
(iii) An apology must be published whenever appropriate.
(iv) Newspapers, whilst free to be partisan, must distinguish clearly between comment, conjecture and fact.
(v) A newspaper or periodical must report fairly and accurately the outcome of an action for defamation to which it has been a party.

2. Opportunity to reply
A fair opportunity to reply to in-accuracies must be given to individuals or organisations when reasonably called for.

★3. Privacy
(i) Everyone is entitled to respect for his or her private and family life, home, health and correspondence. A publication will be expected to justify intrusions into any individual's private life without consent.
(ii) The use of longlens photography to take pictures of people in private places without their consent is unacceptable.
Note – Private places are public or private property where there is a reasonable expectation of privacy.

★4. Harassment
(i) Journalists and photographers must neither obtain nor seek to obtain information or pictures through intimidation, harassment or persistent pursuit.
(ii) They must not photograph individuals in private places (as defined in the note to Clause 3) without their consent; must not persist in telephoning, questioning, pursuing or photographing individuals after having been asked to desist; must not remain on their property after having been asked to leave and must not follow them.
(iii) Editors must ensure that those working for them comply with these requirements and must not publish material from other sources which does not meet these requirements.

5. Intrusion into grief or shock
In cases involving grief or shock, enquiries must be carried out and approaches made with sympathy and discretion. Publication must be handled sensitively at such times, but this should not be interpreted as restricting the right to report judicial proceedings.

★6. Children
(i) Young people should be free to complete their time at school without unnecessary intrusion.
(ii) Journalists must not interview or photograph children under the age of 16 on subjects involving the welfare of the child or of any other child, in the absence of or without the consent of a parent or older adult who is responsible for the children.
(iii) Pupils must not be approached or photographed while at school without the permission of the school authorities.

(iv) There must be no payment to minors for material involving the welfare of children nor payment to parents or guardians for material about their children or wards unless it is demonstrably in the child's interest.
(v) Where material about the private life of a child is published, there must be justification for publication other than the fame, notoriety or position of his or her parents or guardian.

7. Children in sex cases
1. The press must not, even where the law does not prohibit it, identify children under the age of 16 who are involved in cases concerning sexual offences, whether as victims, or as witnesses.
2. In any press report of a case involving a sexual offence against a child –
(i) The child must not be identified.
(ii) The adult may be identified.
(iii) The word "incest" must not be used where a child victim might be identified.
(iv) Care must be taken that nothing in the report implies the relationship between the accused and the child.

★8. Listening devices
Journalists must not obtain or publish material obtained by using clandestine listening devices or by intercepting private telephone conversations.

★9. Hospitals
(i) Journalists or photographers making enquiries at hospitals or similar institutions must identify themselves to a responsible executive and obtain permission before entering non-public areas.
(ii) The restrictions on intruding into privacy are particularly relevant to enquiries about individuals in hospitals or similar institutions.

★10. Innocent relatives and friends
The press must avoid identifying relatives or friends of persons convicted of crime without their consent.

★11. Misrepresentation
(i) Journalists must not generally obtain or seek to obtain information or pictures through misrepresentation or subterfuge.

THE PUBLIC INTEREST
There may be exceptions to the clauses marked ★ where they can be demonstrated to be in the public interest.
1. The public interest includes:
(i) Detecting or exposing crime or a serious misdemeanour.
(ii) Protecting public health and safety.
(iii) Preventing the public from being misled by some statement or action of an individual or organisation.
2. In any case where the public interest is invoked, the Press Complaints Commission will require a full explanation by the editor demonstrating how the public interest was served.
3. In cases involving children editors must demonstrate an exceptional public interest to over-ride the normally paramount interests of the child.

(ii) Documents or photographs should be removed only with the consent of the owner.
(iii) Subterfuge can be justified only in the public interest and only when material cannot be obtained by any other means.

12. Victims of sexual assault
The press must not identify victims of sexual assault or publish material likely to contribute to such identification unless there is adequate justification and, by law, they are free to do so.

13. Discrimination
(i) The press must avoid prejudicial or pejorative reference to a person's race, colour, religion, sex or sexual orientation or to any physical or mental illness or disability.
(ii) It must avoid publishing details of a person's race, colour, religion, sexual orientation, physical or mental illness or disability unless these are directly relevant to the story.

14. Financial journalism
(i) Even where the law does not prohibit it, journalists must not use for their own profit financial information they receive in advance of its general publication, nor should they pass such information to others.
(ii) They must not write about shares or securities in whose performance they know that they or their close families have a significant financial interest, without disclosing the interest to the editor or financial editor.
(iii) They must not buy or sell, either directly or through nominees or agents, shares or securities about which they have written recently or about which they intend to write in the near future.

15. Confidential sources
Journalists have a moral obligation to protect confidential sources of information.

★16. Payment for articles
(i) Payment or offers of payment for stories or information must not be made directly or through agents to witnesses or potential witnesses in current criminal proceedings except where the material concerned ought to be published in the public interest and there is an overriding need to make or promise to make a payment for this to be done. Journalists must take every possible step to ensure that no financial dealings have influence on the evidence that those witnesses may give. (An editor authorising such a payment must be prepared to demonstrate that there is a legitimate public interest at stake involving matters that the public has a right to know. The payment or, where accepted, the offer of payment to any witness who is actually cited to give evidence must be disclosed to the prosecution and the defence and the witness should be advised of this.)
(ii) Payment or offers of payment for stories, pictures or information, must not be made directly or through agents to convicted or confessed criminals or to their associates – who may include family, friends and colleagues – except where the material concerned ought to be published in the public interest and payment is necessary for this to be done.

Published by The Press Standards Board of Finance Ltd., 30 George Square, Glasgow G2 1EG. Registered in England & Wales No. 2554323.

Newspaper and magazine Code of Practice
Source: The Press Standards Board of Finance Ltd.

Read paragraphs 1 to 6 inclusive of the Code of Practice. You are the editor of the local newspaper and you also have children who attend school in the area. You are also a school governor and are keen to maintain the favourable reputation of the school in the community. You have a duty to inform the public of matters of 'public interest'.

GCSE MEDIA STUDIES

Task 1

There is an anonymous phone call to the newspaper, stating that their son was beaten up by a group of girls at the school. Discuss.

(5 marks)

Task 2

A teacher is suspected of having an affair with a student. Discuss.

(5 marks)

Task 3

a How would you discover the truth behind one or both of the stories in Tasks 1 and 2?

(5 marks)

b How would you avoid the charge of harassment or intrusion on the private lives of the suspects, victims, parents or the school?

(10 marks)

c At what point do you think it is in the 'public interest' to publish the story? Would you publish all or any one of these stories?

(10 marks)

Press controls

Other forms of press control are:

- No filming, photography or tape recording in law courts.
- The press can be excluded from the courts by the judge.
- The Official Secrets Act and The Prevention of Terrorism Act can be used to stop journalists revealing the whereabouts of army movements, for example.
- The police can confiscate journalists' material under the Criminal Evidence Act and the Criminal Justice Act.
- Libel is often the main weapon used by people to stop journalists from publishing material. Elton John sued *The Sun* successfully for accusing him of being an alcoholic,

Figure 8.5 PressWise front cover, January 1997
Source: *The PressWise Trust*

and Jason Donovan sued *The Face* for suggesting he was a homosexual.

The Campaign for Press and Broadcasting Freedom and Presswise

The Campaign for Press and Broadcasting Freedom was set up to argue that the public should have a right to legal redress. Campaigners for press freedom also feel that more controls over the press may lead to politicians getting away with actions they do not want the public to know about, for example, public money spent on overseas weapons supply or development.

There is a charity called PressWise which

NEWSPAPER TABLOIDS AND BROADSHEETS

Press Complaints Commission

EMBARGO 00:01 hrs
Thursday 23rd July 1998

Press Release

The Press Complaints Commission has ruled on four sets of complaints relating to payments to criminals. These cover: the serialisation of *'Cries Unheard'* (the story of Mary Bell) by **The Times**; the serialisation of *'The Informer'* by Sean O'Callaghan, by **The Daily Telegraph**; and payments to Lucille MacLauchlan by **The Mirror** and to Deborah Parry by **The Express**. The Commission has yet to determine complaints made about possible payments made by The Daily Mail in relation to the Louise Woodward trial.

The Commission has ruled that none of the payments made by the newspapers breached the Code - which stipulates that payments can be made to convicted criminals provided the material obtained is in the public interest, and payment is necessary to obtain it.

In the case of *'Cries Unheard'*, the Commission found the public interest justification of **The Times** to be 'compelling', and that the serialisation put into general circulation 'material of relevance to a wide range of issues relating to crime and punishment' (paragraphs 3.0 - 3.3).

In regard of the payments to Lucille MacLauchlan and Deborah Parry by **The Mirror** and by **The Express**, the Commission found a 'substantial' public interest justification - not least because the fact that the British Government had been involved in the case made it a matter of legitimate public interest and debate (paras 3.4 - 3.11).

Finally, the Commission found the public interest justification for **The Daily Telegraph's** serialisation of *The Informer* to be 'very strong.' It concluded that the 'book was an invaluable work, and deserved the wide audience that serialisation gave it' (paras 3.12 - 3.13).

The PCC never received a complaint about alleged harassment of Mary Bell and her daughter - without which it was impossible to take any action - but the adjudication makes clear that the Commission had 'a very great deal of sympathy for Mary Bell's daughter' (para 4.1). It would have welcomed a complaint and would have been quick 'vigorously to censure a newspaper if a complaint had been received, backed up by evidence from one of those involved, and a breach of Clause 4 (Harassment) or Clause 6 (Children) proved' (para 4.3).

Finally, the adjudication notes that the Government itself is undertaking a review of the issue of proceeds of crime - which the Commission welcomes. It says that the issue of proceeds of crime 'is a moral and subjective judgement which goes beyond the scope of the Commission and an objective Code at the heart of which is the public interest and the public's right to know. It is a matter of broader public policy for Government and Parliament' (para 6.1).

ENDS

Figure 8.6 The judgements on three cases by the Press Complaints Commission

Source: PCC, 1998

1. Mary Bell, who murdered a young girl and was paid by a writer to tell her story, which was then published in *The Times*. There was a public outcry over this and the press found Mary Bell and discovered that her daughter did not know about the murder.
2. A man tried for terrorist crimes in Ireland was paid for a story serialised in *The Daily Telegraph*.
3. Two nurses who were accused by the Saudi government of murdering a colleague received payment for their story by *The Mirror* and *The Express*. They escaped the death sentence after the British government obtained a clemency plea.

Study the press release giving the judgements on the question of money for stories. Write an essay (maximum of 500 words) in answer to the following question: do you think there is a case for more laws or less to prevent harassment, intrusion or payment of money to the public? A Bill of Rights in 1998 aimed to clarify the limits of journalistic intrusion, however as yet there has been no legislation passed to confirm what these limits are.

publishes material about the media. Their aim is to protect the vulnerable public, but also to allow investigative journalism into public life. As a body devoted to media ethics, they are not in a powerful position. However, in the light of the death of Princess Diana in 1997, the debate about the rights of journalists and the public is still very strong.

Payment for stories

Another area of moral debate is the question of whether people who are criminals or who might be criminals should gain money for publishing their stories.

Ownership

In Britain the print media are dominated by seven companies (as at June 1999). The following ownership figures have been adapted from *The Media Guide, The Guardian*, 1999.

1 News International – 35% of UK newspaper circulation. Owns:

- UK – *The Sun, The Times, News of the World* and *Sunday Times*.
- 40% of BSKY B and News Datacom technology subsidiary.
- US – Fox TV network, television stations across the USA, Fox film studio, Fox video, Fox Interactive, New World Communications Group, FX cable channel, *TV Guide, New York Post, Standard Magazine*, Delphi on line.
- Asia – Star TV satellite to 54 countries, Star movies pay channel, 50% of Indian Zee TV, Asia Sat 2 satellite system, Star Radio, 50% of Pacific magazines.
- Australia – 50% of the newspapers sold in Australia, including *Herald Sun, The Australian Daily Telegraph, Mirror*, stakes in TV stations, 50% of a leading air carrier.

2 Mirror Group – 26% of UK newspaper circulation. Owns:

- *The Mirror, The Sunday Mirror, Daily Record* (Scotland) and *Daily People*.
- 43% of Newspaper Publishing that runs *The Independent* and *Independent on Sunday*.
- Owns Live Television and Wire TV and 40% of Scottish Television.

3 United News and Media – 13% of UK newspaper circulation. Owns:

- *The Express, Express on Sunday* and *The Star*.
- Owns over 80 local newspapers and Miller Freeman magazines.
- Merged with MAI to control Anglia TV and Meridian TV and has shares in Yorkshire TV, HTV and Channel 5.

4 Daily Mail and General Trust – 12% of UK newspaper circulation. Owns:

- The *Daily Mail* and *Mail on Sunday*. The Trust is the second largest newspaper owner, through Northcliffe Newspapers Group. interests in Teletext, local radio, Reuters.
- Owns Channel One and 20% of Westcountry Television.

5 The Telegraph Group – 7% of UK newspaper circulation. Owns:

- *Daily Telegraph* and *Sunday Telegraph*.

6 Guardian Media Group – 3% of UK newspaper circulation. Owns:

- *The Guardian, The Observer*. GMG owns over 50 local papers, several magazines and 15% of GMTV.

7 Pearson – 1% of UK newspaper circulation. Owns:

- *The Financial Times*, Addison Wesley Longman publishers, and Future Publishing Magazines.
- Owns Grundy Corporation in Australia.

Source: Adapted from *The Media Guide: A Guardian Book*, 1999

NEWSPAPER TABLOIDS AND BROADSHEETS

Regional and local ownership

This can be broken down as follows.

Group name	Titles	Weekly circulation
1 Trinity Holdings	121	8,301,337
2 Northcliffe Newspapers Group	56	8,040,969
3 Newsquest Media Group	124	7,653,088
4 Johnston Press	141	4,269,973
5 Mirror Group Newspapers	42	4,219,914
6 Regional Independent Media	33	3,275,611
7 Eastern Counties Newspapers Group	70	3,145,719
8 Southern Newspapers	63	2,708,407
9 Guardian Media Group	36	2,708,407
10 Southnews	54	2,655,744

Table 8.1

Source: Adapted from *The Media Guide*, Steve Peak and Paul Fisher (1999), Fourth Estate

Discuss:

1 Who owns your local daily newspaper?
2 What are its current circulation figures?
3 Obtain a press pack from a local newspaper. Analyse how many people read it from different age groups. Which age group has the highest readership? How does the company gain its revenue?

Specimen Examination Question (OCR)

Section One Question Two: Unseen Printed Text (this question should take approximately 1½ hours of the total 2½ hours)

These Tasks are not actual examination questions. The questions are the sole work of the author and are devised to match the style, mark allocation and format of the relevant question papers from AQA and OCR. They are designed for examination practice. The Tasks are designed to follow the examination paper timings and mark allocations. It is essential that candidates check the specified topics set for the year of their examination, by the examination board. For previous examination papers contact the examination board direct.

The print extracts are from: *The Mirror*, February 26th 1999 and *The Voice*, February 22nd 1999. Advice: study pages 122 and 125 in this textbook.

You will have 30 minutes reading and note-making time.

▶ Before you study the pages read all of the questions first.
▶ Study both pages, including text, headlines, photographs and graphics carefully.
▶ You are to make notes on your answer paper and you should put a diagonal line through your notes at the end of the exam.

a i) What word or phrase would you use to identify this type of newspaper?

(2 marks)

ii) Give reasons for your answer.

(4 marks)

b How are the two front pages similar in the use of the following:
i) the type of language used

(4 marks)

ii) layout, headline and headings

(4 marks)

iii) the use of pictures and captions

(4 marks)

c i) What kinds of audiences are each newspaper aimed at?

(6 marks)

ii) Give reasons for your answers.

(6 marks)

d i) Compare the masthead blocks (where the title of the papers are) of *The Mirror* and the *Daily Mail*. What do the words, typeface and any other information tell you about each paper's image?

(8 marks)

ii) In what ways is the story of Stephen Lawrence presented differently by the two newspapers? Discuss both form and content.

(12 marks)

Extension Tasks

1 **Research** one newspaper's history and how they have adapted to changing audiences.
2 **Track** a major story and see how long it stays in the news. **Assess** why it moves from the front page or out of the paper altogether.
3 **Take photographs** of a group of students, three of which are snatched and three of which are posed. **Select** the best image and crop or enlarge the result using a photocopier. Select the appropriate typeface font and point size. **Create captions** for each photo, for example, the snatched image could be used in a newspaper's negative story, and the posed picture could be used in a newspaper article about the school or college's excellent performance in exams, science, sport or drama.
4 **Research** press agencies such as Reuters and Agence Press France. These are accessible on the Internet. Find out what they do and who they supply news to.
5 **Draw up** a list of possible sources of news and how news comes to the attention of the editors of newspapers.
6 **Create** a press release to encourage the local press to come and take photographs of your event or item (see also Chapter Three).

NEWSPAPER TABLOIDS AND BROADSHEETS

Examination Skills

Knowledge and Understanding

There should be an understanding of the different audiences, both in terms of social group and how audiences are targeted as well as created by newspaper producers. Students should be able to use the technical terms as well as the key words listed at the beginning of this chapter. There should be knowledge of the processes, practices and technology involved in the production of newspapers. There should be a good understanding of the news values that each paper tends to use. Examinations will test the ability to categorise and distinguish the different types of paper through their ownership and by the editorial line taken.

Textual Analysis

Students must have the ability to analyse newspapers, and describe and interpret images, graphics, captions and headings, text and copy. Students should be able to explain the different forms and conventions across a range of tabloid and broadsheet formats.

Practical Work

Students should know how to manipulate finished photographs and crop or enlarge them to suit the paper's ownership, editorial style and audience. Students should be able to understand how typeface font, size and presentation effect the image of the newspaper. The selection of stories for front page mock-ups and production should demonstrate an understanding of the forms and conventions of the format chosen. The use of language and slogans should be appropriate to the type of newspaper.

9 TV hospital dramas and documentaries

REAL BEDTIME STORIES?

In this chapter you will cover: fictional and documentary forms and conventions based on hospitals; types and stereotypes of characters; serials and series, messages and values; audiences; planning a treatment and a title sequence for a new drama.

KW

Series ▪ serial ▪ realism ▪ narrative ▪ types ▪ stereotypes ▪ representations ▪ messages and values ▪ audiences

TW

Settings ▪ *mise-en-scène* ▪ shot-reverse-shot ▪ tracking ▪ dolly ▪ trailer ▪ treatment ▪ episode ▪ voice over ▪ interior/exterior location shooting

POPULARITY

Hospital dramas have been very popular over the last few years. BBC1's *Casualty* has regularly exceeded 17 million viewers. The American drama *ER* is avidly followed in the UK as well as in the United States. There are also numerous documentaries about hospitals, including series about children's and animal hospitals.

Series and serials

A series is a sequence of programmes that has a finite length, for example 6 to 10 episodes for a drama. The serial is a continuous sequence of programmes, such as a regular two or three day weekly soap. For example, the serial *Casualty* has been running for over 13 years.

TV HOSPITAL DRAMAS AND DOCUMENTARIES

Figure 9.1 What is the appeal of watching doctors and nurses?
Source: © *Independent on Sunday*/John Ferrara, 1998

Why the fascination with hospitals?

Perhaps, as with crime films, we like to find out about behind the scenes of life and death situations – medicine also has a certain mysterious appeal. Or perhaps, we like to know that if we were ill and were taken to hospital we would be prepared for it? There are many and complex reasons for liking hospital dramas. There are also reasons for not liking hospital dramas, for example, the sight of blood is too much for some people. Others argue that hospital drama programmes are really another form of soap and that the entertainment factor lies in being able to identify with someone else's daily traumas and celebrations.

Workplace drama

In fact, hospital dramas are not simply about hospitals and the dramas surrounding the emergency care of patients. They are also about the workplace. One aspect of hospital dramas concerns the relationships between the nurses, staff nurses, doctors, porters and management. Other dramas, like the police serial *The Bill*, focus on the working relationships between the officers on the beat, the detectives and their bosses, in an inner city police station called Sun Hill.

Viewers identify with the workplace and see how other people react to typical work situations, feelings and actions. The audience can relate to rivalries, prejudice, competition for promotion, ambition, greed and petty teasing. How do colleagues stick together against their superiors? How is the new recruit treated by the more experienced officers? How do different officers handle the same job? What makes a good day's work or a 'bad day at the office'? These questions all have some basis in the viewer's own reality.

Why do men and women watch hospital dramas?

Read the following account of viewers watching *ER*, taken from an audio-taped transcript (*The Guardian Guide*, 1 March 1998).

ER

The notoriously gruelling episode in which Dr Greene fatally mishandles a problematic birth. Sensitive and self-effacing, Dr Greene is looking endearingly worried, having told the woman whom he eventually kills that all she has is a bladder infection.

Transcript of **three women watching an *ER* episode**:
Jo: Where's George Clooney – he's not in this one at all?

Nicola: Probably off blow-drying his hair somewhere.

Jo: Yes, I notice he never has to wear those shower-cap things they all wear in the operating theatre, so he won't mess up his hair.

Nicola: Anyway, Dr Greene's the best.

Jo and Sarah: No way...

Nicola: No, he's vulnerable without being wimpy. He has a quiet authority; it's like he's sexy because he's good at what he does.

Sarah: Well, he's not very good here – he's the Mr Bean of the emergency theatre.

(This appears to be true. Dr Greene is busy bungling the birth, rushing frantically between mother and baby. With blood spurting everywhere, the patient finally departs, 'What did you use – a chainsaw?', asks Greene's waspish superior. The women watching are similarly aghast.)

Jo: I have to say I think George shows Dr Greene in a bad light. You look at him here and you think, what an idiot – he's just not in control. But there are moments in the current series that show his vulnerability and yet are far more telling of his strength.

Jo: Yeah, right...

Nicola: No, like in the new series. Whether he's dealing with his relationship with Susan or deciding what to do about a patient, you get an insight into what he's thinking. Yet he's more confident and in control – here he is just like a med. student.

Sarah: But the whole show is a soap opera now – the operations are incidental, whereas in this one the medical drama is centre stage and there's virtually no interaction between the characters. I think it's definitely aimed at women. The men are more complex characters now, they've got no history, and that's why they seem sexy.

Three men talk about ER:

Alex: I never wanted *ER* to end once it started. I always fancied Dr Susan Lewis. She's the ultimate babe.

Paul: What are you talking about? She's completely ordinary.

(Meanwhile Paul and Jim revealed why they have no such obsession – the blood. It turns out that they can't even feel their own pulses without losing their lunch. As Dr Greene's patient seems to be bleeding profusely, this causes problems. Paul actually leaves the room.)

Paul (covering his eyes): I can't watch all that blood.

Alex (riveted): Shut up, I can't hear.

(Alex gets quite lost in the details, as the baby's blood pressure drops and he starts reminiscing about the birth of his own baby. At the tear-jerking finale, the men skilfully defuse the situation with hearty coughing and lame jokes.)

Jim: Men like seeing people being machine-gunned and all blown up, but not having strange blood-drenched things pulled out of them.

Discuss and write down your responses to the following questions.

1. In what ways are hospital dramas like soap operas? Consider:
   - characters
   - story line
   - dramatic interaction between characters
   - themes
   - workplace communities
   - the patients and the public

2. Do you agree that hospital dramas are aimed at women only?

3. What qualities do you think men and women find unattractive and attractive in *ER*?

4. How realistic do you think any hospital drama is that you have seen? What makes hospital dramas realistic or unrealistic?

5. What plots do hospital dramas tend to have?

TV HOSPITAL DRAMAS AND DOCUMENTARIES

HOSPITAL DRAMAS

Hospital dramas have developed from the 1960s merry japes of the *Doctor in The House* films, to the city-based realism of 1980s and 1990s in *Casualty* and *Holby City*. Over the years, a number of hospital types and stereotypes have emerged.

Doctors

- The father figure – offers advice and is decisive, calm and unruffled.
- The uncle figure – everyone can talk to him without strings attached.
- The aloof and stern figure – attractive to some women but obsessed with work and does not suffer fools gladly.
- The female doctor who is very professional and has high moral standards.

Nurses

- The women who are saints, unselfish and at the service of others.
- The women who are mother figures, and who listen to the problems of everyone, including the doctors.
- The nervous incompetent who suffers from stress.
- The severe matron who punishes the weak and rewards the strong.
- The flirt who gets her man.

- Male nurses who are caring and sensitive.
- Male nurses who are incompetent and cover up errors.
- Male nurses who are gay and male nurses who are from Afro-caribbean or Asian backgrounds have become more common. Doctors from these social groups and also lesbians are, however, still rarely represented.

---

1 Study an episode of a hospital drama, such as *Casualty*, *Holby City*, *Peak Practice*, *ER*, or *Cardiac Arrest* (re-runs and earlier series can often be seen on satellite or cable TV). Identify the types of characters who are portrayed in these dramas.
2 Make a list of characters and write down their characteristics and attitudes.
3 Compare these types with another hospital drama. Are there any different types of characters? Consider the following:

- managers
- doctors
- nurses
- ancillary staff – porters or cleaners
- ambulance crews

How are hospital workers represented as a group?

To give an example, *Cardiac Arrest* was a hard-hitting six part series reflecting the cynical attitude staff adopted to cope with cutbacks and inhuman, incompetent management.

Cardiac Arrest

Character type	Characteristics and attitudes
Managers	1 New efficiency savings type. 2 Old fashioned fatherly type: 'It'll be alright on the night'.
Doctors	1 Female: realistic, not to be messed around and heart in the right place. 2 Brash and domineering male. 3 Lazy Asian junior doctor, who plays pranks on everyone. 4 Young novice who starts trying to be nice to everyone but ends up being as cynical as the others.
Nurse	Vary in attitude to their job, doctors and patients. Some are very conscientious, others are plain lazy. Nurses and other staff are not the focus of drama.
Ancillary Staff: porters, cleaners, canteen staff, para-medics and ambulance staff	Unlike *Casualty*, the ancillary staff play a very minor role, as the focus is mainly on the nursing staff, doctors and management.
Patients	Patients are not the focus of the drama.

Table 9.1 *Cardiac Arrest*: Character types and their characteristics

TYPES AND STEREOTYPES

Holby City was promoted in press releases and in TV listings magazines as a spin-off from *Casualty*. The cast contained some well-known faces, such as Michael French (played David Wicks in *EastEnders*), Angela Griffin (ex-*Coronation Street*), Phyllis Logan (ex-*Lovejoy*) and Nicola Stephenson (ex-*Brookside*).

The location is set in a cardiology unit in Holby, the unit where *Casualty* patients are sent when they need serious heart operations. The soap was an eight part series and deliberately set out to be linked with *Casualty*. Each episode was an hour long, and dealt with the relationships of the doctors and nurses. Unlike *Casualty*, the focus was on the professionals rather than on the patients, who play a more equal part in the drama of *Casualty*.

> 'We had to make *Holby City* different from *Casualty* or there was no point. That meant that the doctors had to drive the drama rather than work off the backs of the patients. There was no point in making it a homage to *ER*. This is Britain not America. What I noticed when I watched heart surgery during my research was the amazing calm.'
>
> Source: Tony McHale, in *Radio Times*, 9–15 January 1999

TV HOSPITAL DRAMAS AND DOCUMENTARIES

Study the following cast profiles of *Holby City*, a drama that started in January 1999.

What types and stereotypes are there? Are there any types of characters you think are new? Are there any types of real people who ought to be represented, for example, the over 50 year old female? If you think so, explain why.

Consultant
Anton Meyer
This heart surgeon is a perfectionist who doesn't suffer fools gladly. He has high standards and expects everyone to match them. He is played by George Irving of *Dangerfield* fame.

Registrar
Nick Jordan
Meyer's right-hand man is a handsome medic and something of a lady-killer. A perfect role for Michael French, who made his name as love rat David Wicks in *EastEnders*.

Consultant
Muriel McKendrick
Lovejoy's Lady Jane, Phyllis Logan, plays Muriel McKendrick, Holby City's ambitious consultant cardiologist. Autocratic and manipulative, Muriel's single but has an active social life.

Nurse
Jasmine Hopkins
Angela Griffin (*Corrie Street*) plays, Jasmine, a girl from a hippie background who yearns for a conventional lifestyle. But life could well have a few surprises in store for her!

Nurse
Julie Fitzjohn
Jasmine's best friend Julie is played by Nicola Stephenson (Margaret in *Brookside*). She's a busy single mum but is still disappointed when Jasmine pips her to a promotion.

Senior House Officer
Dr Kirstie Collins
Kirstie, played by Dawn McDaniel (*Soldier, Soldier*), is seen as ruthless and aggressive. From a poor background, she has something to prove.

House Officer
Dr Victoria Merrick
Lisa Faulkner (Louise in *Brookside*) plays loner Victoria. She's very bright but plays down the fact that her dad is an eminent surgeon.

TV Quick: Cast and character profiles
Source: *TV Quick*, 9–15 January 1999
© H. Bauer Publishing

NARRATIVE AND PLOT

Typical narratives in *Casualty*

Storyline method

Two or three incidents take place outside the hospital, in the city or the country. Emergency services do their best to contain the injuries and successfully treat them by the end of the episode in situ, or they are ferried back to the hospital for emergency treatment.

At the hospital two or three patients with minor injuries are seen by staff doctors and nurses. Some patients also have personal difficulties and relatives and relationships are put to the test. Nurses and doctors try not to act as social workers but usually end up offering some kind of advice, which is heeded.

During these scenes, the domestic relationships of the staff are also being tested. Issues such as love, hate, death, jealousy, children and work performance are explored, while the characters are under pressure at work. The main message of BBC1's *Casualty* is that they are dedicated public servants and that most of the staff, with a few notable exceptions, do their best to help people recover.

The final section of the programme ends with the struggle to save a life or the death of a seriously ill patient, and the doctors use life-saving equipment on the patient in the emergency theatre.

Locations

Exterior locations, such as quarries and caravans, and the emergency operating theatre provide the high suspense action sequences. Interior locations, such as the reception areas and the nurses' quarters provide the dramatic dialogues and the interactions between people.

Read the following invented sample script:

(Location is in a hospital cubicle, with a bed surrounded by a curtain or next to a blank wall.)
Doctor: So, how did you come to break your arm then, John isn't it?
Patient: Just walked into a door, stupid really.
Doctor: So, was there anyone with you then?
Patient: No, just my mother, that's all.
Nurse: Does she know you are here?
Patient: Yes, no, I mean, she's kind of ... old ... well, I didn't want to upset her. I just want to tell you what a good job you are ... ouch! That hurts!
Doctor: Just sit up a little straighter (taking the elbow and lifting it up a fraction and moving the forearm down a bit without any difficulty). How does that feel?
Patient: Feels OK, it's just down at the wrist it seems to be swollen or something.
Nurse: I'll get something for that, Jane?
Doctor: Yes ... I don't think that there's anything worse than a sprained wrist for the moment – just rest here and we'll be right back. That'll be all for now, nurse.
Nurse: Just sit there – do you want to ring your mother now?
Patient: No, but can I have my walkman – it's on the side there.
Nurse: Yes, of course – let's try to see if we can find it.

(It is found and passed over. Now doctor and nurse are walking out of earshot of patient and stop in the corridor.)
Nurse: Something fishy about his relationship with his mother, you don't think he wanted to get out of the house for a bit, do you?
Doctor: Yes, not so much a Psycho case but a sick case if you ask me. But Jane ... I wondered if ... I was going to ask you if you would like to come and meet my mother this weekend?
Patient: (loud crash and voice calls out) Doctor, Doctor I think I've broken my leg!
(The doctor and nurse look at each other as though doubting the patient, laugh, and then walk fast back towards the patient.)

Read the previous sample script aloud and video it, as if for a hospital drama. Alternatively, read it as if for a radio play, creating sound effects when appropriate. Before you start recording, consider the following:

1 Who is this programme aimed at? Consider age, gender and class.
2 What are the types of people who are playing the doctor, nurse and patient? For example, is the doctor traditionally superior or are they equals in their approach? Is the nurse independent or obedient? Is the patient tough, meek or whining?
3 Plan how you will shoot the scenes to include a background, for example a bare wall or a curtain to resemble the hospital. Ensure that your background does look like a hospital, and not a school. See section following on video methods.

Filming techniques

The following methods of recording scenes on video can be used to film your background for the previous activity.

TV HOSPITAL DRAMAS AND DOCUMENTARIES

Shot-reverse-shot

Use the technique of shot-reverse-shot to film the sequence. This is where you film a head and shoulders shot of the doctor first, recording the speech, then pausing the camera and then filming a head and shoulders shot of the patient. Next film the doctor, then back to the patient, and so on. You will need to stop and start the camera to record the scene as it would be presented in *Casualty*, or *Holby City*. One advantage of using this video method is that the actors only have to remember one line at a time.

Continuous

For an alternative method, video without stopping. Simply try to record as many shots of everyone's faces as possible, when they are talking, but let the camera move towards the subject of the conversations when appropriate, for example the patient's arm.

Create a new hospital drama: write a 'treatment', an outline explanation or description of the following elements:
1 Setting and interior and exterior locations – settings for doctors, nurses, patients and managers.
2 Profiles of the main characters (minimum of five or six main characters).
3 Plots for the first episode.
4 A scene from your first episode.
5 Casting – are you going to use famous people from other dramas or have a completely new set of faces?

Evaluation of a video scene

1 Play back the video you recorded and evaluate the sequences.
Discuss:

▶ What worked and what did not.
▶ How did you make the voices sound dramatic?
▶ What types of shot did you use and did they vary at all in shot, size or angle?
▶ Was the scene better using the shot-reverse-shot method rather than the continuous videoing?

▶ What are the advantages and disadvantages of videoing without stopping?
▶ What are the advantages and disadvantages of videoing one shot at a time?
2 Watch a hospital documentary and study how it is filmed. Are the sequences full of edits? To what extent is the camera left to wonder around freely without interruption? Do you think the camera crew make people perform for the camera? Does the way people appear on the screen feel natural, as though the camera was not there?

GCSE MEDIA STUDIES

HOSPITAL DOCUMENTARIES

Following are three typical documentary TV listings magazine previews, involving hospital related institutions.

1 **Animal ER**, Channel 5, 8.30 pm.
The vets are called out to a pregnant horse entangled in barbed wire at the bottom of a field.

2 **The Coroner's Office**, Channel 4, 9 pm.
A nine year old girl has been killed in a hit-and-run accident in front of her mother, and a 21 year old woman has died of a mystery illness after the local doctor refused to visit. Another day in the twilight world of Birmingham Coroner's office. The bodies are Muslim and according to Islamic tradition should be buried as soon as possible. Dr Richard Whittington is not in the business of rushing his autopsies and sensitive though he is to the need of families to bury their dead in their home country, rules are rules. As the jumbo jets taxi into position, the bodies are finally released and a sigh of relief can be heard from here to Pakistan.

3 **Cutting Edge**, Channel 4, 9 pm.
The story of Friern Barnet hospital. The former mental institution was so large it had its own working farm – and gave birth to the term 'funny farm'. Now it has been transformed into a luxury housing estate. Former inmates of the hospital and present residents describe their feelings about the place.

> **Discuss** the types of drama that can be introduced to the documentaries to interest the viewers in each of *Animal ER*, *The Coroner's Office* and *Cutting Edge*. Study the language of their TV listings previews for clues.

Documentary style

Documentaries on television can be single programmes in slots, such as *Modern Times* or *Cutting Edge*. Alternatively, they can be long series such as *Animal Hospital* or *Children's Hospital*.

Documentaries:

▶ Tend to have a voice over.
▶ Tend to focus on the issues rather than on the character relationships, for example, shocking working conditions rather than a manager's affair with a nurse.
▶ Tend to build up more of a sense of the setting.
▶ Do not have cliffhangers.
▶ Have a serious message.

> **Discuss**: How many of those features do you think apply to documentaries that you have seen?

The fascination with documentaries set in hospitals is in part connected to the success of the hospital dramas, but is also due to the great interest in reality television. The low cost of not having to pay actors and create costly sets makes it an attractive option for television executives.

Camera work

Documentary camera work is not easy to perform without being noticed! The trick is to get close to the subject without them knowing or being aware that you are interviewing them. Trust has to be built up between the subject and the camera crew members. Filming in a hospital is a very intimate experience and the

TV HOSPITAL DRAMAS AND DOCUMENTARIES

temptation to avoid the camera or play act is often very great.

There are at least four techniques for filming documentaries to make them look more 'real':

- ▶ 'Fly on the wall' camera work is designed to appear as though there were no film crew in the room at all; as though they were unseen on the wall, like a fly.
- ▶ Verite camera work is a continuous hand-held shot that simulates the experience of the person looking and walking about the room. Many investigative journalists have to use this technique if they want to gain direct reponse to a question and record it.
- ▶ Secret microphones and cameras have become much more common. Hidden cameras in bags and jackets are used if it is known that the subject does not welcome the prospect of being exposed to the public at a later date.
- ▶ Video diary style is when the camera is given to a person in a particular situation, and they record the experience themselves, talking to the camera that is set up to record them in the corner of the room.

In the case of documenting hospital matters, the camera operator has to be prepared for emotional and stressful scenes. How the public feel about someone filming them depends on the sensitivity of the director and the camera operator.

Production

Dramas require a large number of staff and fixed sets and studios. Crew and staff use up a considerable part of the budget. In addition to the actors and actresses there are: the producer, director, production managers, camera operators, lighting electricians, sound recordist, make-up artists, wardrobe, set designers and props staff.

Documentaries involve a much smaller scale operation. With the arrival of new low light cameras there is often no need for a lighting electrician. A crew may consist of as few people as four in total: the camera operator, sound recordist, production assistant and the director.

Cost

The cost of a documentary, for example, £40,000 for a single hour long programme of *Cutting Edge*, is much cheaper than a wage bill for the staffing of a single episode of *Casualty*. This provides a great incentive for programme makers such as Channel 4 or BBC2 to make dramatic documentaries or docu-soaps, as they are cheaper. Real people can be paid much less than professional actors or actresses. Production costs are therefore much lower on location, as studios usually cost a great deal to maintain for a large cast and varied scene locations.

The docu-soap

The rise of the docu-soap, a highly personality-centred and conflict-ridden documentary set in the 1990s, has led to criticism that the art of documentary making as the representation of real life, has been lost. Makers of docu-soaps claim that real life is dramatic and that if there are real personalities 'out there', then they can only represent them as they are. Classic types are the sweaty, shouting and swearing chefs in documentaries on hotels and cooking. Another type is the endlessly patient and jovial passenger controller of an airport.

SPECIMEN EXAMINATION QUESTION (OCR)

Note: this question is from a 2½ hour paper, with one other question allocated 1½ hours. In section **B**, OCR offers **either** an essay **or** a creative simulation task. These Tasks are not actual examination questions. The questions are the sole work of the author and are devised to match the style, mark allocation and format of the relevant question papers from AQA and OCR. They are designed for examination practice. The Tasks are designed to follow the examination paper timings and mark allocations. It is essential that candidates check the specified topics set for the year of their examination, by the examination board. For previous examination papers contact the examination board direct.

Television hospital drama and documentary
(you should spend an hour on this question.)
Either

1 Essay response – explain how television hospital dramas and/or documentaries set in hospitals use dramatic incidents and a variety of character types to interest their audiences. Discuss with reference to the programme, or programmes, you have studied.

(Total 25 marks)

or

2 Production response – read the following outline for a new television drama and then follow the instructions.
Airport hospital drama
Title: *Morby: a drama series*.
Location: Birmingham Airport.
Time slot: Thursday 8 pm, Channel 5.
Focus: Main focus is the work of the paramedics. Storylines for the first four episodes (two storylines for each programme, plus the staff domestic storyline each week):

Episode One:
Storyline One – animal smuggling and drugs smuggling. The passenger bitten by a 10 year old's escaped pet rat.
Storyline Two – the Nigerian carrier whose stomach contains drugs wrapped in balloons, which are now leaking and making the carrier suffer acute stomach pains.
Hospital staff domestic plotline – the chief nurse orderly who has to make a decision on whether to admit their own 17 year old son into the hospital due to a suspected drugs and drinks excess.

Episode Two:
Storyline One – the drunk (and ill) passengers who express their violence and abuse towards passengers and crew on Flight BA 3216 from New York.
Storyline Two – the check-in desk assistant whose medication makes him aggressive with customers. His short temper contributes to a violent attack on them by a customer who arrives too late to board the plane.
Hospital staff domestic plotline – the nurse whose promotion prospects seem to be undermined by a mysterious hoaxer. They keep ringing her boss claiming that she has a criminal record.

Episode Three:
Storyline One – illegal immigrants stowed on plane. Two Czechoslovakian romanies brought in with a broken arm and hypothermia, caused by holding on to the plane's undercarriage.
Storyline Two – the airline crew's strike and successful claim for more pay. This leads to massive congestion in the waiting areas, accidents and a premature birth.
Hospital staff domestic plotline – the female surgeon whose eyesight is not what it used to be, and her affair with two male staff who are her operating theatre assistants.

TV HOSPITAL DRAMAS AND DOCUMENTARIES

Episode Four:
Storyline One – the reunion of the 70 year old twins separated at birth, who both experience heart attack symptoms minutes before they meet at the exit point from immigration controls.

Storyline Two – the hospital administrator who is going to give up his job. He also has to call a beginning of shift meeting to announce cuts to the staff but cannot face it. He fakes illness at the crucial moment.

Hospital staff domestic plotline – the administrator's gay partner who has decided to force his partner to give up work, has a heart attack at the same time as the 70 year old twins. There are not enough staff around to cope with all three of them. The end of the series sees two interviews for a new recruit to the hospital management team and a new member of the nursing staff.

The hospital team includes: management, ambulance units, auxillary staff (porters, canteen, cleaners), nurses and doctors and reception staff. Airport staff include: administrators, cabin crew, reception staff, baggage handlers, mechanics and shops and services staff. The audience of the show ranges from 12 years of age upwards.

a Devise a title sequence for the series. The images should contain some idea of the different characters and settings of the drama. Draw at least ten frames (and no more than 20 frames) to show the key elements of the programme's title sequence. Include a title for your series. You should indicate key sounds to be heard on the title sequence, for example, music, special effects, voices.

(15 marks)

b Write a commentary (maximum of 300 words) explaining who the audience is for the programme. How will the title sequence attract the audience to the programme?

(10 marks)

Extension Tasks

1. **Design** the front cover of a TV listings magazine and produce an appropriate image (drawn), heading and straplines for the new documentary series described previously. Alternatively, design a cover for the hospital drama you created earlier in this chapter. Produce an appropriate image (drawn), heading and straplines.

2. **Essay**: what are the typical representations of health professionals in hospital dramas? (write a maximum of 700 to 1000 words)

3. **Devise** a ten minute radio phone-in programme, where different members of the class discuss why they think their favourite hospital programme is more realistic than others, for example, *ER* and *Casualty* or *Holby City* and *Casualty*. As a presenter, construct a set of questions covering characters, story lines, settings and themes. Ensure that the speaker identifies him/herself and is not allowed to ramble. Record the discussion on tape and invite another group to comment on your recording. Listen to the tape and write up your comments and observations of the different perspectives. Write about the practical aspect and the decisions you had to make in organising the radio programme, before and during the phone-in.

4. **Compare** an American hospital drama with a British hospital drama, such as *Casualty*. Are there differences in the filming and editing styles? How does each of them attempt to be realistic? Discuss settings, characters and story lines.

Examination Skills

Knowledge and Understanding

Candidates will need to show an understanding of the typical forms and conventions of a hospital drama or a documentary. They should have knowledge of typical representations of hospitals and types and stereotypes of staff, and explore similarities and differences across dramas. The candidate should be able to refer to more than one type of documentary filming style. There should be an awareness of different audiences for different subject material.

Candidates should be prepared (if they choose not to write an essay) to invent a preparatory product such as a storyboard title sequence, a trailer or a scene (cliffhanger) from the programme. Alternatively, there may be a task of writing a treatment or a promotion of the programmes in the form of posters or advertisements.

Students should analyse the relationship between producers and audiences and how hospital dramas satisfy the audience or not. Schedules and target audiences are also areas that students should cover and analyse.

Textual Analysis

Students should be able to analyse the representations, and forms and conventions of hospital drama story lines, *mise-en-scène*, types of characters and their messages and values. They should be able to derive meaning from the messages and values that depict doctors as experts and nurses as carers.

Practical Work

The student should be able to demonstrate a good understanding of the formats for producing storyboards, treatments, scripted scenes, radio programmes and magazine covers. They should know how to annotate a storyboard soundtrack. Candidates will **not** have to be able to draw. The work will need to show good organisation and keen attention to appropriate shape, form and content. The products should show awareness of the institution (real or imagined) in which it was produced.

Menzies or your local paper shop. This type of professional magazine is bought by subscription and is delivered regularly through the post direct to the subscriber. 66% of business area magazines are sent for free, the cost of which is covered by advertising revenue.

The market is broken into mass and specialist interest groups. Specialist interest groups are known as niche markets. Publications range from specialist comics such as *Judge Dredd* to *Flight International* and *Golf Monthly*.

Broad interest magazines made for the mass market, such as TV listings magazines, satisfy a very common need. Mass audiences draw in the widest group of audiences in every demographic group, economically and geographically (see also Chapter 3: Producers and Audiences):

- professional class (for example, ABC1)
- age
- gender
- region

Title	Circulation figures
1 What's On TV	1,765,369
2 Reader's Digest	1,302,659
3 Radio Times	1,400,331
4 TV Times	883,281
5 FHM	751,493
6 TV Quick	740,000
7 Woman	711,133
8 Woman's Own	654,473

Table 10.1 Top Eight Magazines in 1998
Source: Adapted from Audit Bureau of Circulation, 1998

The titles in Table 10.1 can be purchased from shops. They are not free for club members or for favoured retail customers as, for example, with *Sky TV Guide*, *Safeway Magazine* or Cable Guide etc. These are given away as part of the membership service, so they are not in the table.

From the titles listed in Table 10.1, we can see that the types of magazines that are the most popular are TV listings and adult women's mainstream magazines. Following on from these are the teenage women's magazines. Since the 1980s there has also been a rise in the popularity of men's magazines. *FHM* is now one of the best selling UK magazines and has even overtaken *Woman* and *Woman's Own*. There is however, still an absence of any general lifestyle magazine targeted at 11 to 19 year old males.

Launching a magazine

Within a year of being launched, two new magazines ceased by the end of 1998: *Deluxe* and *Stuff*. To launch a magazine in today's market is not always easy. However, despite the competition, a new magazine called *Heat* was launched in 1999.

Heat is a new TV listings magazine with a difference. It aims to be 'a high gloss celebrity-based magazine' published by Emap Metro, which is a sub-division of the Emap parent company. Emap Metro deals with mens' and music and entertainment magazines.

Heat will be, according to its press release and launch publicity pack: 'news-led, packed with snippety items, including lists, facts and statistics – the kinds of things that men tend to feel justifies reading about what is essentially showbiz'. As with *Empire* and to a lesser extent *Q*, *Heat* is not targeted at either sex. The magazine aims to sell 100,000 per week and used TV advertisements from the advertising company, Bartle Bogle and Hegarty to start the promotion. Front covers will include Johnny Vaughan, Will Smith, Jim Carrey, Robbie Williams, George Clooney and Gwyneth Paltrow. It will be competing with *What's On*

TV, *Radio Times*, *Sky Magazine* in the listings, and titles like *FHM*, *Arena* and *Q* in the men's market.

> **Discuss:** what is the unique selling point of a new magazine? Analyse the images and words on the cover, and the editorial inside.

Messages and values

Female magazines

The messages of mainstream magazines are dedicated to the ideal image of a woman who is independent, sexy and looks after her appearance in order to catch a man. Fashion and cosmetics, and advice on relationships tend to dominate teenage female magazines. The ideal woman is often depicted as thin and tall. However, a famous Body Shop advertisement stated, there are only eight women in the world who look like this, and they are top fashion models.

Male magazines

The messages of mainstream men's magazines are focused on the man who enjoys being a lad without a conscience, ogles at women's bodies, drinks large amounts of alcohol, watches football and plays loud music. If he is at all sensitive, he does not want to show it. Men's magazines such as *Loaded* tend to include scantily clad women and articles on sex, football, drinking, fashion and music. The aim is to be wild, witty and to include interviews with the stars.

Alternative magazines

Alternative magazines try to present a different perspective on the world, such as the magazine *Sibyl*. The magazine is not sold in the main distributors such as WH Smiths or Menzies, but is sold by subscription. *Sibyl* is dedicated to women who care about women's issues and politics. *Red Pepper* is a political discussion journal that covers issues which the writers think the current Labour Government does not deal with in terms of socialist politics. These magazines all differ from mainstream magazines, as they express alternative viewpoints and ideas about how men and women should live.

Children's and teenagers' magazines

The children's end of the market includes comics ranging from *Beano*, to teenage comic strip *Dick Tracy*, to graphic comics like *Judge Dredd*, *Love and Rockets*, *Electra* and *Toast*. Some comics cross over into the world of film. The Japanese comic *Akira* became an animated movie, featuring cyber-punk motorcycle gangs doing battle on the streets of post World War 3 Tokyo.

Young people's interest in futuristic stories has now transferred over to Nintendo and Sega games. This has led to a growth in PC games magazines such as *Segapower*, *Bad Influence* and *PC Zone*. Many of these magazines offer free software samples on CD.

Fanzines

Fanzines are an alternative to mainstream publishing. Fanzines are written by the fans. Many fanzines are about music, football and skateboarding and they tend to be sold in the street. For example, football fanzines are often sold near the grounds. Music fanzines are sold at clubs and at venues where bands play. Shops with skateboarding and surfing equipment also have fanzines on the counter. *Blockade* is a fanzine for *Prisoner Cell Block H* fans. It once included a feature on the character of prison officer Joan 'the freak' Ferguson. Copies were available from a PO Box address.

MAGAZINES

As fanzines do not have the benefit of large team of writers and are often written by one or two people, there is very little or no advertising. There is therefore very little incentive for businesses to invest in such a magazine, when only between 50 and 200 copies are likely to be sold.

Format and content

Fanzines are usually the size of an exercise book and are a series of photocopies stapled together. Sometimes they have photographs, however these are only roughly reproduced. There are line drawings and also images recycled from other magazines.

Fanzines do not usually feature articles with famous pop stars. They do however, often express strong opinions about the topics they cover. They are often written without fear of censorship or complaint, as they tend to circulate only in the group of fans who read the 'zine. *Stay Free* is a fanzine produced by one woman from New York, and is dedicated to mocking the advertising industry.

New technology publishing is now thriving on the Internet and major print-based companies have websites. Interactive CD Roms may replace printed materials, but the companies who produce the print versions may be reluctant to lose revenue from advertising. New technology could change the face of newspaper magazine shelves. If not, then it could be that people access their magazines and ask questions and gain advice more interactively using their home computer screens. People may only want to download the pages required, for storage in print form.

Figure 10.1 *Maximum Rock and Roll Drum and Bass*: a mock-up for a worldwide fanzine by Alex Hill

FORMS AND CONVENTIONS

Layout and design

A typical cover of a glossy mainstream lifestyle magazine shows what is inside, but does not tend to include any articles (see Figure 10.2).

Forms and conventions: typical elements

All magazines have some elements in common,

Figure 10.2 A typical cover layout
Source: © IPC Magazines Ltd

MAGAZINES

be it a TV listings magazine or a simple advertising vehicle. Common elements include:

Advertising	Do-it yourself features	Opinion columns
Advice columns	Fiction	Quizzes
Book adaptations	Horoscopes	Reviews
Campaigns	In our next issue	Strips (comic)
Competitions	Letters page	Supplements
Contents page	Lists	Surveys
Covers	Make-overs	
Diaries	Merchandising	

MAGAZINE CONTENT

Compare the following covers and content of the teenage magazines *Bliss* and *J-17*:

1. What are the main elements of the cover headlines?
2. How do they define the age of their audience?
3. Denotate and connotate (see also Chapter 2) the images and printed text on the front cover.
4. What are the differences between the two magazines?

J-17

The magazine *J-17* is a teenage magazine for women, specifically targeted at 13 to 14 year old girls. The straplines on the cover (see Figure 10.3) are that of typical teenage magazine content, with articles on how to get a boyfriend and features such as 'Lads You Don't Date'. The model is dressed in simple clothes and her expression is bright and full of bounce and clean fun just like the image of the magazine.

Much of a typical issue of *J-17* is taken up with film and television celebrity features and, in particular, young men. There is a strapline

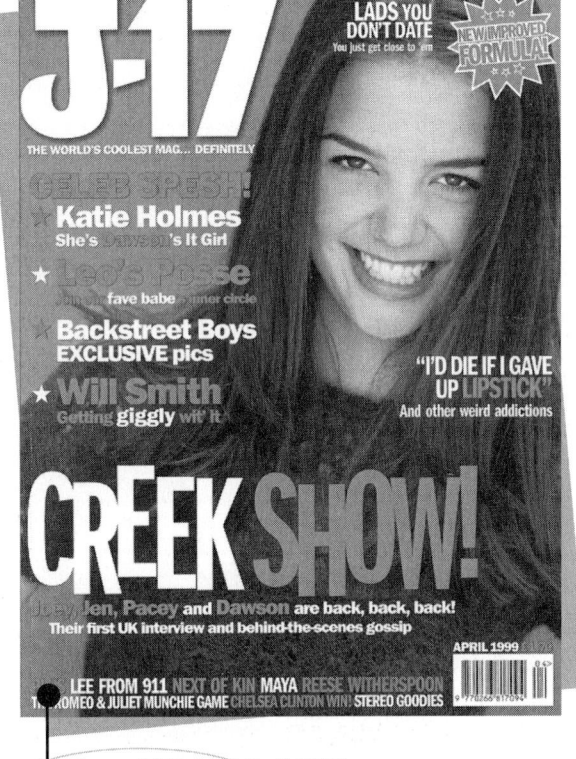

Figure 10.3 *J-17*, April 1999

Source: Emap Élan

on make-up, suggesting that that will be an advice feature. There is also the promise of a competition to win a stereo. Below the masthead is a line that states that *J-17* is the 'world's coolest mag … definitely'.

J-17 had a face-lift two years ago when it wanted to increase the numbers in the lower end of its age range (11 to 13 years), so it lost the word 'seventeen' and substituted the numeral '17'. The slogan still reads: 'New Improved Formula' on the right-hand corner pug.

Bliss

Bliss (see Figure 10.4) is also promising a new look. The image of the model here is more sultry, and therefore a little older in outlook. She, like the model in *J-17*, is staring straight out at the reader. She is wearing a coat, although the image is less clear than on the *J-17* cover.

The *Bliss* cover straplines suggest that a girl's main aim in life is to attract boys: 'How to pull in under 30 minutes'. The age level for *Bliss* would seem to be a bit older than *J-17*, as the latter was more concerned with looking at pictures of men, whereas in *Bliss* it is assumed that girls are more sexually active and assertive.

The main cover headline suggests there will be good advice on how to sort out your life. There is also an article that challenges the myth that women have to be thin, based on another media story about Kate Winslet's professed anger at being accused of being fat. There is an article on animal rights, which appeals to the ennvironmentally conscious girl who reads this magazine. Fashion, beauty tips and free gifts take up 50 pages, so a substantial amount of the magazine is devoted to the improvement of the body and looks. The masthead has a strapline that states: 'The Smart Girl's Guide to Life'.

Images of young women

It is usual for the image of a woman on a magazine such as *J-17* or *Bliss* to be looking directly out at the reader. If you study women's magazines' front covers, you will find that almost all will have a head and shoulders shot, and the woman will be looking directly out, as though looking straight at the reader. The effect of this positioning of the front cover model is to provide an idealised version of what a woman should look like. Over a period of time, seeing models with the same look and the same presentation suggests a stereotype of the kind of person women should identify with.

Figure 10.4 *Bliss*, April 1999   Source: Emap Élan

Advertising

Unlike newspapers, magazines aim to make a

profit through a mixture of cover price and advertising. 66% of business magazines are given free to people who match the publisher's criteria. In this case, revenue comes mostly from advertising. Approximately 78% of revenue comes from display advertising. Magazines have a ready-made pre-defined target audience, so they provide an effective point of contact for advertisers and their target consumers. The following rates for advertising are printed in the *British Rates and Data*.

J-17: June 1997 standard advertisement rates:

Colour page – £14,270

Black and white page – £8,800

The cost of the advertisement is more when the position in a favourable place like the back cover of the magazine where people will see it if is lying on a dentist's table or a waiting room, for example.

Rates for special positions
Inside front cover – £9500
Outside back cover – £9500

Source: British Rate and Data, 1997

The rates above can be compared with those for a comic such as *2000 AD*, which is for 15 to 33 year olds. The rate for a standard colour page is £2000 and the rate for a black and white page is £1700. The reason for the difference in cost is that *J-17*'s circulation figures were 242,516 compared with 28,330 for *2000 AD*'s. *J-17* is read by an estimated 100,000. This figure is calculated by multiplying the circulation figure by 5.5. This gives the estimated number of people who actually read the magazine, as opposed to those that simply buy it in the first place. A magazine may reach homes where there is more than one person, or public areas where several people read them. These figures are important to advertisers who want to be sure they can target their potential product sales to the right people and achieve high circulation figures.

Editorial

In each edition of a magazine, the editor introduces the contents in an editorial feature near the front. An editorial is usually an opinion or an account of the magazine's current position or views on current issues. The by-line indicates that it is the editor's view. He or she speaks to the reader in an informal, chatty manner, often signing off with a handwritten signature.

Discuss:
1 What images of magazines do the editors want to convey in the editorials of *Bliss* and *J-17*?
2 How is language used to make the reader feel at ease?
3 What views of their readers do the two magazines express?

Mode of address

The mode of address is the manner, tone and attitude adopted by the magazine when speaking to the reader. In teenage magazines today, the mode of address is meant to be friendly, in a sisterly or brotherly way. This differs from talking down to the reader, or talking at the reader as if by a news presenter.

Compare and contrast the types of teenagers referred to in the editorials of two women's magazines, such as *Bliss* or *J-17*.

GCSE MEDIA STUDIES

1. Are the two magazine editorial profiles you have chosen different in any way?
2. How do you think their descriptions of the potential readership will attract advertisers?
3. Suggest two or three advertisements that would fit into each of these magazines.
4. Do you think the real readership is the same as the one presented by their profiles? Explain your reasons.

In groups discuss which magazines you or your family purchase. Are there any magazines which everybody reads? Are there magazines which only one person reads? Construct a survey of ten people in a particular group, for example, girls or boys aged 11 to 14 years or girls or boys aged 14 to 19 years.

1. Find out what magazines they like and why.
2. Is there a common response? Are there any big differences in responses?

Study a range of magazines targeted at teenagers aged 11 to 19 years and young adults aged 15 to 24 years. For example, for women: *More, Sugar, J-17, Smash Hits, Marie Claire, Black Woman* or *Red*. For men: *WWF, Hip-Hop, Select, NME, Face, Loaded, FHM* or *Men's Health*.

Discuss the range and variety of interest in the contents, for the audience of each magazine:

a front cover (images, headings, puffs, straplines, and price)
b the contents page (inc. images)
c the advertisements.

Female magazines: facts

Percentage of female readers of magazines

- Women's weekly titles (e.g. *Woman's Own, Bella, Take a Break*): 48%
- Women's glossy, style, fashion monthly (e.g. *Marie Claire, Cosmopolitan, Vogue, Harpers & Queens*): 23%
- Women's general interest monthly (e.g. *Good Housekeeping, Woman & Home*): 19%
- Celebrity weekly titles (e.g. *Hello!, OK*): 31%

Discuss which of the following statements about the absence of a teenage male lifestyle magazine you agree with or disagree with.

1. Ed, age 13 years
   'Basically there's the *Beano* and pornographic magazines and not much in between. I'd like to see stuff on fashion, a problem page, articles about the army, things like that. *FHM* is good, they have pictures of girls without being hardcore porn and *Tropical Disease of the Month* is wicked.'

2. Jonathan, age 13 years
   'Loads of people would read a general magazine if it wasn't too expensive. They should have interviews with famous people and pictures of girls on the front. Some boys might find it too girly and that might put them off. I wouldn't mind a problem page, so long as it wasn't too disgusting. I only read football magazines – other things like music mags and mags with picture of girls are aimed at people older than me.'

3. William, age 16 years
   'I think there should be general magazines

MAGAZINES

for teenage boys, but I am not sure how many people would read them. My friends read *FHM* and *Loaded*, probably because of the naked women. If there was stuff available on things like drugs and more emotional subjects they might read read it – but they wouldn't admit to it.'

4 Mark, age 15 years

'I read *Dream*, it's music with a bit of fashion. There doesn't really need to be magazine for teenagers because they are catered for by men's magazines and specialist magazines.'

5 Emily, age 13 years

'Boys read football magazines and car mags. I get *J-17*, *Sugar*, *Bliss*, *Big*, *Top of the Pops*. They should do something like that for boys because they don't get stuff like gossip and things in the soaps and music and advice. But they're probably happier with football.'

Production activity

Invent a new magazine for boys which targets 11 to 19 year olds. It is to be called *17 Plus*, to attract all males in that age range. Create the following:

1 A mock-up for a front cover, including price, masthead, headline, straplines and layout. There is no need to write any of the articles.

2 Contents page.

3 A list of ten assorted advertisements.

4 Outline what your leading feature and image will be, for the front page.

5 Write your editorial letter introducing the magazine.

MAGAZINE OWNERSHIP

Publishing companies are now often large corporations who own several businesses; some media related and others in completely different business areas, such as the leisure industries.

Most leading magazine titles are owned by a small number of companies. In the consumer sector, IPC Magazines is currently the largest publisher. Reed Business Publishing is the leading business publisher. Both companies are owned by Reed Elsevier Ltd. Other major magazine publishing companies include BBC Magazines, Conde Nast, D.C. Thompson, Emap, G & J (UK), H. Bauer, The National Magazine Company and Reader's Digest. HarperCollins is owned by Newscorp, which is the same company that owns the film company, Twentieth Century Fox and *The Times* and *The Sun* newspapers.

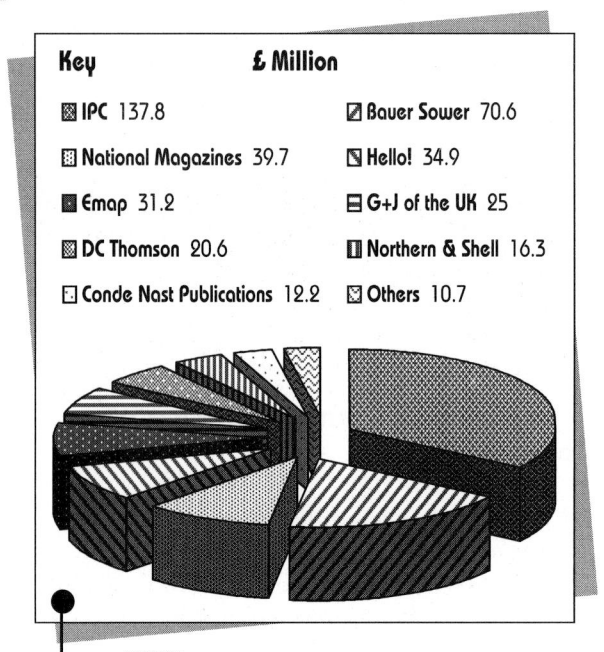

Key   **£ Million**

- IPC 137.8
- Bauer Sower 70.6
- National Magazines 39.7
- Hello! 34.9
- Emap 31.2
- G+J of the UK 25
- DC Thomson 20.6
- Northern & Shell 16.3
- Conde Nast Publications 12.2
- Others 10.7

Figure 10.5 Total retail market share for UK women's magazines (based on cover price revenue)

Source: BMRB/Mintel, 1997

> Research one of the companies listed in Figure 10.5 and find out what they own. What titles do they publish, how much do they cost and what are their best sellers? Most companies have Internet sites to look at, and *The Media Guide: A Guardian Book* is an alternative source of information.

Case Study: Emap

Emap is a large corporation with interests in a wide range of services:

- magazines
- radio stations
- Boxzone: an Internet music website.

Merger

In a recent merger with Petersen in America the development from a niche market magazine company to a mass market company is described in this account of the beginnings of Petersen.

> 'The roots of the Petersen empire can be found in the Auto Performance group with its big hitter *Hot Rod*. The magazine was the original brainchild of Bob Petersen in 1948 and now half a century later it has millions of readers. This year's special anniversary has spawned a host of special one-shots but its the brand extensions that make the eyebrows raise.
> "We sponsor caravans (rallies to you and me), we sponsor races, we have a Hot Rod TV show, we have Hot Rod computer games, we even have Hot Rod Hot Tabasco Sauce."
> Source: Chip Block, on Emap website

Take a look at the Emap website for information on markets and titles.

Emap Radio

Emap Radio has built a substantial presence in local commercial radio in major cities on both sides of the Pennines and in London. The latest addition to their radio portfolio in 1999 is Magic 105.4 FM (formerly Melody FM), in London. This has further enhanced Emap's strategy of forming a stronghold on big city audiences in the UK.

Emap Radio's 18 radio stations have been grouped into 3 radio brands – the Magic Network, Big City Network and Kiss. Each of these brands is targeted at a specific lifestyle within the broader age band of 15 to 44 year olds. The stations are represented by Emap On Air in London and Manchester, as well as local sales teams at each station.

Their portfolio of radio stations, concentrated in the North East, North West, Yorkshire and London, makes them the second biggest independent local radio group in the UK. In 1999, Emap Radio reportedly has a 20.5% share of independent local radio listening hours.

Internet music website

The Broadcasting Bill created the opportunity for Emap to enter other broadcasting areas.

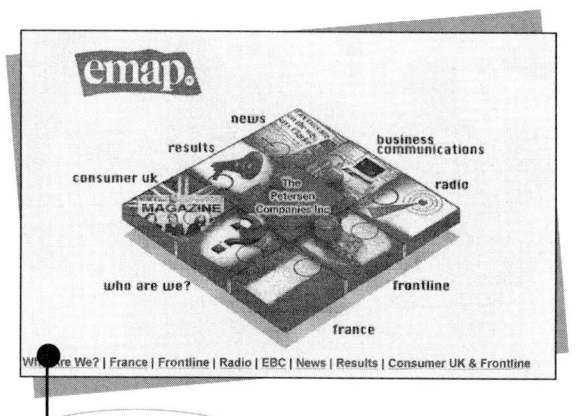

Figure 10.6 Emap on the World Wide Web
Source: Emap 1999

MAGAZINES

This resulted in the acquisition of The Box in 1996 – a unique interactive music television channel controlled entirely by the viewers.

Producing covers: student work

Study the examples of covers created by Media Studies students in Figures 10.7, 10.8 and 10.9.

Figure 10.7

This student was asked to create a new artist and to produce artwork for two different music magazines. She chose to invent a hip-hop artist and placed the image in a more mainstream magazine, like *The Face*.

To produce the image, she took photographs against appropriate backgrounds, having firstly planned out ideas in drawings. Once developed, she enlarged the photographs using a software programme called Photoshop (could use a photocopier for this). Then she cut out (could be scanned) the masthead of the two magazines. Next, she created straplines and cover lines and placed them over the background images.

Figures 10.8 and 10.9

The same process was carried out by another student for the fictional solo artist, Jade. She is

Figure 10.7

Source: © Rachel Stone

Figures 10.8

Source: © Sara Morland

seen to be more at home in the version of a dance, music and club magazine, *Mix mag*, whereas she has been made to appear more glamorous for a version of the more mainstream music magazine, *Vox*.

Figures 10.9

SPECIMEN UNSEEN PRINT QUESTION (OCR)

These Tasks are not actual examination questions. The questions are the sole work of the author and are devised to match the style, mark allocation and format of the relevant question papers from AQA and OCR. They are designed for examination practice. The Tasks are designed to follow the examination paper timings and mark allocations. It is essential that candidates check the specified topics set for the year of their examination, by the examination board. For previous examination papers contact the examination board direct.

Read the following print material and the information before answering the questions. You should spend about 1½ hours on this question and you will have 30 minutes reading and note taking time. Read the print extracts and study all text, headlines, photographs and graphics carefully. Make sure you allow time to study both extracts fully and make notes. You can make notes on your answer paper, however, you should put a diagonal line through your notes after completing the questions.

MAGAZINES

OK!, 12 March, 1999.
Source: © Northern & Shell plc

Profile: *OK!*
Date: March 12th 1999.
Content: 'stars, their parties and homes'.
Circulation: 400,701.
Cost: £1.45 weekly.
***OK!* Contents:**
News and pictures
Hollywood gossip
The exclusive interview: Judy Finnigan and Jerry Springer
Zöe Ball and Norman Cook
Coronation Street's Curly
London Fashion Week
Free Harrod's bag for every reader!
The in-depth interview: Lennox Lewis
Gail Porter
The Mamas and Papas' Michelle Phillips at home
Food: Tessa Peake-Jones
Health: Karren Brady
Esther McVey
Exclusive interview: *Beloved* stars Oprah Winfrey and Thandie Newton
TV listings & coffee break
Horoscopes & celebrity diary
Exclusive wedding day bliss: Jason Lake
Vinnie Jones
World in action

Answer all questions

a What type of magazine is *OK!*?

(4 marks)

Give evidence for your answer for (a)

(6 marks)

b How is the layout and design of the magazine typical of magazines in general? Consider:
   i) typeface
   ii) images
   iii) language
   iv) masthead

(12 marks)

c How is Jerry Springer represented in the magazine?

(10 marks)

d Who do you think is the target audience of *OK!*?

(4 marks)

e Give reasons using evidence from the cover and content list for your answer.

(14 marks)

Extension Tasks

1a Research the following magazines and assess who their target audience is (for example, ABCs, age, gender) and what their readership profile is (for example, lifestyle):

- *FourfourTwo*
- *F1 Racing*
- *Ebony*
- *Sibyl*
- *Amnesty International*

b Analyse the magazine's areas: editorial page, front cover, contents and advertisements: attitude, lifestyle and messages.

2 Design a TV and radio campaign for launching a new teenage male magazine. The advertisement should be no more than 15 frames of a storyboard. The radio advertisement should be about one minute. Provide a short explanation of how the campaign will reach its audience and persuade them to buy the magazine.

3 Create a fanzine web page for the Internet, or a mock-up for one. Research existing web pages for ideas about design and layout. Design features that allow the person browsing to interact. Define the area of interest and explain what type of audience is targeted. What images would you use to attract the audience?

Examination Skills

Knowledge and Understanding

Students will need to have studied the typical features of design and layout of a magazine, ownership and the targeting and construction of audiences. A strong knowledge of typical content and an awareness of alternative approaches to production and layout will also be useful.

Textual Analysis

Students will need to demonstrate skills in interpreting images and text. They will need to be able to denote and connotate the front page as a whole, and in its different parts: images, headlines, cover lines, masthead, etc. Attention should be paid to the use of colours, typeface and language on the front cover of a magazine. The institutional style, messages and values and audiences should be brought out by analysis of visual and written content and mode of address. For example, an analysis of *What's on TV?* (front cover) could be:

> What's on TV? Uses the BBC publicity department's photographs of well-known soap stars to promote the introduction of the hospital drama, Holby City. The characters look straight at the camera as though they want to appear friendly to the readers. The female's smiling look suggests enthusiasm and dedication to her job. The man is smiling a little but his look is one of determination and self will. One associates the clothes they both wear with hospitals.

Practical Work

In the AQA examination, practical skills using knowledge of layout and typical content on cover and in content lists will be required. Questions on set topics such as sport or TV drama may, for example, require the student to create mock-ups of a TV listings page. Mock-ups (hand drawn, rough layouts) will be asked for, including: straplines, headlines and a

MAGAZINES

rough idea of image size and typeface size, font style and colour. The use of promotional texts such as radio advertisements, full page advertisements in other magazines or television advertisements may be part of the creative element of an AQA style question. Institution and audience should be defined by the visual, typographic and colour styles. Contents lists, straplines, mastheads and the tone and manner of address should convey the type of institution and its intended audience.

11 Advertising: standards and controls

WHO'S IN CONTROL?

In this chapter you will study where advertisements are placed, their different purposes, and the creative approaches that producers adopt. The case studies provide analysis of audience responses by the industry regulators: the Advertising Standards Authority, Independent Television Commission and the Radio Authority. The main assignment is to produce a mock-up and a pitch for an advertisement brief, in the role of a creative advertisement agency.

KW

Representation ▪ bias ▪ sexist ▪ racist ▪ ageist ▪ controls ▪ positioning.

TW

Creative dept. ▪ media planners ▪ copy ▪ advertorial ▪ masthead ▪ tag line ▪ camera ready ▪ typeface ▪ demographic ▪ psychographic

WHAT ARE ADVERTISEMENTS?

One definition of advertisements by the Advertising Association is:

> Advertisements are messages, paid for by those who send them, intended to inform or influence people who send them.

There are three points to consider in this definition. Firstly, all advertisements contain a message which may be expressed in words as a slogan – for example, 'Kill Your Speed'.

Secondly, advertisements are paid for by advertisers. The cost of an advertisement in glossy magazines, for example, means that advertising is a major source of income (approximately 40%) for magazines. Advertising also provides money for the television channels which carry the advertisements. Advertising is therefore a commercial business, as opposed to 'free' publicity created by press releases or photo opportunities.

Thirdly, advertisements have a purpose to persuade or raise awareness of the existence of their product in the people whom they target. The advertising for the new *Star Wars* film, released in 1999, was claimed to have achieved a massive 80% public awareness, months before its actual release.

WHO ADVERTISES?

In the UK a range of advertisers exist, many of them are small businesses who try to promote themselves. Bigger companies will buy in an advertising agency to create the messages in the relevant media. Famous advertising agencies such as Saatchi and Saatchi, and Bartle, Bogle and Hegarty became successful over a period of years and command respect from companies looking for national coverage and high impact campaigns.

The Government also spends considerable amounts of money on advertising. By 1989, the Government had become the nation's largest advertiser, as a consequence of its record spend on advertising in excess of £98 million (M. Scannell, 'The impact of marketing and public relations in modern British politics', unpublished Ph.D. thesis, 1991). In September 1989, the advertising campaign to promote the privatisation of electricity cost £76 million. The highest commercial advertiser spent no more than £12 million total in that year.

Government advertisements fall into two types: information (for example, tax returns or child benefit) and persuasive (for example, to warn the public not to drink alcohol and drive).

Other groups of people who advertise include some political parties and also pressure groups, such as Amnesty International, Oxfam or the National Society for the Prevention of Cruelty to Children. Individuals also advertise their second-hand goods in newspaper or magazine 'classifieds', usually for free.

Advertising media

More than half of the money spent on advertising in the UK is spent on the press – newspapers, magazines and trade directories. The second most important advertising medium is television, accounting for 27% of advertising money. TV advertising is more expensive than in newspapers, therefore only the bigger companies can advertise on TV regularly.

Direct mail

Direct mail is advertising material sent straight through the letter box into people's homes. It is usually described as 'junk mail', and 11% is spent on this type of advertising in the UK.

Others

Outdoor advertising such as billboards, bus shelters and buses account for 3% of the costs. Radio advertising is cheap and 2% of advertising costs are spent on this medium. Cinema advertising reaches a tiny 0.5%, though this is a relatively young audience.

GCSE MEDIA STUDIES

1 Watch the advertisement breaks before and after the regional evening news. **Make a list** of all the advertisements in these breaks. How many are about national products? How many are products or services from local companies? How many trailers or 'teasers' are there for programmes on that channel later? Are there public information programmes produced by the Government?

2 Now watch the advertisements in a break during a soap opera (6.30 to 8.30 pm) **Compile a list** of advertisements. **Compare** the breakdown of these types of advertisements with those in your first list. Do the two lists differ in content and if so, how do they differ or not? Do they suggest a different type of person is watching for each slot in the schedule? If so, who are these people?

Study the list of advertising media below:

Billboard	Electronic mail	Point of sale
Brochure	Facsimile	Poster
Catalogue	Insert	Press general
Cinema	Leaflet	Regional press
Circular	Magazine	Transport
Direct mail	National press	
Directory	Packaging	

Write down three advantages and disadvantages of the following: television, newspaper, radio, billboard, direct mail.

ADVERTISEMENT PRODUCTION

Creative department

An advertising agency's creative department actually produces the advertisements. The department is run by the agency's creative director. There is often a series of creative teams, each consisting of a copywriter and an art director. These two work together on words and pictures. Some agencies have their own art studios, though most now have artwork created by outside studios. Illustrations, photographs and typesetting have to be produced and checked ready for printing by the team. If the advertisement is a television promotion, then actors, actresses and props have to be organised for the television studios.

Copy

Copy is the term used for all the words in print or voice-over, and the printed words in television and cinema advertisements. When the copy is put together with the artwork, the printed material is then described as 'camera ready'. This means the artwork can be photographed for the final film negative before printing many copies in the chosen format.

Editorial

An editorial is usually a leading article and has the writer's by-line attached to the top of the piece. An editorial can be any piece of writing in the newspaper or magazine that expresses the paper's viewpoint. Editorial pieces are usually confined to the main feature articles and the headlines. There is also often an editor's comment column inside the paper.

Advertorial

An advertorial is a mix of an advertisement and an editorial. The use of advertorials is very common in local newspapers. In exchange for purchasing advertising space for a product, the paper will provide free space to the advertiser, in an article about the product itself. The article will never be critical about the product; if anything it will be positive. The newspaper gains advertising revenue and the producer of the goods gains free advertisement space.

Estate agents, for example, who wish to sell an expensive house, will often be regular buyers of newspaper space to advertise their properties. The articles next to these advertisements appear to be neutral at first, when talking about a 'charming new housing estate'. However, when you read to the end of a piece, it is clear from the telephone number and the contact name of the estate agents that the piece has been used to promote the properties on behalf of the estate agent.

Media planners

Media planners help advertisers place their advertisements in the best slots in the breaks between television programmes. They preview as much of the television programmes as possible, by looking at the television listings and watching what is in the programmes they are going to advertise alongside. The media planners then purchase blocks of time from the TV broadcasters. Advertisements shown only regionally are much cheaper than a guaranteed slot in the national independent network.

Summary of production process:

▶ Strategy development.
▶ Copywriting.
▶ Design and art direction – creating image and layout.
▶ Production of print adverts, including illustration and photography.
▶ Production of TV and radio spots.
▶ Media buying.
▶ General coordination, planning and budgeting.
▶ Public relations.

ADVERTISING CONTROLS

The Advertising Standards Authority (ASA)

The Advertising Standards Authority was established in 1962 to provide independent scrutiny of the system of self-regulation of advertisements. Self-regulation meant that the industry itself checks its own standards. The aim is to ensure that the system operates in the

ADVERTISING CODE

Principles

2.1 All advertisements should be legal, decent, honest and truthful.

2.2 All advertisements should be prepared with a sense of responsibility to consumers and to society.

2.3 All advertisements should respect the principles of fair competition generally accepted in business.

2.4 No advertisement should bring advertising into disrepute.

2.5 Advertisements must conform with the Codes. Primary responsibility for observing the Codes falls on advertisers. Others involved in preparing and publishing advertisements such as agencies, publishers and other service suppliers also accept an obligation to abide by the Codes.

2.6 Any unreasonable delay in responding to the ASA's enquiries may be considered a breach of the Codes.

2.7 The ASA will on request treat in confidence any private or secret material supplied unless the Courts or officials acting within their statutory powers compel its disclosure.

2.8 The Codes are applied in the spirit as well as in the letter.

Figure 11.1 ASA Code guidelines
Source: © *The British Codes of Advertising and Sales Promotion*, CAP

ALCOHOLIC DRINKS

46.1 For the purposes of the Codes, alcoholic drinks are those that exceed 1.2% alcohol by volume.

46.2 The drinks industry and the advertising business accept a responsibility for ensuring that advertisements contain nothing that is likely to lead people to adopt styles of drinking that are unwise. The consumption of alcohol may be portrayed as sociable and thirst-quenching. Advertisements may be humorous, but must still conform with the intention of the rules.

46.3 Advertisements should be socially responsible and should not encourage excessive drinking. Advertisements should not suggest that regular solitary drinking is advisable. Care should be taken not to exploit the young, the immature or those who are mentally or socially vulnerable.

46.4 Advertisements should not be directed at people under eighteen through the selection of media, style of presentation, content or context in which they appear. No medium should be used to advertise alcoholic drinks if more than 25% of its audience is under eighteen years of age.

46.5 People shown drinking should not be, nor should they look, under twenty five. Younger models may be shown in advertisements, for example in the context of family celebrations, but it should be obvious that they are not drinking.

46.6 Advertisements should not feature real or fictitious characters who are likely to appeal particularly to people under eighteen in a way that would encourage them to drink.

46.7 Advertisements should not suggest that any alcoholic drink can enhance mental, physical or sexual capabilities, popularity, attractiveness, masculinity, femininity or sporting achievements.

46.8 Advertisements may give factual information about the alcoholic strength of a drink or its relatively high alcohol content but this should not be the dominant theme of any advertisement. Alcoholic drinks should not be presented as preferable because of their high alcohol content or intoxicating effect.

46.9 Advertisements should not portray drinking alcohol as the main reason for the success of any personal relationship or social event. A brand preference may be promoted as a mark of the drinker's good taste and discernment.

46.10 Drinking alcohol should not be portrayed as a challenge, nor should it be suggested that people who drink are brave, tough or daring for doing so.

46.11 Particular care should be taken to ensure that advertisements for sales promotions requiring multiple purchases do not actively encourage excessive consumption.

46.12 Advertisements should not depict activities or locations where drinking alcohol would be unsafe or unwise. In particular, advertisements should not associate the consumption of alcohol with operating machinery, driving, any activity relating to water or heights, or any other occupation that requires concentration in order to be done safely.

46.13 Low alcohol drinks are those that contain 1.2% alcohol by volume or less. Advertisers should ensure that low alcohol drinks are not promoted in a way that encourages their inappropriate consumption and should not depict activities that require complete sobriety.

---

public interest. The ASA is independent of the Government and the advertising business.

How much control does the ASA have?

A number of sanctions exist to counteract advertisements and promotions that conflict with the Advertising Codes:

1 The media may deny access to space.
2 Adverse publicity may result from rulings published in ASA's monthly report.
3 Trading sanctions may be imposed or recognition revoked by the advertisers, promoters or by the agency's professional association.
4 Financial incentives provided by trade, professional or media organisations may be withdrawn.

The ASA deals with the following:

▶ Advertisements in newspapers, magazines, brochures, leaflets, circulars, mailings, catalogues and other printed publications,

facsimile transmissions, posters and aerial announcements.
- Cine film and video commercials.
- Advertisements in non-broadcast electronic media, such as computer games.
- Viewdata services.
- Mailing lists, with the exception of business to business.
- Sales promotions.
- Advertisements and promotions covered by the Cigarette Code.

The Committee of Advertising Practice (CAP) is the self-regulatory body that devises and enforces the Codes. CAP's members include organisations that represent the advertising, sales, promotion and media businesses.

Broadcast commercials are the responsibility of the Independent Television Commission and the Radio Authority.

Independent Television Commission (ITC)

The ITC monitors television advertisements and decides which advertisements should be withdrawn, according to the ITC Code of Advertising Standards and Practice. In 1997, the ITC received 5,337 complaints about 1,529 television advertisements, of which 73 were upheld. This still constitutes a very small proportion of the total population of the UK.

An example of a complaint received about an advertisement was for Lucozade Low-Calorie drink. It featured two stock comic characters from the adult comic *Viz*. The ITC received 309 complaints about the negative stereotyping of overweight women and bad language.

> 1 Select two magazines, one aimed at a female reader and one aimed at a male reader.
> 2 How many advertisements include images of women? What ideas about women do they represent? Repeat the same for the advert aimed at men.
> 3 Do you think the representations are realistic, idealised or restrictive?

Complaints

In 1997, the ASA received a total of 10,678 complaints, of which 454 related to sexism in advertisements. 59 complaints were upheld, relating to seven advertisements. This compares with 12,055 complaints received in 1996, of which 846 related to sexism in advertisements. 211 complaints were upheld, relating to 17 advertisements.

Offence

Research into advertising in the UK carried out by the ASA draws the following conclusions. The British public found the main causes of offence to be:

- Setting a bad example to children.
- Being disturbed or unsuitable for children.
- Featuring bad language.
- Being shown in the wrong place, so that children can see it.
- Being in bad taste.
- Being sexually explicit.
- Containing violence.
- The portrayal of women.

Source: Adapted from *ASA Annual Report 1998*

Taboo subjects

Taboo (or completely 'no-go') areas for advertisers include death, religion and bad language.

Case examples: complaints made to the ASA

Studying test cases on the regulation of the advertising industry can reveal how commercial factors work to combine messages and values for the purposes of selling products.

---

1 Read the examples of print-based advertisements which follow. Discuss the contents of the advertisements as they are described in the wording of ASA's adjudications and verdicts.
2 Study the verdicts. What is your opinion of the verdicts? Give reasons for your answer.

Complaint: Objection to an advertisement, in the Dandy, for Cheestrings, that was in the form of a comic strip. The page was headed 'ADVERTISEMENT' and stated "Cheestrings. Present Strings at a Birthday Party' in the top left-hand corner. The complainant objected that, although the page was headed 'ADVERTISEMENT', to a child it was not clearly differentiated from the editorial content of the comic.

Adjudication: Complaint not upheld. The advertisers said the advertisement was designed to convey the message that Cheestrings could be used in an alternative, fun way and was one in a series that had run in the Dandy and Beano comics. They said they designed and researched their advertisements with both parents and children, which had shown that children of six to 12 years old could easily distinguish the advertisements from the editorial. They pointed out that the regular editorial features and characters would be familiar to readers and believed that the 'Strings' character would not be confused with Dandy characters. The Authority considered the advertisements would be recognised by children as advertisements and were unlikely to be confused with the editorial content of the comic. It did not object to the approach.

Source: ASA

Complaint: Objection to an advertisement in the Guardian for Q magazine. The advertisement was headlined 'Jesus! It's Madonna WORLD EXCLUSIVE INTERVIEW!'. The complainant objected that the reference to Jesus was offensive.

Adjudication: Complaint not upheld. The advertisers apologised for the offence they had caused and said they had withdrawn the advertisement. The publishers did not comment on the complaint. The Authority considered that, although the advertisement's play on the names Jesus and Madonna was unlikely to cause serious or widespread offence to readers of the Guardian, it asked the advertisers to take care when using this approach in the future.

Source: ASA

Case: examples using the ITC's Code of Advertising

---

1 Read the following complaints about advertisements.
2 Discuss and write down what you thought were the reasons for the complaint. What were the reasons for each verdict?

Nature of Complaint

Advertising for The Mirror claimed 'Tomorrow, the Mirror is just 10p' and repeated variations of that claim a number of times. The complainant objected that he had been charged more and, when he contacted The Mirror Group, had been told that the offer applied only at selected outlets. He had not seen any qualification on the commercial.

Assessment

The ITC found that the advertising had run only in certain regions and that it had carried superimposed text which read 'Price reduction only in restricted parts of Yorkshire, Tyne Tees, Granada & Ulster TV regions. Usual price 32p. No purchase necessary. Details from Mirror Group offices.' The agency explained that the 10 pence price was only available from independent newsagents in the regions listed or from newsagents belonging to groups whose shops were all within those regions. (In other words, if even one branch of a chain was outside the four regions, none of the branches would have sold the paper for 10 pence.) However, the text was not held on screen for as long as the ITC's rules require, was in small type and for part of the time was against a confusing background of newsprint. The ITC judged that the text was too hard to read.

In any case, the ITC judged that, even if it had been legible, the disclaimer had not given viewers a sufficiently accurate indication of the availability of the offer. Given the absolute nature of the main claims, the ITC concluded that the advertising had been misleading.

The advertising ran for a short time only.

Decision

Complaint upheld.

Source: ITC

Nature of Complaint

Advertising for Sky's Movie Channels featured ordinary people quoting famous lines from various films. One was 'You're only supposed to blow the ****** doors off' (Michael Caine in The Italian Job). Some complainants objected in principle to the use of swearing in television advertising. Others were concerned about scheduling when children were likely to be watching.

Assessment

The ITC recognised that, for some viewers, any swearing in advertising is unacceptable but did not consider that most viewers would find this use of a relatively mild swear word inherently offensive, particularly since it was used in a relevant context. The ITC did, however, accept that parents were entitled to expect that television advertising should not appear to endorse or encourage swearing and, for this reason, instructed the BACC to restrict the commercial to post-9pm.

Decision

30 Complaints upheld on grounds of inappropriate scheduling

18 Complaints not upheld

Source: ITC

GCSE MEDIA STUDIES

Case Study: alcohol

> 1. Study the Advertising Standards Authority's guidelines concerning advertisements about alcohol.
> 2. Read the Advertising Guidelines and the specific guidelines for alcohol printed by The British Code of Advertising Practice analyse on behalf of the ASA on page 171.

Sponsorship

Television sponsorship has increased considerably as rules have relaxed about what can and what cannot be shown. Beamish Stout sponsors *Inspector Morse*, Stella Artois sponsors *Film on Four* and Cadbury's Chocolate sponsor *Coronation Street* on ITV. Masthead programming is now allowed on all ITC licensed services other than Channels 3, 4 and 5. Masthead programming is programming that uses the editorial and production resources of a magazine title.

ANALYSING STILL ADVERTISEMENTS

For any print advertisement, there are three areas that can be analysed:

- Languages and categories
- Audience
- Messages and values

Study the leaflet in Figure 11.2 and answer the following questions relating to it.

Languages and categories

How is the meaning presented in Figure 11.2? What effect does the presentation have? What does it mean and what type of advertisement is it?

Text

Consider brand name and slogan when analysing advertisements. How does the slogan in Figure 11.2 relate to the image and the graphics? It is also important to consider typefaces, point size and the use of upper or lower case letters.

Figure 11.2 A leaflet linked to several advertisers through film promotion tie-ins
Source: [Nestlé]

ADVERTISING: STANDARDS AND CONTROLS

Technical codes

How was the leaflet made? Analyse the image in Figure 11.2 in terms of: lighting, cropping, enlargement, colour and text (typeface and point size).

Audience

Who is the leaflet in Figure 11.2 directed at and how has this been achieved? Who produced it and for what reason?

Messages and values

What is the overall message of the advertisement in Figure 11.2?

Advertising

The most commonly used typefaces are:

- Futura
- **Franklin Gothic**
- **Bembo**
- Garamond
- Goudy

It would be useful to study some advertisements to see which typefaces are used.

Target audience

In defining a product there needs to be research into who will buy it. Questionnaires will aid this process. Refer back to demographic groups in Chapter Three.

Research questionnaire one

Use the following check list to produce a questionnaire for a chosen target audience.

1 Demographic group:
- Sex
- Age range
- Cultural or ethnic group
- Marital status
- Household size
- Occupation type
- Home owner or renting
- Income range
- Other

2 Psychographic
The most important values are:

- Home, family, career, spirituality, adventure, honest, spiritual, status.
- Hobbies, interests.
- Greatest concerns, for example, crime, the environment.
- Religion.
- Political affiliation.
- Spending habits.
- Amount of spare time.
- Voluntary work.

Research questionnaire two: media usage

Use this checklist for a telephone interview for a face-to-face questionnaire.
Name and age
1a TV (yes/no)
   At these times/days......................
   b List all TV channels and programmes you think your target audience watches.
2a Radio (yes/no)
   At these times/days......................
   b List all radio stations or types of radio stations.
3a Newspapers (yes/no)
   b List newspapers you think your target group reads (daily, weekly, local, regional or national).
4a Magazines (yes/no)
   b List all magazines you think your target group reads (regional and national).
5a Does your target use the Internet (yes/no)
   At these times/days......................

6a Music – what type of music does your target group listen to?

b In which medium do they listen to music (Radio, CD, Audio-cassette, TV programme)?

7 Of the above media which media do you think are best for reaching your target group? List all that apply, but star those which are outstanding.

Positioning

In advertising psychology, every person can be 'positioned' in terms of their attitude. For example, a 'couch potato' or a 'get up and go' person. Review also Chapter Three for ideas on audiences. You need to define your typical consumer's attitude before deciding where and how to construct the images. Draw up a list of statements or points based on the information in Questionnaire Two, and decide which media will suit them best. If they do not watch TV, then there could be a great deal of money saved.

Advertising slogans

Here are some popular slogans:

▶ L'Oreal – Because I'm worth it.
▶ Kit Kat – Have a break, have a Kit Kat.
▶ Honda – First the man, then machine.
▶ Galaxy – Why have cotton when you can have silk?
▶ Levis – Original.

> Watch and make notes on the key slogans of some television advertisements, and collect some magazine slogans which you find effective.

ANALYSING TELEVISION AND FILM ADVERTISEMENTS

1 Study the example of a Fairy advertisement (page 182). This is how a creative agency would plan it. Notice how the words in the text explain the lighting and camera movement.

2 Watch an advertisement and draw the main shots (frames). Use simple line drawings – you do not have to be an artist. Write down the script and the elements of the *mise-en-scène*: lighting camera shot size, angle and movement.

a Analyse the advertisement: denotation and connotation of image and sound. **Denotation**: What is in the frame? **Connotation**: What do the sounds, shots and signifiers suggest to you? How do these ideas relate to wider ideas in society?

| ADVERTISING: STANDARDS AND CONTROLS |

Visual Instructions	**Soundtrack**
 It is now morning and the woman is in medium shot wearing a dressing gown. She cringes and takes the dish and dunks it. She passes the pan onto the next frame.	Music slow
 When she pulls her hand back she discovers, to her surprise, a bottle of Fairy.	Music speeds up Voice: *But now it is easy due to best ever Fairy!*
 Then we see a close up view of the Fairy bottle saying 'New – Best Ever'.	Music still speeding up
 The woman turns to the camera with a pleasantly surprised expression on her face. She looks at the camera directly – a close up of just her head.	Music now quick and happy

Figure 11.3 Fairy Liquid Storyboard student work: denotation of advertisement

Source: © Judah Shostak-Reilly

SPECIMEN EXAMINATION QUESTION (AQA)

These Tasks are not actual examination questions. The questions are the sole work of the author and are devised to match the style, mark allocation and format of the relevant question papers from AQA and OCR. They are designed for examination practice. The Tasks are designed to follow the examination paper timings and mark allocations. It is essential that candidates check the specified topics set for the year of their examination, by the examination board. For previous examination papers contact the examination board direct.

Paper Two controlled text (4hrs)

Advertising Brief
From: The Government's Central Office of Information
To: Agency

Produce a competitive bid for a £2 million campaign to prevent drinking and driving in the over 45 year old age bracket. Research has shown that younger generations have, on the whole, responded well to not drinking and driving. However, there is a hardcore group of men who do not heed any warnings, maintaining the 'there's nothing wrong with one for the road' attitude. The TV advertisement will only run once over two weeks, and is best placed in the run up to Christmas. The poster or posters can accompany the timing of the television drink and drive advertisement warning.

Previous campaigns have tended to show the effects of the accidents and portrayed the victims as they are today. The images have been hard-hitting. Do the public need a new approach?

Task 1

a Describe what you think are the key features of Government advertisements?
b Government advertisements are often produced by advertising agencies. Describe the process of creating an advertising campaign for a client.
c What are the advantages and disadvantages of television, radio or posters in launching an effective media campaign?

(30 marks)

Task 2

Devise a trailer for TV and the cinema.
Either
a Draw, design or describe a cinema trailer in storyboard format (not more than 10 frames). Make sure you fill in all the storyboard frames and annotate them indicating a soundtrack, lighting, camera movement, voice-over and props.

(25 marks)
or
b Design a poster campaign. Make sure you design and annotate the image, layout and typeface. Consider the target audience — if they are over 45 years old, how will you interest them without making it easy for them to reject the message?

(25 marks)

Task 3

Use plain sheets for parts **b** and **c**. You will need to use the radio or to help promote your campaign.
Either
a Create a radio advertisement to go out on

ADVERTISING: STANDARDS AND CONTROLS

local radio, lasting 30 seconds and drawing people's attention to the campaign (30 seconds equals 90 words maximum). Remember to use other sound effects as well as voices.

or

b Suggest other ways in which you might promote your campaign.

(30 marks)

Task 4

Write a letter to the Central Office of Information explaining:

- ▶ The key features of your campaign and the ideas and effects intended in the sound and images and text used in the poster.
- ▶ The characters or figures, and the types of males they represent.
- ▶ The forms and conventions you have used.
- ▶ The precise method of targeting the audience – messages in typed text and in visual codes.

(15 marks)

Extension Tasks

1 Research the responses to any advertisements you think are controversial, such as Benetton, Tango or Hooch. Produce a demographic and a psychographic questionnaire to use before asking questions. Analyse (300 words) your findings and explain what it is that people object to or why they do not mind.

2 Produce an advertisement for a film trailer on the radio (30 seconds) for a new audience.

3 Research the ITC (http://www/itc) and ASA websites (http://www.asa.org.uk) and study the previous year's findings for a particular product (perfumes) or a criteria (language). Report your findings on paper or in another medium, such as news print or radio.

4 Make a new advertisement by redesigning an existing print advertisement product, to target a new audience.

5 Select any magazine and carry out an analysis of how many advertisements contain males or females as the main figures. How are they represented?

Examination Skills

Knowledge and Understanding

Examiners are looking for a good degree of knowledge about regulation and control by the main governing bodies: ASA, ITC and the RA. There needs to be a good understanding of the process, as well as the huge financial implications of advertising in any medium which carries it. Strong understanding and application of the audience concepts of demographic and psychographic will produce the best answers.

Textual Analysis

There should be sound denotation and connotation of an advertisement. The best approach is to describe and then analyse the ideas associated with the image, its construction and the connection with the words. The time and the place where these advertisements can be seen or viewed can greatly affect their impact.

> Task 1 asks you to identify typical features of government campaigns. The truth is, that tactics have changed over the years. With Aids health promotions,

the initial method was to stereotype girls and boys into fixed roles and behaviours. The Aids' television and poster advertisements of the mid-80s depicted boys who 'coped' with their heroin addiction by saying 'I can handle it', in a kind of macho stance. Girls were shown as being body conscious, so all reference to drugs was about how bad it makes you look ultimately.

With drink advertisements, there have been at least three types of tactics in the annual campaign against drinking and driving. The first was to show that the driver might be killed in a horrific car crash. The second was to show the effects of driving on the victim's family. The third was to show the enduring effects on the victim of the car crash, after being severely injured by a drink driver.

Practical Work

The composition of words into slogans and catch phrases is one half of the task of producing a poster. The creation of an image is targeted at the audience, but also builds the imaginary audience into the image itself. The layout, design and the typeface all require thought and considered selection. The image itself needs to cover gesture, poses, expression, clothes and props. An awareness of who owns the product and how the producer includes a logo is also desirable.

12 Sport, game shows and chat shows

GAME, SEX AND MATCH

This chapter covers sport, media, money and technology. The massive amount of money that can be made from sport has changed the way sport is run and the way it has been experienced over ten years. Now, with the introduction of new technology, there are new ways of viewing and paying to be sports spectators. This chapter is about how spectator sports are presented, including sporting events, game shows, confessional shows and quiz shows.

KW

Spectator ▪ spectacle ▪ pay-per-view ▪ subscription ▪ digital ▪ personalities ▪ celebrities ▪ 'live' ▪ pre-recorded ▪ audiences ▪ virtual reality games

TW

Highlights ▪ photography ▪ replay ▪ commentary

WHY WATCH SPORT AND GAMES?

Action and violence

The 1975 sci-fi film *Rollerball* is set in the future, where sport is completely dominated by media. Violence is banned from society, except in sport. The rollerball game is a violent cross between ice-skating and American football. All the action and violence of the rollerball game is captured on camera and the audience watches as avidly as if it were the National Lottery. In the film, the television audiences enjoy the cruelty of the physical combat and some of the casualties in the game die. This is reminiscent of sports in Roman times, when if gladiator fights did not end in several deaths, the spectators were disappointed.

Drama

Some of the reasons why people watch television sport are no different than when watching a television drama. Most sporting games involve a contest between two sides: teams or individual competitors. There is conflict, tension and drama, and by the end of the match one side wins or there is a draw. Some individuals are singled out as heroes, and there are often villains to criticise.

In the 1998 football World Cup, the England football player David Beckham became the English side's public villain for being sent off and reducing the team to ten men, and therefore potentially allowing England to lose. Michael Owen was seen as the hero because he was only eighteen and he scored a spectacular goal. Sporting commentators use dramatic language, which makes the event sound like a story or a film narrative, using phrases such as a 'fascinating spectacle', 'a fight to the finish' or a 'gripping finale'.

Figure 12.1 David Beckham: the media must have their 'villains'
Source: Press Association *Daily Mail*, 26 February 1999

The spectator who uses radio or television enjoys sport because of the skills of the team or the individual, the drama and changing fortunes, the attack and the counter-attack.

SPORTS MEDIA

Which media can audiences view or obtain information from about sport?

Some examples are:

- Television
- Newspapers
- Radio
- Teletext
- Fanzines
- Books – autobiographies, novels
- Advertsing
- Sponsorship
- Films
- On line Internet
- In person

SPORT, GAME SHOWS AND CHAT SHOWS

1. Study a TV programme listings page from a newspaper or magazine. How many different types of sports can you identify?
2. Compare the BBC's sports output with that of Sky Sports 1, 2 and 3.
3. How many hours for the different types of programme format can you identify over a period of one week?

	BBC (hrs/week)	Sky Sports (hrs/week)
Live events		
Pre-recorded events		
Chat shows		
Documentaries (pre-recorded)		
Quiz shows (pre-recorded)		
Others		

4. How much of BBC1's sports output is live?
5. Is there a difference between Sky's and BBC1's types of sports television programmes?

BSKYB

As a commercial provider, Bsky B sells advertising space in order to fund sports programmes and staffing. The influence of BSky B on sport has been dramatic.

In 1989, BSKYB was created as the first UK satellite station. It began with five channels and increased to over 40 by 1996. In 1994, BSKYB paid over £300 million for exclusive rights to the Premiership football league. This effectively ended the BBC's control of broadcasting all the top live football matches.

BSKYB's investment has totalled £1.5 billion since it started investing in sport in 1989, when it started its satellite Sports Channel. Initially, the subscription fee for Premiership viewing was over £5.99 but by 1999 this rose to £24.99.

In 1999 however, the Football Premiership turned down Rupert Murdoch's bid to renew total exclusive rights to broadcasting top level football.

SPORTS ISSUES

The effect of corporation takeovers on sport could be to bring it increasingly under the control of a few companies who have media ownership. Investments have been made in the following ways:

- High salaries earned by top players, agents and managers.
- Ten new stadiums built between 1989 and 1999.
- International sports stars joining football clubs in other countries (Chelsea's own football team has nearly 90% of foreign nationalities).

Sport	Annual income men (£)	Annual income women (£)
1 Formula One	8.1 million	n/a
2 Football	2.0 million	n/a
3 Tennis	1.9 million	1.5 million
4 Horse racing	1.1 million	1.1 million
5 Athletics	up to 1.0 million	up to 1.0 million
6 Snooker	500,000	13,000
7 Golf	470,000	90,000
8 Cricket	300,000	n/a
9 Rugby	72,000	n/a
10 Rowing	2,000	2,000

Table 12.1 Salaries of those at the top of their profession

Source: AXA

Sporting values

Fair play and gamespersonship are values associated with sport. As in cowboy films the audience expects to see that the baddies are punished and the virtuous are rewarded. The sporting world is now highly professional and in some sectors like football, at the top level sports people are very well paid.

Audiences also watch the way that sports stars behave in private and in public. There are numerous newspaper reports about corrupt footballers, managers, and officials and their sex lives, because they are in the public eye and these items sell newspapers. More specific sports world issues such as performance enhancing drugs, violent fans and who owns teams, are also covered in TV documentaries and radio features.

Celebrities

Professional athletes and commentators at the top of their profession are now seen and heard as frequently as soap stars and politicians, in advertisements, on television, radio, or in magazines and newspapers. Eric Cantona, the footballer and poet, promoted EuroStar travel to France. In real life Cantona attacked a spectator who was calling him racist names by jumping into the crowd. The EuroStar advertisement's image of the poet and peaceful man was quite different from his previous image as a kung fu kicking footballer. Gary Lineker, in contrast, is known as a clean, honest player, who jokingly promotes Walkers crisps by stealing crisps from other famous people. Vinnie Jones appeared in the British film, *Lock Stock and Two Smoking Barrels* (1998), because his already established 'tough guy' image suited the crime theme in the film.

Real life

The ordinary spectator gains enjoyment from watching live TV because it is one of the forms of television in which one cannot predict what happens next. This expectation of surprise and real life drama is shared by other 'live' programme formats, although these can be pre-recorded. These programmes also involve a kind of game: including contestants, presenters as 'referees' and studio audiences as 'spectators' with voices.

GAME SHOWS AND CHAT SHOWS

Chat shows, confessional TV shows such as *Kilroy, Ricki Lake, Vanessa, Trisha* and *Oprah Winfrey*, and quiz shows such as *Who wants to be a Millionaire?*, involve strong elements of tension and surprise because they are or appear to be depend on human success or failure.

SPORT, GAME SHOWS AND CHAT SHOWS

Structure

The programmes are not scripted, or so we are led to believe. After they have been recorded live, edited and shortened to fit the programme length, they still create the sense that no one can tell how the participants or members of the 'crowd' will react at any given time. Similar to sporting events, in confessional TV shows or competitions, such as *Blind Date*, the viewer is presented with a contest between the participants which depends testing the knowledge, skill or calmness of the participants who are placed under pressure. The difference is that for most sporting events the professionals play to earn a living, whereas in confessional or quiz shows, ordinary members of the public perfom for the thrill of being on television or to win prizes.

Budgets

Game shows can afford to give away large prizes because there are no lavish sets or 'stars' to pay for. The budget is mainly spent on the prizes, the staff salaries and the presenter(s). A presenter like Angus Deaton on *Have I got news for you?* can be paid around £18,000 per show.

The crowd as 'performer'

Confessional TV shows also get the studio audience involved in cheering, booing and commentating, so that they become part of the action. This can be likened to televised sport for mass audiences. In confessional television shows such as *The Jerry Springer Show*, the audience is encouraged to respond to what the programme guests say. Sometimes this can lead to fights between members of the audience. This makes the programme appear more unpredictable and even adds to its appeal, although programmes are rarely broadcast if matters get out of hand. In contrast, other programmes with big audiences such as the *National Lottery* have audiences who only clap or cheer when they are told to by the studio managers.

1. **Study** a number of chat shows, confessional shows and programmes which involve participants and an active studio audience.
2. **Examine** where the cameras must be positioned in order to film the presenter, the audience and the participants.
3. To what extent is the audience allowed to speak out and do its own thing? How much time does the programme spend on shots of the audience, and what they do and say?
4. Is what you are seeing the whole event, and if not, how much of the real event might have been edited out? How can you tell?
5. **Study** the camera positions and sound coverage of the audiences and participants in a sporting event like Wimbledon, American or English football. Are there differences of approach in how the crowd is used? How is the crowd used to create atmosphere? Are they just used as background? Do members of the public get asked their views on the game?

Real danger

Whether pre-recorded or live, game shows and sports programmes promise surprises and even danger. Both sporting professionals and members of the public perform on their 'stages' before our eyes. Most television programmes are shortened and edited before they go out on air, however, live radio and television offers the danger, the thrills and the mistakes, the recoveries, the jubilations and disappointments of real life.

> Watch a sport on TV where there is a high chance of failure, such as a motorbike rally, skateboarding, skiing or horse jumping. Study how the commentator talks about failures or disasters. To what extent does the commentator have to make the accidents sound less bad than they actually appear on screen?

Theatre of cruelty

Some sports programmes emphasise danger or pain, such as wrestling or extreme sports. These tend to be broadcast on dedicated channels or shown only occasionally. In wrestling, the loser is often seen to be hit over and over again, in different ways. This is part of the show, in which the audience is seen to enjoy the spectacle.

Wrestling is an unusual sport as most of the action is faked. Even though the audience is aware of this, they enjoy the sight of strong men or women 'acting' out a body contact fight. It disputed that much of a wrestling show is arranged in advance, including the final outcome. Ringside audiences and fans of *WWF* (*World Wrestling Fanzine*) claim not to mind whether a match is fixed or not.

Extreme sports

Extreme sports programmes cover activities such as tobogganing, skateboarding or bungee-jumping, and these have a greater factor of risk and failure built into them. Twenty years ago these sports would not have been considered worthy of attention. However, thirty years ago snooker and darts were not considered worthy, but now they are highly popular television sports.

SPORTING PROGRAMME CONTENT

Title sequences

Most television sports title sequences convey considerable energy and wit. The pace of the editing for the title sequence of *Match of the Day* is quick and dramatic; the camera work is varied with sweeping pans and zooms, together with a soundtrack which is highly energetic and dramatic. The shots are of famous football players waiting in the changing rooms or displaying their skills in scoring goals, and shots of mass cheering from the grounds.

Study a number of sports programme title sequences. See how they create a sense of audience expectation for their particular sport:
1 Denotate and connotate their images and sounds.
2 Look at the following elements and analyse how they are presented.
   a Drama
   b Characters
   c Celebration or disappointment
   d Sound voice-over
   e Soundtrack music and effects

Highlights

Much of television sports programming is prepared earlier than its time of transmission. The highlights of each game on *Match of the Day* last between fifteen minutes and half an hour. How far do you think these programmes represent what actually happened in the game? What do you think was left (edited) out? Why do you think these sections were edited out?

1 Go to a game of sport: for example, volleyball, swimming competition, football or rugby. Record it on video or audio-tape. Make a shot list and create a rough edit plan. The edit plan shows the shots in the order you want.
2 **Edit** your footage down to ten minutes. What did you leave out and what did you keep in?
3 Was there a need for a voice-over? How does the target audience for the product affect what is said in the voice-over commentary?
4 How could you make your final video sequence video or audio-tape to look and sound professional?
5 How would you film a long-distance running race, bicycle race or ski jump, using only one camera? What difference would having two cameras make?

Replays and slow motion

Action replays are an essential part of modern sports programmes. They allow audiences to see action again, which they cannot see if they are at the ground or track (although many stadiums do have large screens to replay scenes). Cricket also uses the 'third umpire' to judge whether a player is run out or not. It is important to be able to view a sporting event from as many different angles as possible.

Studio critics are asked to commentate over a replay so that the whole sequence can be enjoyed and analysed over again. Use of the replay of the goals and, for example, the idea that goal scoring in football is the best part of the play, have been criticised for making games seem more exciting than they really are. In the real game there often long periods when the play is not exciting. Boredom, however, is not an experience programme makers want their audiences to have. The TV audience is therefore always given a highly selective view of what actually happened.

Technical elements

Cameras

Most large sporting events use more than one camera to record the event. In football matches there are two goals to record, plus the two lengths of the pitch. In reality there are many more angles to cover.

Voice-over

Like any piece of live radio or television sport (swimming, acrobatics, hockey, rugby league), the action is presented through the voice-over of the commentator. Commentators provide background information about the players or the athletes, and warm the audience up before the game or race. Once the game is under way, the action is dramatised by the increasingly excited voice-over. This keeps the tension flowing until there is a surprise, a goal or a win; the voice is then jubilant, and then quiet and calm again. Some sports, such as cricket, do not lend themselves to fast talking and the tone of the voice is more reflective and casual.

1 **Watch** a ten minute section of a football, tennis or swimming match with the sound turned down. See how much you can understand without the commentary. What can't you understand without the help of the commentator? Is there any advantage in not being able to hear the commentator?

2 **Review** the discussion in Chapter Seven about presenters' clothes, tone of voice, use of language and content. How do sports commentator's present themselves? Are they emotional and do they get carried away? Are they quiet and more informative, and less inclined to show their personal bias? Which style do you prefer: emotionally charged or calm and informative?

3 **Listen** to a BBC Radio 5 Sports programme or any local sports commentary live and watch any television commentator on the same sport. What do the presenters do differently on the radio in terms of:

▶ content
▶ explaining visual detail
▶ expressing their own reactions
▶ soundtrack effects

Figure 12.2 Des Lynam – a well-known and popular sports presenter
Source: © BBC Photograph Library

Personalities

Radio and television presenters provide the links between the sport and the commentaries, conducted in interviews with studio experts. Presenters become personalities and their image is created to make audiences identify with them and the channel they work for. Famous football presenters like Desmond Lynam are well-known for their smooth and calm manner. The voice of Murray Walker, the motor car racing commentator, who, after many years, moved from BBC1 to ITV, has become associated with the world of motor car racing.

FINANCE AND THE SPORTS MEDIA

Sport is a very profitable industry. It is now possible to pay for some television sports channels by subscription or on a pay-per-view basis.

Publishing

Men's enthusiasm for football is expressed in different media, notably, through comedians

SPORT, GAME SHOWS AND CHAT SHOWS

such as David Baddiel and Frank Skinner. There are many autobiographies on famous football clubs and stars, and now there are books about female football fans also.

Sports fanzines

The biggest area of writing has been by the fans, in the fanzines. The format used to be A5 and the 'zines were photocopied and stapled together. Now the Internet has drawn in the 'zines onto web sites, and so the format has changed. The editorials of 'zines tend to be outspoken on the fans' point of view of their club. They often criticise the management or the players. 'zines express personal opinions, and so the rules of professional journalism do not always apply.

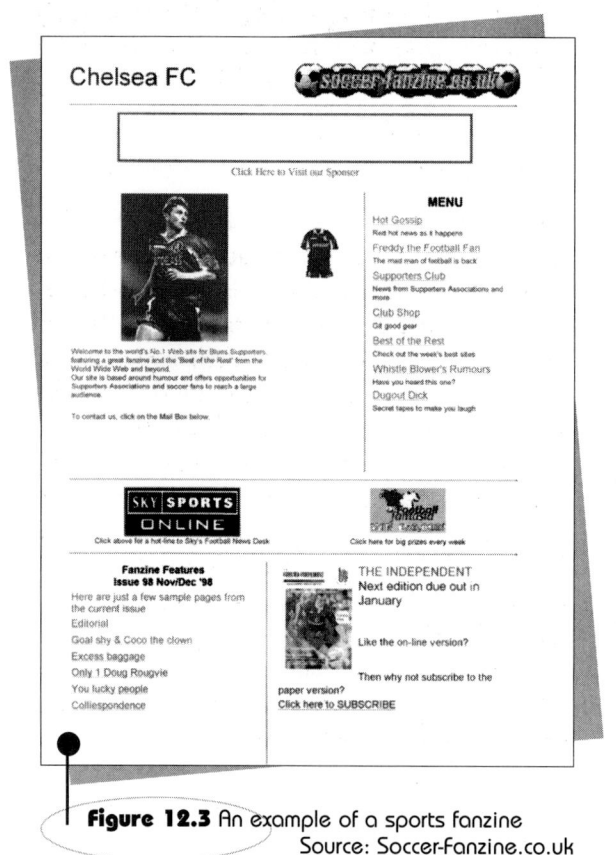

Figure 12.3 An example of a sports fanzine
Source: Soccer-Fanzine.co.uk

Home viewing

Subscription

Subscription television is where a customer pays a regular amount of money on an **annual** basis and in return is provided with all the services on that channel.

Pay-per-view

Pay-per-view occurs when the viewer pays a one-off amount to watch an event. Popular sports, especially boxing, which have a worldwide interest but that people cannot afford to travel to, are obvious targets for pay-per-view. The promoters know this and can make the live boxing fight exclusive to paying viewers. The rest of the viewers have to wait for the highlights after the event has finished on the same channel, or watch on other channels.

		Date	Revenue £ million
1	Evander Holyfield v Mike Tyson	June 97	1.99
2	Mike Tyson v Evander Holyfield	Nov 96	1.60
3	Mike Tyson v Peter McNeeley	Aug 95	1.58
4	Frank Bruno v Mike Tyson	Mar 96	1.36
4	Evander Holyfield v George Foreman	April 91	1.36
6	Mike Tyson v Razor Ruddock	June 91	1.23
7	Bruce Seldon v Evander Holyfield	Oct 90	1.06
7	Brude Seldon v Mike Tyson	Sept 96	1.00

Table 12.2 World's top pay-per-view sports events
Source: Gould Media, *The Guardian*, 12 March 1999

Advantages of pay-per-view

In the UK football is one of the sports where fans often live a long way from the place where their team plays, or the home fan does not want to travel a long distance for away matches. Many Londoners support Northern teams and the opposite also applies.

Approximately seven million English and Welsh fans claim to support Manchester United, Liverpool or Newcastle. 95% have never visited a football ground and would prefer to watch it at home. Pay-per-view is aimed at the viewer who does not want to subscribe all season, but might want to watch the occasional match at home.

Disadvantages of pay-per-view

The disadvantage of pay-per-view is that supporters have to pay to watch a match they might previously have watched for free on other terrestrial channels. The long-term view is that, although large clubs will prosper, the smaller clubs will suffer. Smaller clubs with low attendance gates will not be selected over those with high attendances, as this would not make much money. The rich clubs will get richer and the poorer clubs might not even survive.

New technology and the future

Current satellite systems and the new digital boxes which come with the next generation of video recorders and televisions allow the viewer to press a button and pay to view there and then. The pay-per-view customer can also, with some packages, choose which camera angle and position they want to watch from. TV companies now use many cameras at the ground and the viewer selects where they want to view different sections of the match from. Formula One motor car racing crosses many countries every year and this is a typical example of being able to see a 'live' broadcast of an event.

In Spain on 14 March 1999, Canal Satellite Digital broadcast the football clash between Barcelona and Real Madrid. This game attracted 295,000 paying customers. The game reportedly generated an income of £2.5 million, of which £1.15 million was divided between the two clubs. Canal Satellite deployed 150 personnel, 18 cameras, six commentators and an airship for the match. However, restricting the game to pay-per-view customers caused a storm of protest among the public. Politicians promised to change existing regulations to protect games of 'national interest'.

In the UK, there are approximately 18 million football fans in England and Wales. Pay-per-view is predicted to bring in 280 million for Premiership clubs by the 2003–2004 season. Clubs could also earn a further £240 from selling a 'television season ticket', offering a package of 60 live games per season to their fans. That compares with the £135 million the entire Premiership received from Sky Sports for live rights in 1999.

'Free to air'

The problem with one company achieving great success is that other companies may lose money. The other major issue is then whether any major sports events will be seen on 'free to air' channels. Free to air is the term given to non-commercial stations such as BBC1. The BBC traditionally broadcast all the big events 'live' every year, however, Formula One, football and rugby union are now often shown on other channels. Among the events that the BBC have held onto are Wimbledon, Test Cricket and the Oxford versus Cambridge boat race.

In the USA, one solution has been to allow all American football games to be shown free on television, funded by expensive advertising between the breaks. Television rights and merchandising are shared equally around the National Football League's 30 teams.

SPORT, GAME SHOWS AND CHAT SHOWS

Digital

Ondigital is a new digital service company combining the two major ITV companies, Carlton Communications and Granada. They compete for audiences by using digital means of transmission and therefore can expand the number of channels available. With the merging of the Internet and television, it is possible for the public to replay their own recordings and then watch a football match in different ways using different camera angles and commentaries.

The theory is that ability to replay a game or show from almost any angle will eventually be in the hands of the home spectator rather than the television producer.

SPORTS SIMULATION (AQA)

Your Premier division football club, Grandchester United, is about to be taken over by Glaxa, a large insurance company. Glaxa are working with Earth, a large cable company. Earth have a very large share of the UK cable market. This will mean that you will only be able to see the matches on television on a pay-per-view or subscription basis. You could always buy an expensive season ticket and go to the matches but you can't always get to the away matches. On the other hand, the club has a shortage of European players, so the takeover would enable you to buy some world class players.

However, you have decided to launch a media campaign to resist the takeover, arguing it is in the interests of the club's fans to prevent the takeover occurring. Answer the following tasks in order.

Paper Two controlled text (4 hrs)

Task 1

a Explain the typical features of presentation in BBC's or ITV's television sports programmes? Comment on aspects of the following: studio, presenters, live action, graphics and special effects. Refer to one or more types of sports.

(30 marks)

Task 2

Either

a Script a local radio news item about the problems of the potential takeover bid by Glaxa. Include both positive and negative points of view. (1–2 minutes long: average 3 words per second.) Use the radio script pro-forma provided.

or

b Design (in a sketch) a web page for a club fanzine called *On the Spot*. Your page should include a space for the club's fans to express their points of view. Explain the details of your page, in writing.

(20 marks)

Task 3

Either

a Produce a local evening newspaper (regional newspaper) item: indicate contents of a photo (a very rough sketch), caption, headline, and text of 100 words (the masthead is not necessary). The editor's view of the issue may be biased in one way or another.

or

b Design a poster which expresses your views on whether the club should be taken over by Glaxa or not. You have paid for advertising space in your local paper for a full page spread. Include a slogan, written text and images.

(30 marks)

Task 4

Write a letter to the fans in the clubs' fanzine explaining why you think Grandchester United will not benefit from the takeover by Glaxa and Earth. Explain the points for and against, and argue why you think your point of view is best.

(20 marks)

Extension Tasks

1 **Research** broadsheet and tabloid newspapers for examples of stories in the main section on sporting personalities. How are they presented? What angle do they take? Produce a fanzine version of the same event: describe layout, content and images.

2 **Watch** another country's presentation of a sporting event, for example, Italian football. Study the commentator and commentary style, the content and tone, the camera positions, and movements and shot sizes, the use of crowd's participation, the studio experts, the soundtrack and the title sequence.

3 **Video** a table tennis match from the viewpoint of one player. Evaluate its strengths and weaknesses. To what extent can you produce something of interest, which is not conventional, using two or three cameras?

4 **Video** a football match that is also going to be broadcast on the television. Record your own commentary at the same time. Compare the results with that of the televised commentary. Is your version of the match similar or different to the television or radio commentary? How would you improve yours or their commentary?

Examination Skills

Knowledge and Understanding

To answer a question on sports and the media you should become familiar with the main organisations and media products involved in the big money business of sports media (the BBC and other international organisations such as Bertlesmann and American news companies). There should be a good knowledge of the different ways in which live and pre-recorded television sports events are sold, presented and distributed. The range of media, sports journalism and radio, for example, should be studied to gain an understanding of forms and conventions of sports presentation, reporting, commentary and analysis. Alternative media products such as fanzines and community cable should also be explored. Terms such as pay-per-view and subscription will need to be used to indicate some of the different ways in which sport is financed and consumed. There should be an understanding of the relationship between the sponsors and the sporting organisation's commitments to advertise products. Students should understand the different presentational formats and styles of reporting in all media.

Textual Analysis

The analysis of television and radio sport should tackle standard conventional formats of programmes. The title sequences, presenter, commentator, the crowd and the participants are all actors in the sporting 'drama'. Discuss the denotative and connotative associations with sounds and images. In radio, the structure and the format of the sports programme should be studied: music, interviews, reports and commentators. Identify institutional elements of branding, logos or lettering, voice or soundtrack.

Comment on Task I: TV Sport presentation styles

The studio presentational style of Des Lynam on BBC1's Match of the Day football programme is relaxed and yet authoritative. He usually wears a jacket and tie and looks straight to the camera for the links. He is usually accompanied by two or three 'experts' who are often ex-players. They are usually seated behind a desk, making them appear more authoritative. The same format also applies to the commentaries on tennis or Olympic sports. The anchor presenter makes comments, provides information and tries to tease comment and predictions out of the studio panel. There are often links to the pitch where an on-the-spot commentator gains, in close-up or medium shot, immediate post-match reactions from the players and the managers. Throughout the game, the crowd is usually seen and heard in the background 'en masse' but not usually interviewed as individual commentators.

Practical Work

Producing simulations of professional products for sports requires careful thought. The use of a commentator is a convention which could be broken. With one camera, the use of zoom, pan and movement tracking around the game should be used carefully, to sustain interest. The edited version should demonstrate a logical sequence, for example, the football in the goal mouth comes after the person kicks the ball, not before! Radio lends itself more easily to the constraints of non-professional sports reporting. Utilise the soundtrack of the crowd and the participants of the game itself.

13 New media and old

INTO THE NET AND ONTO THE ROM

In this chapter you will study the past and present of media technologies and their applications. A number of questions about the future and present are asked: what can technology now offer, for whom is it produced, who owns it and how can it be used? Who controls the content of the Internet?

KW

Standalone ■ networked ■ on line ■ E-mail ■ digital ■ analogue ■ interactivity ■ convergence ■ regulation and control

TW

Satellite ■ cable and terrestrial ■ Rom ■ Ram ■ DVD ■ World Wide Web ■ Internet ■ Intranet ■ nonlinear editing

TO BOLDLY GO . . .

At the turn of the twentieth century, in 1900, the world had just begun to experience the wonders of film. At that time, no one quite anticipated the major impact cinema would make on our everyday lives. In fact, the invention of the submarine and the expansion of cities were viewed as greater subjects of interest. In a similar fashion, the turn of the twentieth first century has seen major technological changes which have affected all the traditional media sectors.

Communications media were separate until recently. Today, the television, cinema, music, radio, print (papers, magazines and comics), computer games and software, on line computing, advertising, and news gathering industries do not exist in isolation. With the invention of the computer, digital technology and new ways of using the telephone, new technologies are now transforming each medium.

COMPUTERS

There are three forms of computer systems:

- standalone
- networked
- on line

Stand-alone

First, there is the stand alone computer, which uses discs, DCD-Roms and hardware disc drives. Most people use computers for word processing and need to keep their information stored on separate discs from the hard drive. The hard drive is the internal processor that runs any programmes sent to its memory.

The computer's RAM (random access memory) is activated by a 'floppy' programmed disc, containing information and interactive material. The ROM (read only memory) part is memory that can only be read from. Microwaves have computer chips which are run on ROM, so that instructions work when the power is switched on. Most computers now accept CD-Roms, which allow image and text files and multimedia texts to be easily read.

Networked

The second type of computer is the networked computer, where information can be sent from one computer to another when they have been linked up. Many schools and colleges and workplaces are networked so that information can be easily circulated. A small group of computers can be linked and closed off to other computer access. This is called an 'Intranet'. In businesses, many professional accountants or legal professionals will set up their closed circuit of computers into a Intranet, to maintain confidentiality.

Internet

The third type of computer system is the global Internet. The Internet is a collection of computers linked together around the world. The World Wide Web (WWW) is a collection of machines running software for sending graphics across the Internet.

As an Internet user, you give yourself a name which becomes your URL (Uniform Resource Locator). For example, a typical address would be: http://www.yourname@aol.com.uk. The address can also be contacted to activate your web page if you were to create one. Some people create more than one address if they wish to discuss different topics, for example, *Titanic*, sci-fi films or Indie music. The address length is less daunting than it seems, as the structure of the different segments of the URL can be broken into four parts:

- **http** equals hypertext (special code to enable transfer from part of the web to another)
- **www** equals World Wide Web
- **yourname** is the network name you have
- the last section tells you the Internet service provider, for example aol (America Online) and the country or place you are sending the message from.
- **com** equals company, and the uk equals United Kingdom(Au = Australia, etc.)

The Internet is now a major form of communication and information exchange, as it is immediate and cheap in comparison to phone bills. The E-mail (electronic mail) messaging system has created a whole new phenomena of newsgroups, chat groups, net 'zines and personal communication links between people who have never met each other, from all over the world.

Convergence

Traditional media companies have joined up with computer on line services, software companies and telephone companies. This means that, with a few exceptions, a few large companies now control almost every aspect of media production, the products, the means of distribution and the point of sale. The word convergence describes how the different media meet in one point.

In the home, the broadcast media of television and radio will link with the fax, the phone call and the electronic message, through one central point – the computer screen. From one screen people will be able to interact with:

- television and radio and television
- information
- home banking
- shopping
- games and events
- E-mail

Big businesses are investing in as much of the following as possible:

- Newsgathering media, TV stations, information and news suppliers, newspapers.
- Telephone services.
- On line computer networks and software.
- Broadcasting networks and systems of delivery.
- Copyright purchases of photographic and moving images, music, arts.
- Rights to events, such as world boxing matches, UK football, USA American football and basketball.

The company that wins the race to control all of these sectors could become extremely rich and powerful.

Your local newspaper may belong to one of the bigger organisations, such as Trinity International Holdings or NewsQuest. The television franchises are owned by a small number of organisations who also own papers and radio stations.

Research your local TV company and radio and newspaper companies. What is the parent company called? What else do they own in other media and other businesses?

FORMATS

Film

Film conventionally used 35 mm celluloid to project images onto cinema screens. However, film can now be distributed in various formats. Today it can be:

- Transferred onto digital versatile disc (DVD).
- Bought as video tape in 'sell-through' shops like Woolworths.
- Broadcast via satellite, cable or terrestrial aerials on television.

NEW MEDIA AND OLD

The UK digital highway is shared through six multiplexes. Multiplexes combine all the inputs into one signal. Viewers then access the bundle of signals according to which supplier they use. A different decoding box will also be needed for each supplier. The revenues for the suppliers will be made from selling TV set-top boxes, the programme subscriptions, the pay-per-view programmes.

Sky Digital

Sky Digital is owned by BSKYB. Sky Digital transmits on 200 channels and carries BBC1 and BBC2 and Channels 4 and 5. In addition to the usual Sky channels, Sky Digital will also screen Manchester United football matches.

Online Digital Terrestrial

Online Digital Terrestial is owned by Carlton and Granada. It includes 30 channels, 15 of which are free.

Cable and Wireless

Cable and Wireless is a cable channel that aims to provide Sky Digital's programmes on its network.

BBC

The BBC have joined up with the international company Flextech, and their programmes are shown on Sky and Online Digital.

Equipment

Seven manufacturers are developing television sets with an integrated set top box: Toshiba, Panasonic, LG, Grundig, Amstrad, Sharp and Samsung.

Shopping

Today, there is much talk of a revolution in information, entertainment and financial systems and how this revolution will change our lives. Already it is possible to buy goods through a home computer and shop in a 'virtual space' on screen, which looks like a shopping area. The purchasers select goods by clicking on the mouse. The on line computer and the television set are two pieces of modern technology that link TV, computer games, teletext, E-mail, films and sport on demand.

Convergent services

Examples of the way computers, media and telephones have crossed over are:

- Internet services are delivered to TV sets via systems such as Web TV.
- E-mail and World Wide Web access via digital TV decoders and mobile phones.
- Web-casting of radio and TV programming on the Internet.
- Music publishing on the Internet.

Example 1: Music

The rock artist David Bowie produced an album that he then placed on the Internet as an on line CD. Both audience participation and commercial gain could result from this arrangement. This is what he believes could happen in the future:

> The users can decide on the packaging themselves. Hundreds of ideas have come in, of photographs, tickets, and memorabilia collected by fans of the tour I just did. Users could download a selection of these images and make their own booklets, printing it out, putting it in a case and eventually downloading the album itself from the internet.
>
> Source: David Bowie, in *The Guardian*, 15 January 1999

Individual music artists who wish to publish on the Internet run the risk of upsetting their record companies. However, the cost of buying a CD could become far cheaper if local stores were sent the soundtrack down the Internet. They could then write their own discs, thus reducing packaging costs. The discs would consequently be cheaper.

In March 1999, Sony began distributing music via satellite to specially designed television set-top boxes. Subscribers to Sony's multi-channel digital satellite service can download CD-Roms to mini discs, CD-Rom or re-writable DVD. The competing format is MP3, a particular type of compressed information file that compresses the information so it can be transferred more easily. Customers will need specially designed set-top boxes to download MP3 files.

Example 2: Television

Television formats are also transferring onto the Internet. Mark Lamarr, a music and television comic, is working, in 1999, for AOL (America Online) to reproduce the 'chat-with-celebrities-net-show' formula that Oprah Winfrey ran successfully in the United States.

Example 3: Radio

Blur 'web-broadcasted' a 45 minute Radio 1 concert on their official website.

Example 4: Advertising

In March 1999, BSKYB failed to win access to the new digital service of ITV 2 on satellite. This was a disappointment to them, as they could therefore not gain the additional advertising revenue. ITV could regard this as a potential loss to BSKYB.

Shortly after the case of BSKYB and ITV, Granada and Carlton were warned by the ITC for refusing to carry an advertisement for Sky premiere's football channel Sky Sports:

ONdigital owners warned over BSkyB ad

GRANADA and Carlton were yesterday handed a formal warning by TV regulators in the latest round of the tit-for-tat war over digital television, *writes Steve Busfield.*

The Independent Television Commission said the two ITV companies and their licensees which run ONdigital, the new digital terrestrial service, had unreasonably discriminated against BSkyB by refusing to carry a Sky Digital advertisement for Premiership football, exclusively shown on Sky Sports channels.

The companies had claimed the advert's words "football on Monday nights" constituted a specific invitation to view.

But the ITC noted the licensees had carried an ONdigital advert for the Mike Tyson-François Botha heavyweight boxing bout that contained a much more specific invitation.

The previous day the ITC had ruled against Sky in a row over whether the satellite broadcaster should be given transmission rights to the new digital service ITV2.

Source: *The Guardian,* 25 March 1999

Example 5: Multimedia

Previously, television production companies would offer broadcasting, video production and post-production facilities. For example, the production company Victoria Real has five trading areas:
1 Broadcasting and video production – television and corporate videos.
2 Post-production facilities – television, film and graphics.
3 Interactive programming and advertising – interactive television.
4 World Wide Web – web pages.
5 Real products – software products.

The idea of a television company now seems old-fashioned. With the rise of video games, interactive television and CD-Roms, an approach to the information world is no longer confined to a series of half hour television programmes. Different levels of involvement and more direct electronic forms of text, visual and aural communication are now possible. On the other hand, the chance to explore the Internet across nationalities may not seem so exciting if we have to pay a high price for it. Another doubt is whether the drive towards convergence actually means sameness and not the diversity we might have hoped for.

Regulation and control

The content of all digital services must comply with published codes on programme content, advertising and sponsorship, technical standards and subtitling. Therefore, new digital television services will still have to comply with the controls, according to whether they are terrestrial (land-based), satellite or cable. The BBC, ITV, Channel 4 and Channel 5 have to follow guidelines on the number of hours they broadcast of factual and fictional programming, and community and public information services.

Practical production guide

Every Media Studies syllabus includes practical assignments for coursework. There are full-scale productions and there is practical work, which involves a low level of technology.

▶ **Production work** is the production of media texts for specified audiences using appropriate equipment and resources.

▶ **Practical** work means activities such as storyboarding and scripting, which are a necessary part of the production process.

PROFESSIONAL VERSUS AMATEUR

Examiners do not expect students to produce magazines, video and radio products to the same level of expertise as the professionals. If you are fortunate enough to have colour desktop publishing, inkjet or laser printers and television or audio-recording studios, then this will improve the quality of your finished products. However, no student is marked down for not having these facilities. It is important to state in your writing what equipment you used so that an examiner can make a judgement about how well you have managed with the equipment you have available.

Criteria

Examiners are looking for your ability to use the conventional forms and conventions of any medium. For example:

▶ Does your product show awareness of the typical layout and content of a broadsheet or tabloid newspaper?

▶ Does your video storyboard for an advertisement make sense as a promotion as well as a sequence of images and sounds?

In addition, the examiners are looking for a demonstration of how audiences are targeted. This can be achieved by way the form and content of the media product has been presented. You will need to provide further evidence of this in the critical commentary.

Practical activity

Producing a storyboard is an example of small-scale practical work. In the real world of television and film, a storyboard is a vital planning format for imagining how the shots and sounds will appear when sequenced together. A storyboard should be well annotated and carefully presented (see Chapter Two: Languages and Categories). On its own, a storyboard does not fulfil the requirements of a complete assignment. A storyboard should be accompanied by, for example, an analysis of mainstream product(s) and a critical commentary.

Practical production

Alternatively, practical work can involve media technology in a larger-scale project. For example, you can use a video camera or an audio-tape recorder to record a news bulletin presentation. The AQA production assignment is intended to incorporate the use of a larger scale practical and technical element.

Example production sheet

Subject: 'Moviewatch-style' television film review
Medium: Video (television)
Names of people in group: Funmi, Kamaljit, Jo, and Matt
Equipment and materials needed: Video camera, chairs, posters, editing facilities.
Treatment: We are making a 'Moviewatch-style' review of the latest Indian/Pakistan/Hong Kong film video releases. The video sequence will be about five minutes long and will include our views on one film in particular and a general overview on several Asian (mainly Indian) films. The presenter will act in the style of Johnny Vaughan, but will be female. The guest panel who will comment on the films will be one Pakistani, one Indian, one Hong Kong Chinese student and one Caucasian. We aim to show what films are on offer to the community in which we live which are very popular but are not much talked about on programmes like *Moviewatch*. The camera work will be hand-held and the editing will involve lots of unusual angles and fast pans. The panel will have strong opinions which should differ greatly. The edited version will have clips from the films we have been talking about.
Dates for recording: January 20th and 27th 1999
Date for editing: February 3rd and 10th 1999.
Date for critical commentary deadline: February 20th 1999
Select medium: Video for television

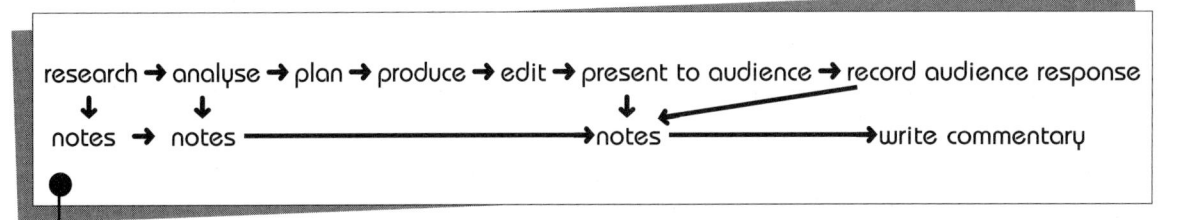

research → analyse → plan → produce → edit → present to audience → record audience response
  ↓   ↓   ↓
notes → notes ─────────────────────────→ notes ─────────────────→ write commentary

Figure 14.1 Diagram of the production process

Critical commentary

All individual and group practical products need to be explained in a critical commentary. For any media product produced for mass media consumption or for an individual's Media Studies practical production assignment, the same questions can be asked. The critical commentary should explain the process of producing the product and its production (30% of the words). The major part of the commentary (70% of the words) should cover the areas raised by the following questions.

Critical commentary and planning questions

Question	Concept area
▶ **Why the product is produced?** (e.g. an advertisement is used to promote and sell another media product, such as a TV programme)	Messages and Values
▶ **What format is chosen?** (includes visual and/or aural elements, e.g. documentary)	Languages and Categories
▶ **What form, style and design ideas are presented?** (e.g. *The Big Breakfast*: youthful presenters, colourful sets, loud and brash music, bright strong graphics, jerky camera with deliberately exaggerated zooms and pans, short, comical, briskly presented items)	Languages and Categories
▶ **Who exactly is it targeted at?** (e.g. *TFI Friday*. ABC1s aged 15 to 24 males and females)	Producers and Audiences
▶ **How is the audience constructed?** (i.e. included in the mode of address or the positioning? *The Big Breakfast*: friendly, chatty, youthful presenters who use jokes which a younger audience might not understand. Puns, jokes and games, competitions, music and films for younger audience.	Producers and Audiences
▶ **Is the product effective and successful with its audiences?**	Producers and Audiences
▶ **Is the producer satisfied with the end result?** What would they do to improve it?	Producers and Audiences
▶ **Who is the producer?** (e.g. an advertising agency called Believe, or a newspaper called *Eyewash*?)	Producers and Audiences
▶ **Who financed the product?** (e.g. the company Microsoft, by a sponsor, by actual sales or by the Government?)	Producers and Audiences
▶ **What ideas do you associate with the signifiers?** (e.g. dark clouds over castle signifies horror genre)	Messages and values
▶ **What attitudes and values about society and people does the media product contain?** (e.g. advertisement depicting sunlit breakfast cereal in perfectly tidy kitchen with two smiling children; mother and father suggests an ideal family event)	Messages and Values

Coursework requirements: by examination boards

Each examination board also has an end of year timed examination paper. Check your specific syllabus for details. Note also that individual examination syllabus requirements may change so check these yearly.

AQA

- Coursework: 50%
- Three assignments: 25%. A commentary of 1000 words should accompany each assignment.
- Production and evaluation: 25%. A supporting evaluation account of about 1000 words must accompany the production work. Of the four assignments, the practical projects should be presented in at least two media.

OCR

Coursework: 50%
Either
- Three pieces of practical work, plus three 500 to 750 word evaluative commentaries.

or
- Two pieces of practical work, plus two 500 to 750 word evaluative commentaries and one essay task (1000 to 1500 words).

or
- Two essay tasks (1000 to 1500 words each) and one piece of practical work, plus one 500 to 750 word commentary.

If candidates attempt more than one piece of practical work it is recommended that one should be a group project. If two practical media are attempted they should be presented in at least two media.

WJEC

- Coursework: 50%. Candidates are required to submit three pieces of work. Production work should be supported by evaluation.

Practical assignments

The following are examples of low technology practical assignments with small-scale products:

1 a Analyse existing newspapers and explain how the audience is targeted in the content and form of the paper.
 b Storyboard ten frames of a regional TV advertisement for a new youth section of a local newspaper.
 c Evaluate the process of devising the storyboard. Denotate and connotate the sequence of images and sounds. How does the sequence target its audience?

2 a Analyse the typical features of a music magazine and how it targets its audience.
 b Produce a rough pencil drawing of the cover page of a special 10th anniversary edition of a magazine and its contents list, including headlines, masthead and cover lines.
 c Evaluate the process of devising the magazine. Denotate and connotate the form and content of the magazine and explain how it targets its audience.

3 a Identify radio advertisements and explain typical features of a range of radio advertisements.
 b Produce a radio script (maximum of 30 seconds) to promote a particular evening's episode of a well-known television soap.
 c Evaluate the process of devising the radio script. Denotate and connotate the form and content of the radio promotion and explain how it targets its audience.

Example of a critical commentary for an assignment

(Refer also to the images produced by a student on page 20 of Chapter Two: Languages and Categories.)

This extract from a critical commentary explains the meaning of the source image as well as one of the three products the student made from it, by cropping the photograph and placing it in another context.

The image originated from the front page of *The Guardian*. The article was about an item of topical interest involving the late Lady Diana. This came to light at the Labour Party Conference a month after her death, in 1997. When Clare Short had a picture taken at Brighton beach she was representing the Government's view of dangerous weapons which she feels should be outlawed.

The image denotes a middle-aged woman holding up two objects. These objects look very much like lethal weapons used in a war situation. There is a sign next to the woman which is indicating that there are dangerous mines around. In the background there is what looks like the sea.

The image connotes that the woman is campaigning against dangerous mines. This might indicate that there are unexploded mines around the coast of Brighton although they are not. Her expression suggests sternness and hostility. She is disapproving very strongly of the weapons. Her posture and the way she is holding the weapons suggests that she feels very strongly and doesn't really want to hold those weapons. This is because she is holding the weapons far enough away from her body so she feels safe. Her hands are only holding the weapons tight enough not to drop them. Her clothes connote safety and protection. The sign is red, this usually connotes danger.

The words anchor the picture by giving it some kind of meaning. For example, we can get some feed back from the picture, for example we know it is about dangerous mines and that the Labour Party have promised to sign the treaty on banning landmines. The campaign is for outlawing dangerous weapons and Lady Diana was associated with it.

The picture is representing a very strong and in depth topic. By the way Clare Short is holding the objects, along with her facial expressions, you immediately get the impression that it's a very serious matter which is undergoing a great deal of investigation.

Invented image and context of image A (Chapter Two: Languages and Categories)

Image A denotes an unusual object which looks like a designer beaker or jam jar. This is mainly because the object has what seems to be a bottom and a lid. The only difference is that the top part of the object is very strange and unusual.

The image could be an object for a photographic competition or a piece of abstract art work. This is partly because there is a hand in the background holding the object up. This also could connote an unidentified object.

The photographer wanted to aim specifically at the object and not at the person. This is shown by a close up on the object. This allows the picture to have a much more specific meaning or aim. The camera position obtains a front on view of the object and gets a good concept of the picture. The lighting throughout the picture is very pale and really only gives us a bold outline of the object. Because of the way the picture has been photographed we don't really know if the object is round, flat or square. I feel by the picture being in black and white and blown up (using a photocopier) so that it loses detail, you get a feeling of uncertainty about the precise details of the images.

The captions of the picture are designed to create a feeling of mysteriousness. This was done using objects which have not been proved to exist. You would expect to find this type of article in a space magazine or an *X-Files* magazine. The new image which I have created has been changed considerably from the original image. I have done this by taking the original dangerous references away and introducing a feeling of sci-fi-mystery.

The audience which I have targeted the magazine article for will range between 12 to 26 years of age and possibly upwards, because the subject matter appeals to the unknown fans, of this age group.

Technology used: photocopier, enlargements, word processor with range of fonts incorporated.

PRODUCTION

Examples of typical productions are:

1. Make a 30 second television advertisement for a new perfume, directed at 25 to 35 year olds.
   Write a critical commentary explaining the research, the process of production, ownership, the form and content, audience of the advertisement.
2. Produce a first edition cover and contents list for a new music magazine.
   Write a critical commentary explaining the research, the process of production, the campaign to launch the magazine, ownership, the form and content, and audience of the advertisement.

Guidelines for producing a **Video**

There are three stages in the process of making a video: pre-production, production and post-production (see Figure 14.1).

Pre-production

Treatment

The success of a video depends on planning out as much of the filming and the editing before starting. You need to share and brainstorm ideas. Once you have decided on the content of the video, you must decide on how you will treat the subject matter. You should write a short summary explaining what your video is about, at what time of day the programme will be shown, and what format and style it will take. This summary is otherwise known as the 'treatment'. The treatment should include:

▶ A brief outline of the piece.
▶ Who might take part in it.
▶ What places or events you will include.
▶ The style and tone of your piece.
▶ The format.

GCSE MEDIA STUDIES

Pre-production → Treatment → Research → Recce → Script/Storyboard → Shooting script → Practice

↓

Production → Technical check-up and practice → Recording → Logging → Transcribing

↓

Post-production → Edit plan → Rough edit → Voice over and music → Music and effects → Final edit

↓

Audience responses

Figure 14.2 Guidelines for producing a video

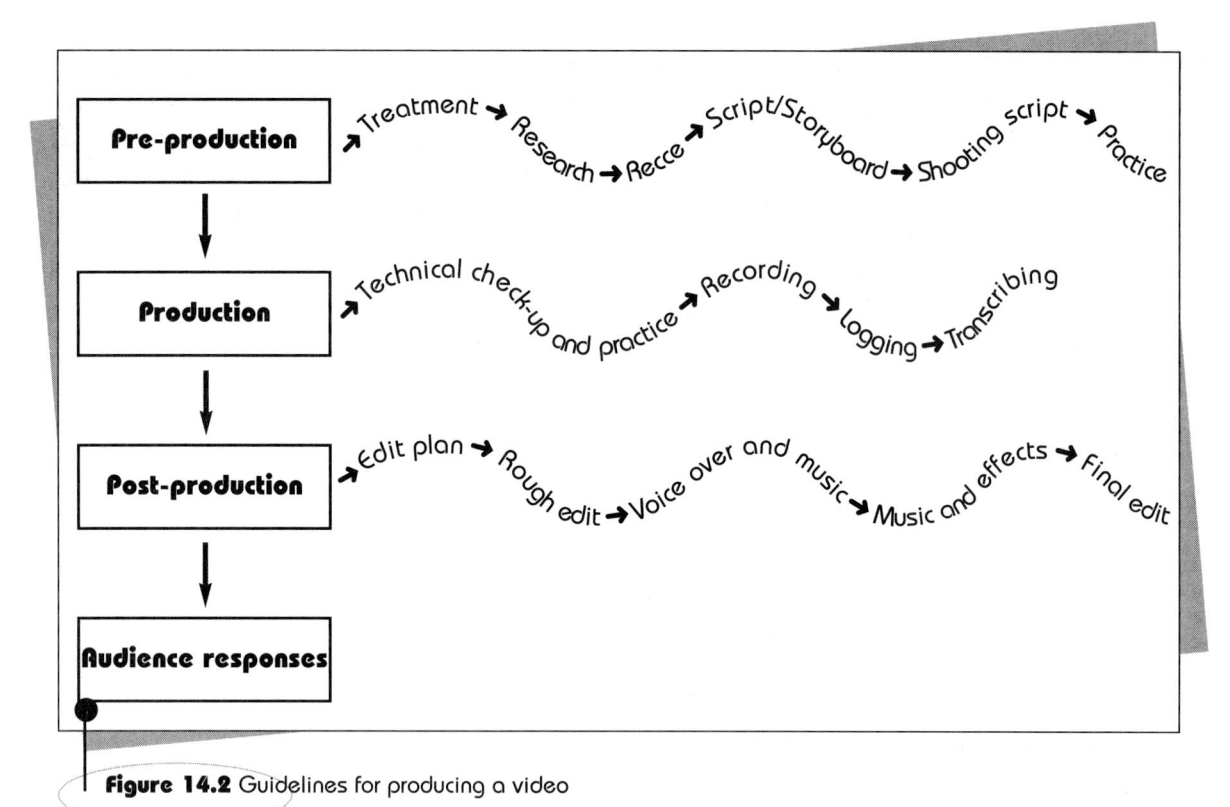

Concepts

Remember to answer these main questions:

- Who is it for and when will it be shown? (Audience)
- Who made it? (Producers)
- What do you want to say? (Messages and Values)
- What forms and conventions do you want to use? (Languages and Categories)

Research

Fiction

If you are making a drama or a fictional video then you will need to write a script. This details the structure of the programme. A script will show the order of the programme's elements and contain: questions, speech drama, location settings, props and sound effects. See AQA's pro-forma for a script, in the Appendix. These blanks are what you will be provided with in the examination.

Factual

If you are making a factual programme, you will need to think more about how to organise your interviewees and record questions that make sense. You will need to write a script showing the content of the video sequence.

Storyboard

A storyboard is a series of sketches of each frame of the film you are going to write. Storyboarding allows you to plan how to film the shots in each section of your film. It can be tempting to simply pick up the video camera and shoot whatever is in the frame. You need to become familiar with how to use the tripod and experiment freehand with the cameras. However, it is important that you have a clear idea about how many shots you will need to film each section from your idea. You will need to make decisions about:

- tripod or hand-held camera
- shot size
- shot angle
- shot movement
- shot background and foreground
- props and clothes

Pre-production check list

1 Check that everyone knows what they are doing and that they are committed to turning up and bringing their props or piece of equipment to the place where you are videoing.
2 Check you can use all your equipment before you go out. Check also that your equipment works. Check the batteries are fully charged up. There is nothing worse than finding out you have no power left.
3 Check you have enough video tape.
4 Arrange to meet at the location half an hour before videoing starts.
5 Try to rehearse the camera movements and shots without recording, so you have a practice run.
6 Allow ten seconds running in time, once you have pressed the record button. Allow ten seconds running out time, once your scene has finished. (By carrying out the previous two instructions you can edit two sequences together so they lock securely onto the control track, without jumping and ruining the edit.)

Mikes

Test out the sound before you start. If you are using the built-in microphone, make sure you are not too far away from the speaker or actors or actresses. If you are using a hand-held mike, make sure you are pointing it in the right direction, to avoid picking up any irritating noises.

Recording

Make sure your tripod is level and make sure the microphone is working. Be brave enough to record more than one take of the same shot. This covers you in case one of your take does not turn out well.

Post-production check list

Logging and labelling

Once you have shot a scene, make sure you label the tape and log the scene on a logging sheet. This will help later when you are editing, as you will often need to find a particular scene quickly from the tapes you have videoed.

Edit plan

Once you have filmed, view your material and make a list of the sections you want to edit together, specifying counter numbers. This paper edit should briefly describe the sequence, the tape and the duration of the piece.

Edit the sequences according to your paper edit. Show your rough edit to friends and teachers. Gain reviews and responses from different audiences, at home and at school. Write these responses down to include them in your critical commentary. Finally, edit and change anything you think is not what you really want.

If you have the technical facilities, place music and titling over appropriate sections. Place credits at the end, remembering to include any special thanks to people who helped.

Guidelines for producing a radio programme

The process of producing a radio programme is very much the same as for video. All of the stages of video pre-production, production and post-production can be followed. The main consideration in radio is in finding the best sounds to create atmosphere, how much sound is needed and how the presenter makes the medium exciting, live and immediate. The script layout can follow the format below.

Many students choose radio because it is in some ways an easy medium to carry around and obtain material. Radio can use music, sound effects, different locations and a range of opinions in depth. However, it is important to check that you have the facilities to achieve what you want. Most schools and colleges have audio-cassette recorders and some have full mixing desk facilities. If you only have an audio-cassette recorder then you will have to record all your sound 'live'. Any music and speaking will have to be faded in and out as you go along.

Treatment

The treatment should include:

- A brief outline of the piece.
- Who might take part in it.
- What places or events you will include.
- The style and tone of your piece.
- The format.

Concepts

Remember to answer these main questions:

- Who is it for? (Audience)
- When will it be broadcast? (Audience)
- Who made it? (Producers)
- What do you want say? (Messages and Values)

The forms and conventions may vary according to whether it is, for example, Radio 1, Kiss FM or a local independent or alternative radio station. Your radio script might look like this:

Sound	Dialogue	Other information	Timing
Intro: music fade out	This is your only real local alternative radio station bringing you views and news which are different. Oh yes, and there's music as well as chat and gossip. Today, we have in the studio three experts on alternative fashions and why we can't get enough of the style and fit of clothes that we really, really want. If you want to phone in your opinions on fashion, avoid the queue get in your view now by phoning this number ...	Laughter in background	9 secs 13 secs
Music starts to fade up			10 secs total

Figure 14.3 Sample radio script

Magazine or newspaper front cover production

(Refer also to Chapter Eight on Newspapers, and Chapter Ten on Magazines, for layout and content)
The layout and design for a newspaper and flatplan usually takes the form of a series of roughs, showing headlines, spaces where the photographs fit in and the column divisions where the text is allocated space.

Producing a web page

A web page is basically a word-processed page with links. HTML (Hypertext Mark-up Language) is the code which allows these links to be made.
Software resources: Adobe PageMill, Microsoft Front Page, Claris Home Page, Netscape Communicator, Internet Assistant.

Plan on paper the layout of image and text for your page on paper. Consider the following:

▶ Who is your audience?
▶ Write, draw and gather content.
▶ Format.
▶ Assemble page.
▶ Publishing the page.

Scan in your images or use a digital camera. Save the images in JPEG format. Type in the text for your web page. Arrange the layout of the page according to how you want it to look and then save your page as a web page (this may involve saving as 'web page' or as 'Save as HTML').

To publish on the Internet, you will need to run some FTP software (File Transfer Protocol).

Next let people know what your URL is – this is the address of your web page.

Which medium?

Finally, have you chosen the right medium? Selecting the right medium for the right topic depends on the following:

▶ Who will consume it?
▶ Is the topic best suited for that medium?
▶ Financially, it is more viable for one medium or the other?
▶ Is the subject local, regional or national?

Decide which medium suits the following tasks:

1 A documentary followed by a phone in chat show on whether genetically modified foods should be sold in shops. National audience, mainly over 15 year olds.
2 Underage drinking. In-depth interviews with local people about attitudes to under age drinking. Regional and local, 12 year olds and upwards.
3 A campaign to build a new bypass or to pedestrianise a part of a town or city. Regional, over 35 year olds.
4 A consumer guide to 'what's on': reviews and previews about entertainment in the area. Local, youth, 15 to 24 year olds.

How much do I know?

Use the following questions to test your knowledge of important facts from each chapter. The answers are printed in the *GCSE Media Studies Teacher's Book* (ISBN: 0340 730374).

Music: Chapter 5
1. Who are currently the five major companies in the music industry?
2. Name two labels from each company.
3. Who still continues to buy vinyl records?
4. Name two departments in a typical major music company.
6. What is synergy?

Film: Chapter 6
1. What is a unique selling point (USP)?
2. Name five major studios.
3. Name two distribution companies.
4. What is the BBFC and what does it do?
5. What is a shot-reverse-shot?
6. What is a tag line?

Television and Radio: Chapter 7
Television:
1. What is the watershed?
2. What is the ITC?
3. What is the BSC?
4. What does 'hammocking' mean?
5. Name six news values?
6. Name one supplier of news.

Radio:
1. What is the RA?
2. Which TV channel organises its news teams to produce television and radio from the same material, i.e. a bi-media approach?

Newspapers: Chapter 8
1. What is a masthead?
2. Name six newspaper companies (note that this is not necessarily the same as the title of the newspaper).
3. Give five reasons for declining circulation figures of national newspapers.
4. What type of power does the PCC have, to control the press?
5. Describe a constraint which newspapers have in their reporting from courtrooms.
6. What is the ABC and what does it provide?

TV Hospital Dramas and Documentaries: Chapter 9
1. Name at least two hospital dramas.
2. Describe what happens in a cliffhanger.
3. What is a serial?
4. Name two types of filming techniques that are associated with making documentaries look real.
5. Describe three ways in which documentaries differ from dramas.
6. Name a documentary programme series from one of the TV channels.

Magazines: Chapter 10
1. What is currently the top selling TV and radio listings magazine in the UK?
2. Which publishing company also owns Kiss FM?
3. What is the word given to describe an article written by the editor, which passes comment?
4. What is a niche magazine?
5. Name ten typical features in the contents of a magazine.
6. What is the circulation figure of a magazine (as opposed to its readership figure)?

HOW MUCH DO I KNOW?

Advertising: Chapter 11
1 Name six places where advertisements can be found.
2 What does the ASA do?
3 What is BRAD?
4 What does the ITC monitor?
5 What is an advertorial?
6 What is copy?

Sport, game shows and chat shows: Chapter 12
1 Name two television programmes, of any type, which have sponsorship logos in their title sequence or in the break points of a programme.
2 What is subscription TV?
3 What is the difference between live and pre-recorded highlights of a sporting event?
4 Name two UK newspapers owned by the owners of Sky Sports 1, 2 & 3?
5 Which company currently owns the rights to televise Formula One car racing?
6 Why is sport such a lucrative money maker for television companies?

New media and old: Chapter 13
1 What does WWW mean?
2 What do the initials DVD stand for?
3 What is a back catalogue (music industry)?
4 Explain what pay-per-view means.
5 What is the benefit of an ISDN line?
6 When did the BBC start its first regular TV broadcast service?

Media studies concepts

Demonstrate your understanding of Media Studies concepts by writing your definitions of each of the following:

1 Languages
2 Categories
3 Producers
4 Audiences
5 Messages
6 Values

Resources

Your learning resources centre or your local library should have most of the following newspapers and books.

General: all media

1 'Media Guardian' section of *The Guardian* on Monday – articles, facts and figures. Covers soaps, advertising, newspapers, magazines, documentaries, dramas, institutions, future of broadcasting.
2 Media section of *The Independent* on Wednesday.
3 Media sections of Sunday broadsheets.
4 Review section in *The Guardian* on Friday – useful for latest film, video and music reviews.
5 'The Editor' – a supplement in *The Guardian* on Saturday – the world's media, surveys of news coverage, media Internet sites, magazine reviews.
6 *The Media Guide: A Guardian Book* – published every year. Contains a directory of who is who in media businesses and statistics on films, television, advertising, newspaper circulation and magazines.

Researching information

When asking for information from organisations, remember that most of the people who answer the phone are very busy and are often part of small office teams. Ask precise questions, such as: 'Can you send me your information/press pack or annual report about your organisation?'. If more than one person in the class is covering the same topic get one person to write on behalf of everyone else and share the copy.

Advertising

1 Advertising Standards Authority (ASA) – 2, Torrington Place, London WC1E 7HW. Website: http://www.asa.org.uk
2 Independent Television Commission (ITC) – 33, Foley Street, London W1P 7LP. Website: http://www.itc.org.uk

Book publishing

Major book publishers now have their own websites. You can look at these to see how they design web pages and promote their books. Some feature an organisational map of what departments and businesses they own, and sometimes an end of year accounts report.

Film

1 *The BFI Film and Television Handbook* – a yearly review of film box office and television viewing figures. Published by the British Film Institute, 21, Stephen Street, London W1P 1PL.
2 *Sight and Sound* film magazine – published monthly by the British Film Institute. Serious film reviews and full synopses, credits and reviews of all film and video releases.
3 *Empire* and *Total Film* are mainstream magazines which contain information, gossip and reviews on film releases.
4 British Board of Film Classification (BBFC) – 3 Soho Square, London W1V 6HD.

Film Internet sites:
Ain't it cool news –
    http://www.aint-it-cool-news.com
Bollywood –
    http://www.alt.movies.Indian
The Cinema Connection –
    htttp:/media.socialchange.net.au/CinemaConnection/
Cinema Sites –
    http://www.cinema-sites.com
Filmworld –
    http://findafilm.com/html/thisweek.html
Hollywood On-line –
    http://hollywood.com

RESOURCES

Internet Movie Database – http://www.imdb.com
Motion Picture Release – http://www.tvgen.com
Moviefinder – http://moviefinder.com
Premiere magazine – reviews and news from America http://sites.premiere.com
Hollywood Reporter magazine – reviews and news from America http://sites.hollywood.com
Yahoo Entertainment Movie and Film Links – htttp://www.yahoo.com/Entertainment/Movies…and…Films
Hollywood film studios all have their own sites.

Music

1 British Phonographic Industry (BPI) – 25, Savile Road, London W1X 1AA.
2 On line music – TOTP Charts (BBC Online site) and Pepsi Charts (Channel 5).
3 Music press – magazines such as *Smash Hits* or *Select*.
4 Music Internet sites:
There are a wide variety of dedicated sites to bands and performers.

General music information and links to other music sources of information – http://dotmusic.com/artists
The Knowledge (independent labels/artists) – http://www.knowledge.com
Some music magazines also have websites (*NME*, *Q*, *Rolling Stone*).
The major music companies all have websites promoting their products (EMI, Virgin).
Artists such as Peter Gabriel or David Bowie are creative artists as well as musicians, and often also have their own sites – http://www.DavidBowie.com

Newspapers and Magazines

1 Audit Bureau of Circulations (ABC) – Black Prince Yard, 207–209 High Street, Berkhamstead, Herts HP4 1AF. Website: http://www.abc.org.uk
2 Campaign for Press and Broadcasting Freedom – 8, Cynthia Street, London, N1 NJ
3 Newspaper Society – Bloomsbury House, 74–78 Great Russell Street, London WC1B 3DA.
4 Press Complaints Commission (PCC) – 1, Salisbury Square, London EC1 8AE.
5 Newspaper and magazine Internet sites:
http://www.telegraph.co.uk
http://www.pa.press.net
http://www.the-times.co.uk
http://www.record-mail.co.uk
http://www.reednews.co.uk
http://congleton.guardiangrp.co.uk

For links to UK local newspaper websites, check out the sites of publishers such as Emap, Reed, Thompson and Northcliffe.

Radio

1 IRN – radio and news agency. 200, Grays Inn Road, London WC1 X 8XZ. Website: http://www.irn.co.uk
2 Radio Authority (RA) – Holbrook House, 14, Great Queen Street, Holborn, London WC2 5 DG.

Television

1 British Broadcasting Corporation (BBC) – covers BBC radio and television. Portland Place, London W1A 1AA.
2 *Broadcast* magazine – contains audience ratings by programmes, films, children's TV, drama, sport, plus channel-by-channel overview.
3 Broadcasting Standards Council (BSC) – 7, The Sanctuary, London SW1P 3JS.
4 Independent Television Commission (ITC)
5 ITV (Network Centre) – 200, Grays Inn Road, London WC1 8HF.
6 Radio Internet sites:
http://www.spinner.imagineradio.com
http://www.radio.yahoo.com
http://www.radio.lycos.com
http://www.rollingstone.com

Examination Boards
1 Assessment and Qualifications Alliance (AQA) – Devaf Street, Manchester M15 6EX.
2 Southern Examining Group (SEG) – Stag Hill House, Guildford, Surrey GU5 5XJ (Publications Dept).
3 Oxford and Cambridge Royal (OCR) – 1, Hills Road, Cambridge, CB1 2EU. Media Studies Subject Officer: Birmingham Office, Mill Wharf, Mill Street, Birmingham B6 4BU.
4 Welsh Joint Education Committee (WJEC) – 245, Western Avenue, Cardiff CF5 2YX.

Glossary

The conceptual glossary which follows contains media studies terms. Technical terms are explained in the text of each chapter (see also Index).

Anchor Words or captions used to 'hold down' the meaning of a photograph create an 'anchor'. Without captions or words, the meaning of an image is more open to interpretation.

Audience In media studies, the term audience is used to describe more than the common sense idea of a group of people who sit in the cinema seats. An audience can also be defined by different criteria: social, demographic, psychographic or cultural. Audiences are targeted by media producers and can also be constructed. Audiences have different uses, needs and expectations of media.

Category The media can be divided into different categories by technological differences, including radio, film, television and magazines. Media can also be labelled in terms of their form, for example, documentary, fiction, news or light entertainment. They can also be labelled in terms of their type, genre or style, for example, horror or crime films, or quiz and soap opera TV programmes.

Code A code is a system of meaning which is understood within a social group or a society. In the western hemisphere, values and ideas about society are conveyed in the audio-visual media. For example, Rembrance Day, marking the end of the 1914–18 war in the UK, is represented visually by poppies and barbed wire. In film, the haunted house settings provide the visual code for the horror genre.

Connotation Connotation is a secondary level of meaning by which codes and conventions are interpreted. It is different from denotation, which describes factually what is in the image.
Connotative meanings link ideas associated with the image from outside the text. See also denotation.

Construct All fiction or factual media products are artificially created. Therefore, all media texts are constructs. What the media depict is only a representation of imagined or real life. There is no such thing as a natural 'effect'.

Conventions A convention is any agreed or established way in which the elements of a medium's language is combined to create meaning or an effect. A typical convention of game shows is to include bright flashing lights and showbizzy sets, and a loud participating audience. A typical convention of a horror film is to see an open window, the curtains blowing and the moon covered by a dark cloud.

Denotation Denotation is the common sense descriptive level of meaning in an image or sound. See also connotation.

Genre The term genre is usually associated with different 'types' of film – adventure, comedy or western, for example. The word can also be applied to television, for example, game shows, thrillers or soaps.

Icon Originally an Eastern European Christian painting depicting God or Jesus. Today, the term icon is used to describe someone or something which has achieved almost god-like status. In the world of politics or music the fans often 'worship' their idols so much that these people become icons.

Ideology The system of beliefs found in the values and messages of a media product. These values might be found in the messages which makers of the products want to convey: 'buy these trainers, be cool'. The product might reflect the values of the society and the time in which the product was made, for example patriotic second world war films.

Institution Institutions are organisations which produce media texts, with production facilities, finance, distribution, exhibition, technology, and associated messages and values. It is a term used to describe not only large organisations such as the BBC, but also social institutions such as the church or the state. The term also applies to the different producers in the production process. For example, an advertising agency produces an advertising campaign for the Government's Central Office of Information.

Languages Languages are the forms and conventions belonging to each medium. For example, in film, the formal elements include the visuals (type and size of shot, framing and composition and lighting) and the soundtrack (speech, sound effects, atmospheric sound and music).

Mass Mass media texts are deliberately designed to appeal to the widest number of people.

Mise-en-scène A French term, meaning everything which is placed in and associated with the frame (shot) of the camera: props, dress, scenery, camera angle, shot size and movement, lighting, colours, acting.

Narrative The structure of the story line or organisation of the media product. The plot of *Cinderella* is usually told as the fairytale describes the events. The narrative is how the events are told. It is also possible to talk about the narrative structure of non-fiction texts such as television news programmes.

News values The factors and criteria by which news producers decide the selection and order of the news. The word is a media studies term not used by the professionals in everyday discussion.

Niche Niche audiences are small and select in terms of social or interest group. For example, the financial news section of a television breakfast news programme is aimed at business men or women. A niche audience is a small segment or corner of the whole market.

Polysemic A visual image which contains several meanings, especially if there is no caption or heading to anchor it.

Producers The makers of the media texts include not only the artists, directors and production crew but also the people who plan, distribute and market the film. For example, a television programme broadcast by the BBC might be made by an independent television company on behalf of the BBC.

Representation A media text contains representations of people, events and places which the producers have produced to communicate with their audiences. The media text is by its very nature a constructed, second-hand and partial version of real or fictional life. A media text contains dramatised action or actual events through its medium. For example, television and its means of presentation is broadcasting.

Sign A sign is an element of the image which contains a reference to some other idea in reality. For example, the British flag connotes national identity. The term 'signifier' is used to describe the object which contains a 'sign' of meaning.

Text All media products which can be interpreted and 'read' are defined as 'texts'. Films, posters and trailers are all media texts which belong to the cinema industry. Toys used for tie-in product merchandising are not media texts.

Appendix

TASK NUMBER

STORYBOARD SHEET
Directions, dialogue, camera, music, special effects (sfx)

Do not write in this margin

TASK
NUMBER

STORYBOARD SHEET
**Directions, dialogue, camera,
music, special effects (sfx)**

Do not write
in this margin

TASK NUMBER

STORYBOARD SHEET
Directions, dialogue, camera, music, special effects (sfx)

Do not write in this margin

TASK
NUMBER

STORYBOARD SHEET
Directions, dialogue, camera, music, special effects (sfx)

Do not write
in this margin

PRODUCTION SHEET

MEDIA: FILM, TELEVISION OR RADIO

Special instructions Vision	Special instructions Sound	Dialogue	Other information Setting, interior, exterior, action	Timing

PRODUCTION SHEET

MEDIA: FILM, TELEVISION OR RADIO

Special instructions Vision	Special instructions Sound	Dialogue	Other information Setting, interior, exterior, action	Timing

PRODUCTION SHEET

MEDIA: FILM, TELEVISION OR RADIO

Special instructions Vision	Special instructions Sound	Dialogue	Other information Setting, interior, exterior, action	Timing

PRODUCTION SHEET

MEDIA: FILM, TELEVISION OR RADIO

Special instructions Vision	Special instructions Sound	Dialogue	Other information Setting, interior, exterior, action	Timing

Index

advertising
    added value 62
    advertorials 174
    agencies 172
    analysis 179–81
    bias 61
    controls 43, 174–8
    creative 173–4
    ideologies 60–61, 62–3
    magazines 161–2
    media 172–3
    'on behalf of' 63
    propaganda 60
    resources 219
    synergy 80
    targeted 180–81
Advertising Standards Authority (ASA) 43, 174–7
alternative media 45
anchorage 19–20, 21, 222
archetypes 56–7, 144
audiences 45–6, 222
    constructed 47–8
    demographic groups 48–9, 180–81
    engagement 50
    identity 50
    loyalty 41
    participation 190
    and producers 6, 7–8
    segmentation 49
    social values 49
    target 7, 21, 49–50, 117

BBC 33, 36, 38
    Producer's Guidelines 40–41
bias 61
Bliss 161
British Board of Film Certification (BBFC) 40, 43, 98
British Rates and Data Handbook (*BRAD*) 47
Broadcasting Act 1990 38
Broadcasting Standards Commission (BSC) 42

cable television 38, 202
Campaign for Press and Broadcasting Freedom 135
captions 19–20

cartoons 6–9, 11
categories
    and languages 6–7
    media 5, 23, 222
CD-ROMs 200, 203, 205
cinemas 97–8
circulation, newspapers 46–7, 130–31
codes 11, 222
computers
    Internet 200–1
    networked 200
    stand-alone 200
connotation 19, 222
construction 222
controls
    digital services 206
    film classification 40, 43, 98
    press 44, 133–4, 136
    radio 43
    television 40–41, 42–3
    video classification 43, 44
conventions 222
    newspapers 11, 13
    radio 11
    soap operas 11
convergent media 201, 204–6
Crimewatch UK 54–5
critical commentaries 21, 209
cross media links, films 91
cycles of production 34, 38–9, 86–7, 110–14

demographic groups 48–9, 180–81
denotation 18–19, 222
Diana, Princess of Wales 7–8, 19, 136
digital
    radio 203
    television 37, 196, 202, 203–4
distribution 38, 40
distributors 96
docu-soaps 150
DVDs 201, 203, 205

editing, films 30–31
editorials 7, 162, 174
'effects' debate 9

electronic press kits [EPKs] 91
Emap 165
ER 142–3
exhibition
   films 87
   television 38, 40

fanzines 12–13, 157–8, 194
filming
   close up 30
   continuous 148
   cross-cutting 30
   hospital documentaries 149–50
   long shots 30
   medium shots 30
   shot-reverse-shots 148
films
   adaptations 28–9
   budgets 94–6
   cinemas 97–8
   classification 40, 43, 98
   costs 101–2
   cross media links 91
   cycle of production 86–7
   directors 96
   distribution 87, 96
   early 27–8
   editing 30–31
   exhibition 87
   financial cycle 87
   genre 24–7, 96, 98
   horror 24–5
   ideas for 87–9
   independent 91–2
   marketing 89–92
   mise-en-scène 88, 99, 223
   narrative 27–30
   new formats 201
   posters 92–3
   press releases 91
   resources 219–20
   rights 87
   science fiction 98–101
   soundtrack 29
   stars 94–6
   structure 28
   teasers 91, 92
   tie-ins 90–91
   unique selling points 97
forms and conventions
   magazines 158–60
   newspapers 13
   television 23

genre 23, 222
   film 24–7, 96, 98

hammocking 41
hoaxes 55–6
hospital documentaries 149–50
hospital dramas
   filming 147–8
   narrative 146–7
   popularity 141–3
   stereoypes 144–6

icons
   objects 15, 16–17
   people 14–15
ideology 60–61, 222–3
images 6–9, 14, 19–21
Independent Television Commission (ITC) 42, 176–8
inheritance 41
institutions, media 21, 34, 36, 223
Internet 70, 200–1, 204–5, 206
intranet 200

J-17 160–61

landmine campaign 18–19
language, and catagories 6–7, 10–11, 223
Lawrence, Stephen, enquiry 122, 124, 125, 126–7
leaders, newspapers 7

magazines
   advertising 161–2
   circulation 46–7
   content 160–63
   editorials 162
   forms and conventions 158–60
   launching 156–7
   mass market 155–6
   messages and values 157–8
   music 77–9
   niche market 155–6
   ownership 164–6
   resources 220
   targeted 157
Men in Black 1997 102–3
mass marketing 155–6, 223
mass media 44
media
   institutions 34–5
   language 10–11
   studies 5–6
   texts 5, 10, 22–3, 55–6

INDEX

messages and values 6, 8–9
   added value 62
   alternatives 61–2
   bias 61
   ideologies 60–61, 62–3
   magazines 157–8
   propaganda 60
   social value 62
mise-en-scène 88, 99, 223
modes of address 162
Mojo 78
music
   see also recording companies
   awards 77, 79
   band marketing 74–5
   charts 68–9, 75, 80–81
   image 70–71
   industry statistics 73
   mainstream 68–9
   marketing 76–8
   new media 203
   play lists 76
   press 77–9
   press releases 81
   radio 68–9, 74–5
   resources 220
   sales 76, 79–83
   segmentation 77
   unique selling point 82
   videos 75

narrative 27–8, 223
national identity 62, 63–4
news
   balance 115–16
   choice of medium 109
   questioning 116–17
   relevance 114–15
   values 114–17, 223
news values 132–3, 223
newspapers 11
   see also press
   broadsheets 7, 13, 121, 131–2
   circulation 47
   controls 44, 133–4, 136–7
   cost 131
   distribution 7–8
   editorials 7
   exclusives 122, 123
   format 121–6
   forms 13
   headlines 11
   kickers 122, 123

   leaders 7
   marketing 131
   mastheads 122, 123
   news values 132–3
   ownership 137–8
   photographs 127–8
   pugs 122, 123
   resources 220
   sales 8, 129–31
   tabloids 7, 13, 121–2, 131–2
   target readership 131–2
   typeface 127
niche marketing 155–6, 223
niche media 44

OFTEL (Office of Telecommunications) 42
ownership 38–9

photographs
   analysis 17–21
   captions 19–20, 21, 128
   cropping 20–21, 128
   posed 127
point of interaction 38, 40
polysemics 17, 223
post-production 34, 214
pre-echo 41
pre-production 34, 212–14
Press Complaints Commission (PCC) 44, 133–4, 136
press releases 35, 81, 91
producers, and audiences 6, 7–8, 223
production 34, 38–9
   critical commentaries 209, 211–12
   cycles of 34, 38–9, 86–7, 110–14
   radio 215
   sheets 208
propaganda 60

radio
   analogue 203
   controls 43
   conventions 11
   digital 203
   music play lists 76
   production 215
   resources 220
   sexism 74
reconstruction 54–5
recording companies
   artist and repertoire (A&R) 72
   independent labels 72–3
   sales 76, 79–83
   statistics 72, 73

strike force 72
structure 71
representation 53–4, 223

satellite television 38, 202
science fiction films
    characters 99
    genre 98–9
    iconography 100
    mise-en-scène 99
    plot and sources 99–100
    situations 99
serials 58, 141
series 58, 141
shots
    close up 30
    long 30
    medium 30
    shot-reverse 148
signifiers of meaning 14, 223
Smash Hits 78
soap operas
    conventions 11
    place 59
    realism 57–8
    stereotypes 58
sports
    celebrities 189, 193
    danger 190–91
    earnings 188–9
    finance 193–5
    media 187–8
    television 188, 191–3
    values 189
    voice-overs 192
Star Wars 1977 102
stars, films 94–6
stereotypes 55, 56, 58, 145
style 222
symbols 14
synergy 80

target audiences 49–50, 117, 180–81, 222
target readership 131–2, 155–7
teasers, films 91, 92
Teletubbies 39–40
television 11
    see also advertising; hospital documentaries; hospital dramas; television news
    audience loyalty 41
    BBC 33, 36, 38, 40–41

BSkyB 188, 205
cable 38, 202
chat shows 189–90
controls 41, 42–3, 177–8
digital 196, 202, 203–4
distribution 40
forms and conventions 23
'free to air' 195
game shows 189–90
independent 38, 42, 176–8, 205
Internet 205
music 75
ownership 39
pay-per-view 194–5
production 39
replays 192
resources 220
satellite 38, 202
schedules 40, 41
signature 107–8
SkyDigital 37
slow motion 192
soap operas 11, 57–9
sport 188, 191–3
subscription 194
terrestrial 202
watershed 41
television news
    agenda setting 108
    cycles of production 110–14
    format 13
    gatekeeping 111–12
    news values 114–16
    scheduling 112
    sources 111
text 10, 223
tie-ins, films 90–91
typefaces 127, 180

unique selling point (USP) 82, 97

values, and messages 6, 8–9
videos
    classification 43, 44
    music 75
Voice of Listeners and Viewers (VLV) 43

web page production 216

youth culture 69–70